God So Loved, He Gave is a work of rare theological and spiritual perceptiveness. As it conducts its readers through the movement of God's ways with the world, it invites them to contemplate the divine works and to be formed in godliness by them. This is practical Christian divinity at its best: intellectually astute, humane, and animated by the gospel's generosity.

—*John Webster, professor at King's College, University of Aberdeen, Scotland*

Kelly Kapic has given us a forceful presentation of our universe ruled by a magnificently giving God. It is a scholarly and deeply thoughtful presentation that is, at the same time, vividly inspiring. It will help you to think magnificently of God and of what your life can be in his universe. Stepping into a life of giving love is the only reasonable response since that is how God is and how he has made us.

—*Dallas Willard, professor of philosophy at University of Southern California, author of* The Divine Conspiracy *and* Renovation of the Heart.

The Heidelberg Catechism tells us that "it is impossible that those grafted into Christ by true faith should not bring forth fruits of thankfulness." Kelly Kapic's book shows why. It shows biblically and theologically that anyone who grasps the nature of God and of his gospel will live a life poured out in acts of generosity, especially to the poorest and most needy. I'm glad to recommend it.

—*Tim Keller, pastor, Redeemer Presbyterian Church, New York City*

God So Loved, He Gave is an amazing book. In it Kelly Kapic deftly moves from our being recipients of all God's generous gifts through Christ to our being stewards of God's gifts as we share them with others. This book is both encouraging and challenging. It should be read attentively and prayerfully.

—*Jerry Bridges, author of* The Pursuit of Holiness

God So Loved, He Gave: Entering the Movement of Divine Generosity is a must read. Jesus himself said it is more blessed to give than to receive. Entering the movement of divine generosity is what we all ought to be concerned about. This is a great book; it is beautifully written, practical, helpful, and biblically sound. I encourage all Christians, particularly those seeking to experience the blessings that come out of generosity, to read this book. The blessings we receive from generosity are not limited to strictly financial blessings, but often are the blessings of love and encouragement that we get from sharing our lives with others. These blessings are more precious than silver and gold.

—*Dr. John M. Perkins, founder and president emeritus of the Christian Community Development Association of the John and Vera Mae Perkins Foundation*

God So Loved, He Gave is an eye-opening exploration of the boundless dimensions of God's heart for the world. Simultaneously it raises the bar for how God's image-bearers join him in big-hearted, open-handed, selfless generosity of our resources and of ourselves to the world he loves. Kelly Kapic has gifted us with a thought-provoking, deeply needed vision of our calling to gospel living.

—*Carolyn Custis James, author of* Half the Church

Here is a rich portrayal of redemption! In *God So Loved, He Gave* we are challenged to don the familiar story of salvation as a vestment more precious than the king's crown jewels. As we robe ourselves, we take delight in the story's often surprising and baffling, but always precious, truths. Sparkling quotes enliven each chapter.

—*Bruce K. Waltke, author of* An Old Testament Theology *and professor emeritus of Old Testament, Regent College, Vancouver, BC*

This fine book is an elegant portrayal of a marvelously generous God, who calls his people to show forth his generosity in a world that he sent his Son to redeem.

—*Richard J. Mouw, president of Fuller Seminary and professor of Christian philosophy*

Our cultural environment seems to assume a world as a given rather than a gift, as debt rather than exchange, as limited resources rather than "enough to go around." How refreshing it is to step into the world of the triune God, who not only gives it all but creates a new society that anticipates his everlasting shalom. Kapic leads us into the breathtaking vistas of this new creation, with beauty and wisdom. This book itself is a welcome gift to Christ's body.

—*Michael Horton, J. G. Machen Professor of Systematic Theology and Apologetics, Westminster Seminary, California*

In this book Kelly Kapic uses his considerable wisdom and skill to unpack the story of God's generosity and what it means to belong to and follow a generous God. At stake is nothing less than what it means to follow Christ faithfully in today's world. Kapic is a clear communicator who cherishes Christ, cares for the church, and conducts all the right conversations across the fields of biblical theology, systematic theology, historical theology, and practical theology. The result is a rare combination—a robust, warm-hearted, accessible book that glories our generous triune God and instructs and inspires readers throughout the church.

—*Justin Taylor, managing editor, ESV Study Bible*

Many books today address the practical questions of stewardship and generosity. But few do this while making the crucial connection between the gospel and giving. I highly recommend *God So Loved, He Gave* for every recipient of God's grace who desires to become a participant in divine generosity.

—*Howard Dayton, cofounder of Crown Financial Ministries; founder of Compass-Finances God's Way*

To belong to one who truly loves me is bondage sweet, for true love frees its object to delight in its greatest joy—which is to please one's lover. Such a paradox for the mind is readily deciphered by the heart and is explored with charming writing, winsome freshness, and gospel zeal by the well-read Kapic. A once-common hymn declared that those who know the old, old story best long to hear it like the rest. Kapic's book demonstrates that one who knows the gospel well can tell Jesus' story very, very well—so well that we will delight to be owned by the One who gave himself for us.

—*Bryan Chapell, president, Covenant Theological Seminary*

God So Loved, He Gave

entering the movement
of **divine generosity**

God So Loved,
He Gave

Kelly M. Kapic
with Justin Borger

ZONDERVAN®

ZONDERVAN.com/
AUTHORTRACKER
follow your favorite authors

ZONDERVAN

God So Loved, He Gave
Copyright © 2010 by Kelly M. Kapic

This title is also available as a Zondervan ebook. Visit www.zondervan.com/ebooks.

This title is also available in a Zondervan audio edition. Visit www.zondervan.fm.

Requests for information should be addressed to:

Zondervan, *Grand Rapids, Michigan* 49530

Library of Congress Cataloging-in-Publication Data

Kapic, Kelly M., 1972 –
    God so loved he gave : entering the movement of divine generosity / Kelly M. Kapic with Justin Borger.
        p. cm.
    Includes indexes.
    ISBN 978-0-310-32969-5 (hardcover, jacketed)
    1. God (Christianity) — Love. 2. Generosity — Religious aspects — Christianity. I. Borger, Justin. II. Title.
BT140.K37 2010
241'.677 — dc22   2010010827

All Scripture quotations, unless otherwise indicated, are taken from *The Holy Bible, English Standard Version,* copyright © 2001 by Good News Publishers. Used by permission. All rights reserved.

All Scripture quotations labeled NIV are taken from the Holy Bible, *New International Version®, NIV®.* Copyright © 1973, 1978, 1984 by Biblica, Inc.™ Used by permission of Zondervan. All rights reserved worldwide.

Any Internet addresses (websites, blogs, etc.) and telephone numbers printed in this book are offered as a resource. They are not intended in any way to be or imply an endorsement by Zondervan, nor does Zondervan vouch for the content of these sites and numbers for the life of this book.

Cover design: Rob Monacelli
Cover photography: Biwa Inc./Getty Images
Interior design: Mathew VanZomeren

Printed in the United States of America

10 11 12 13 14 15 /DCI/ 22 21 20 19 18 17 16 15 14 13 12 11 10 9 8 7 6 5 4 3 2 1

To Tabitha
During the writing of this book you walked
through cancer with courage and grace,
and through it all you gave the rest of us an authentic glimpse of
him who is the Giver of life.
You are the most stunningly beautiful gift I know.
Kelly

To my grandparents
William and Helen Cross
who embodied the words of Jesus,
"It is more blessed to give than to receive."
Justin

Contents

Living in the Gifts:
Cross, Resurrection, Church

Preface

LET ME TELL YOU A STORY. . .

While it may be a familiar story, how well do we know it? Many people believe that this story is the most important story in the world. The characters and main events of the narrative are commonly known, but do we really understand it?

This is the story about God. This is the story about everything that exists. This is the story about humanity. It is this grand narrative that I want to tell you about, even if you have heard it a thousand times. For what we discover in this story inevitably surprises, baffles, and sometimes even offends both those who are near and those who are far away.

But I believe that if this story is understood, and if we have the courage to believe it, everything looks different. God looks different. You and I look different. Everything about this world looks different. And yet, the point of the story is not merely to change our thinking, but to liberate our lives.

Here is how it starts . . .

From all eternity God not only has existed, but he has lived in perfect fullness, joy, and delight. At some point the eternal God then did the unfathomable — he created everything out of *nothing*, out of no-thing. For he alone existed until he spoke with creative force and brought that which was not into being. Whether one thinks of sand or stars, trees or people, God created all that is not God. All that has come into existence owes its ultimate reality to him.

As Creator, God is the King and owner of all things. God himself is the artist of this diverse, beautiful, and dynamic world, so this world should reflect the brilliance and contentment of its Creator.

However, unlike lifeless statues made by a sculptor, living and free people were created by God. Out of God's own freedom he made creatures in his image; he created us to walk with him, to commune with him as we enjoy his presence and blessing. But we have rejected his love and his lordship, which has resulted in death and disaster. We have turned from the One to whom we belong. As a result of our sin and rebellion the great song of creation turned into a deafening moan. This rejection of God's kingship caused a rupture in the entire cosmos, for, if you could hear it, even the rocks and the trees began to cry out against this fissure between the Creator and his creation.

What could be done? God could have decided simply to crush his creation as a frustrated potter crushes a newly formed jar that is disappointing, deciding to start over from scratch. But God took another way.

In the pages that follow you will read the story of divine generosity. When captured by the depth of God's gifts in the gospel, we discover that he frees us to participate in his work of grace, hope, righteousness, and love. This is the generous life; this is what *belonging* to God is all about.

We have written this book in the hope that as we learn to dwell in the good news of belonging to God, we will grow in the freedom to give ourselves to God and others in ways that are impossible for those who treasure their lives as their own. We hope people will discover in this book how, in God's strange economy, to live with God as the Master is not suffocating, but is the very thing that will finally allow us to breathe deeply and live courageously. We invite you to "take hold of the life that is truly life" (1 Tim. 6:19 NIV).

part one

From Belonging to Bondage

The Ewe Lamb
What Went Wrong?

AND THE LORD SENT NATHAN TO DAVID. He came to him and said to him, "There were two men in a certain city, the one rich and the other poor. The rich man had very many flocks and herds, but the poor man had nothing but one little ewe lamb, which he had bought. And he brought it up, and it grew up with him and with his children. It used to eat of his morsel and drink from his cup and lie in his arms, and it was like a daughter to him. Now there came a traveler to the rich man, and he was unwilling to take one of his own flock or herd to prepare for the guest who had come to him, but he took the poor man's lamb and prepared it for the man who had come to him."

Then David's anger was greatly kindled against the man, and he said to Nathan, "As the LORD lives, the man who has done this deserves to die, and he shall restore the lamb fourfold, because he did this thing, and because he had no pity."

Nathan said to David, "You are the man!"

(2 Samuel 12:1 – 7a)

Every man has a property in his own person; this nobody has any right to but himself.

John Locke[1]

Know that the LORD, he is God! It is he who made us, and we are his!

Psalm 100:3

My existence is not something I have or possess. It comes to me, without my having any say about it, from another as a gift. In the strictest sense, I am but do not have my own existence.

Luke Timothy Johnson[2]

As the perfect one, God sheds himself abroad. His perfection is unhindered self-possession and self-enjoyment that includes (but is not exhausted by) infinite generosity.

John Webster[3]

God owns by giving.

M. Douglas Meeks[4]

chapter one

All Things Belong to God

We Belong to the Lord

I remember asking my son, who was five at the time, about his day. Jonathan didn't think very long before he smiled and piped up, "I learned something. Do you want to hear it?"

"Yes," I replied.

"You can't serve two masters."

That made me smile. Clearly that morning his class must have looked at Matthew 6:24: "No one can serve two masters, for either he will hate the one and love the other, or he will be devoted to the one and despise the other. You cannot serve God and money."

I was impressed with what he learned, and I thought our conversation would move on, but Jonathan asked: "Do you know what a master is?" Intrigued, I wondered what he might say. "Owner" was his simple reply. Satisfied that he had taught me enough for one evening, he returned to his dinner in hopes of getting dessert. But even as he moved on, I found myself taken aback by his simple but deeply insightful answer—okay, he was probably just repeating what he learned in class, but coming from the mouth of a child it felt profound. Was Jonathan right?

In 1563 some ministers produced a catechism in Heidelberg, Germany, to teach the essential truths of the Christian faith. The first question in the catechism moves us to the heart of the matter:

Question 1: What is your only comfort, in life and in death?

Answer: That I *belong*—body and soul, in life and in death—not to myself but to my faithful Savior, Jesus Christ.... (emphasis mine)[5]

But Don't We Own Ourselves?

Our passion to possess, however, jeopardizes this joy of belonging to God. Especially in the affluent West, our sense of self can become so wrapped up with the idea of self-ownership that the thought of belonging to somebody else—including God—looks like a threat and not a hope. Fearing to give, we grasp ever more tightly. We constantly clamor for our "rights" and cling to the impression that we own our bodies, our money, our ideas, our time, our property, and everything else we can manage to slap our name tag on. But more than anything else, we feel sure that we own *ourselves*.

John Locke (1632–1704), the English philosopher and political thinker, helped shape this modern mentality, arguing that self-ownership is an incontestable human right:

> Though the earth and all inferior creatures be common to all men, yet every man has a property in his own person; this nobody has any right to but himself.[6]

The loss of self-ownership, whether to states or to other people, led to all kinds of abuse in Locke's world. Fears of such abuse are woven into the fabric of many contemporary political and social ideals.

In fact, today it seems offensive, maybe even anti-American to be told that there may be a problem with the idea that we own ourselves. After all, how can we ever downplay the great wickedness of slavery in America's past? Without question, this historical evil that darkens our history makes it almost impossible for us to conceive of the idea of being "owned" or having a "master" as a good thing. But is it possible that lives lived under the impression of self-ownership might actually harm both ourselves and others?

There still remains an underlying problem that can be hard for us to recognize, much less admit. We live under the burden and illusion of *self-ownership*. Think of commercials that tell women that at forty-five years old they should still look twenty-eight, and if not, it is their fault for not buying the product. Parents are promised their children's future success if they will only purchase the newest educational video and attend every extracurricular sporting activity. From the clothes we wear to the food we eat, the reality is that convention, society, and a complex of other competing forces own us. We are owned by our possessions; owned by those around us; owned by people we have never met but who exert incredible power over our lives in some of the most subtle and sinister ways.

So we enter into the myth of self-ownership, and we cannot hear the good news. I will never forget when we lived overseas and I spoke with a British friend about his recent visit to New York City. Discussing his time in the States he said, "Americans are funny, because most of them pride themselves on being free, with everyone living just as they want. Yet, the truth is," he continued, "everywhere in New York I went I saw people wearing uniforms. A child of six years old and a man in his fifties looked the same, each wearing baggy Levi's, a t-shirt, and a ball cap." His point was that their freedom was illusory.

The concept of freedom can be deceptive, and in truth pure self-ownership is impossible and a lie, because we are always owned. The question is not *if* you will be owned, but *to whom* will you belong? We are called to choose this day whom we will serve (Josh. 24:14–15). Will you belong to the true Owner or to competing powers? Deep down we sense we are owned and we rage against this, but in the process we end up serving degrading masters rather than the Lord of love.

Embracing God's Ownership as Good News

The great tragedy of this possessive way of thinking about ourselves is that it causes so many to reject the gospel itself, the good news that we are not our own but have been "called to *belong* to Jesus Christ" (Rom. 1:6, italics added).[7] The gospel tells us that we have been "bought with a price" (1 Cor. 6:19–20) and that God has "set his seal of ownership on us" by his Holy Spirit (2 Cor. 1:22 NIV). "The God of Christians," Blaise Pascal once said, "the God of Abraham, the God of Isaac, the God of Jacob … is a God of love and of consolation: he is a God who fills the soul and heart of those whom he possesses."[8] But when we think of ourselves as our own personal property, it becomes difficult to embrace God's ownership as good news. After all, how can the gospel be "good news" when it calls us to deny the very thing we see as our ultimate possession? If we are ever going to appreciate this liberating truth of belonging to God, we must first be reminded of God's original relation to creation.

God's Gift of Creation

From the nebulae in outer space to our personal savings accounts—God owns *everything*. As the Dutch statesmen Abraham Kuyper (1837–1920) famously put it, "there is not a single inch on the whole terrain of our human existence over which Christ ... does not exclaim, 'Mine'!"[9] As we will see, this expansive view of God's ownership is found not merely in a few obscure passages of Scripture, but it is an ever-present assumption throughout the whole Bible.[10] Fundamental to the reality of God's ownership of all things is the truth that he alone is the Creator of everything that exists.

God Created out of Freedom, Not out of Need

We cannot rightly conceive of the gift of creation until we first recognize that God's creative actions are *free*. By definition, gifts are unnecessary. God did not have to create. If we are ever to understand the joy and power of human liberty, we must first gain a better appreciation of God's glorious freedom. It is out of divine freedom that God creates — nothing forced his hand.

Creation was not made in order to perfect something lacking in God.[11] As A. W. Tozer reminds us, "To admit the existence of a need in God is to admit incompleteness in the divine Being. *Need* is a creature-word and cannot be spoken of the Creator. God has a voluntary relation to everything He has made."[12] Acts 17:24–25 confesses this truth:

> The God who made the world and everything in it is the Lord of heaven and earth ... he is not served by human hands, as if he needed anything, because he himself gives all men life and breath and everything else. (NIV)

This does not mean that God is distant or unconcerned, but the exact opposite inference is more fitting. The God who did not need to create, who is eternally complete in himself, is the God who *does* create, who continues to uphold what he created, and who takes a personal interest in each life and molecule of creation.

God Created out of His Triune Love

God's generosity flows out of his love, and thus we must ask a few key questions about his love. Did God need to create in order to experience love? Does God only *become* loving after he creates, when there is something to love? Actually, no.

Scripture affirms that "God *is* love" (1 John 4:9, 16). Love is a perfection of God's being, which means it is not something temporary or accidental to him. All of his being is of love. To speak of God apart from his love is to speak of someone other than God.

How, then, is it possible that God loves before there is a creation? Simply put, the God who creates is Father, Son, and Holy Spirit, one God existing in perfect unity and love in a triune manner. Pope Benedict XVI, reflecting on John's comment that "God is love," says it well:

> Here we find ourselves before the most dazzling revelation of the source of love, the mystery of the Trinity: in God, one and triune, there is an everlasting exchange of love between the persons of the Father and the Son, and this love is not an energy or a sentiment, but it is a person; it is the Holy Spirit.[13]

Here Pope Benedict reflects a long Christian tradition, which sometimes spoke of the Father as the Lover, the Son as the Beloved, and the Spirit as the Love between them.[14]

Although analogies between God's love and our love have significant problems, one thing in Scripture is clear: the eternal God is love. Divine and eternal love is then unfolded and directed toward creation from the Father through the Son in the Spirit.[15] God does not need to create in order to experience love, because the triune God exists in love within himself. He creates as an outworking of that eternal love. C. S. Lewis summarizes the point well: "God, who needs nothing, loves into existence wholly superfluous creatures in order that he may love and perfect them."[16] God creates out of the overflow of his eternal triune love, and we were made to enjoy and respond to this very love.

God Created for the Purpose of Celebration

Centuries ago theologians claimed that the end or goal of creation was the glory or celebration of God (*gloria* or *celebratio Dei*).[17] Creation's existence is meant both to bring God glory and enable all his creation to enjoy him. All things were made to reflect and express the Creator's beauty and majesty. Consequently, while creation's primary end is God's glory, the secondary end is humanity's good. "Yahweh's good intention," says Walter Brueggemann, "is a place of fruitfulness, abundance, productivity, extravagance—all terms summed up in the word *blessing*."[18]

People were made to love the Creator, partly by taking pleasure in the rest of creation and by faithfully participating in it. Not surprisingly, then, God's first command to the man and woman he creates begins with a call to "be fruitful ..." (Gen 1:28). Humanity was to reproduce, to enjoy and share the gifts of God in creation, and to live in joyful response to these blessings. The goal of creation was quite simply *celebratio*—celebration; this word was also used in the history of the church to describe a feast or sacred function that people participated in.

Notice that the Bible itself regularly calls people to celebrate God and his work in the world through Sabbaths, festivals, and feasts.[19] In part, these events reminded them of God's goodness as the one who makes all things and from whom all things come (1 Tim. 4:4). This God could be trusted not merely for the past, but for the present and future (cf. 1 Tim. 6:17). Even to this day, there are churches around the world that still have "Harvest Sundays" and the like, which serve as reminders of God's faithful lordship over all things.[20]

Such events serve to bring us back to rightly recognizing the Creator. Many of us have lost that sense of connection between food and the earth. The easy access to grocery stores and restaurants, and our distance from farms and the raising of animals can create the illusion that food and water are guaranteed. We take it as a given that they will be there. In truth, they are "given," but given by the Creator and Sustainer of everything. They are gifts.

The whole of creation was made to celebrate God, to feast on his graciousness, and to return to him in praise.

All That God Created Was Good

Because all things come from God, creation is inherently good (Gen. 1:31). The story of creation in Genesis 1–2 repeatedly makes the assessment that every step and element of God's creation is all good. The light, dirt, and seas were wonderfully good; the vegetation, stars, birds, and animals were delightfully good; humanity, the great climax of creation, was likewise unequivocally proclaimed by God to be good (Gen. 1:4, 10, 12, 18, 21, 25, 31). Although people have sometimes treated aspects of the material world as intrinsically bad, Genesis unflinchingly reminds us of the original wholeness and glory of the earth. In the beginning *everything* was made good, including humans, their bodies, and their relations with God, each other, and the world. We were designed to live in harmony with the rest of creation.

Further, creation is not good merely because it is intricately engineered or beautifully put together, but because it comes from a good God. Creation is a *gift* through which we enjoy the Creator himself (cf. Ps. 19:1–2; 1 Tim. 6:17). Thus, to delight in elements of creation should provoke us to celebrate the creator God. Whether you eat or drink, do all things to his glory, recognizing his lordship over it all (Eccl. 2:24–26; 1 Cor. 10:31). All that is comes from God, and thus it displays God's generosity. In truth, nothing can be earned nor can demand be made of it—everything points back to the reality of gift. As Walter Brueggemann has explained,

> There is a givenness to be relied on, guaranteed by none other than God. That givenness is here before us, stands over us, endures beyond us, and surrounds us behind and before.... The most foundational experience is the daily experience of *life's regularities*, which are experienced as reliable, equitable and generous.[21]

When this fundamental orientation of praise for God's generosity is forgotten, great tragedy and disillusionment occur.

God's Ownership Confronts and Comforts Us

On the one hand, it would be a lie to suggest that the idea of God's absolute ownership is not somewhat offensive to our modern sensibilities. As James Luther Mays says, "The declaration that the Lord is owner is an intentional denial that anyone else is."[22] That is offensive. Note 1 Corinthians 4:7, where Paul asks, "What do you have that you did not receive? And if you did receive it, why do you boast as though you did not receive it?" That too is offensive and deeply humbling.

On the other hand, God's ownership—or our belonging to God—is deeply comforting. Especially in the face of scarcity, hardship, struggles, and darkness. As Regina Spektor, a thoughtful contemporary musician observes in her powerful song "Laughing With," there is a paradox that happens when we are desperate.[23] Whether we are at a hospital, in the trenches during wartime, or wondering where our next meal is going to come from, in such times we don't find ourselves laughing at God. We long for his care and provision. Yet when things are going well, when laughter fills the air, then we somehow think the idea of God can be hilarious. Spektor has it just right. When we are faced with our vulnerability, with our lack of power and control, with our great need—in those times our hearts often ache with the longing to belong to One who can be trusted, who is truly sovereign and good even in the midst of our fears.

This is why the covenant relationship God shares with his people, combined with the great covenant summary we find repeated throughout the Bible, hinges on the idea of belonging:

> I will take *you* to be my people, and I will be *your* God.[24]

The essence of the covenant is this relationship of his being ours and our being his. Similarly, the great priestly benediction of the Old Testament begins with this blessing of belonging:

> The LORD *bless* you and *keep* you....[25]

Thus, when rightly understood, belonging to God brings, not personal privation, but peace and protection to God's people. As Zacharias Ursinus, coauthor of the sixteenth-century Heidelberg Catechism, has said: "We are his property; therefore, he watches over us as his own, so that not so much as a hair can fall from our heads without the will of our heavenly Father. Our safety does not lie in our own hands, or strength; for if it did, we should lose it a thousand times every moment."[26] God's ownership cuts both ways, it confronts us even as it comforts (cf. Job 41:11; Ps. 100:3; Isa. 43:1; Ezek. 37:27).

Creation Was a Gift Calling for a Response

God creates and thus owns, not as a tyrannical agent seeking to seize power, but as a benevolent Lord who makes in order to give. In other words, God freely creates out of his delight to share his own goodness with others. God is full and he makes full. Thus, as he creates, he invites us to enjoy the feast and to extend his gracious hospitality and care to others; in this way we are images of our Creator.

Ancient monarchs would often send out images or statues of themselves to the various regions over which they ruled.[27] These images represented the king. When someone saw the image, they were to remember that the land was actually under that monarch's authority. Furthermore, it was the monarch alone who was thought to be made in the god's image—he *alone* represented the god(s). In this respect Scripture highlights a radical, even revolutionary, break from its ancient Near Eastern context. For the Bible makes it clear that not merely the monarch, but every person on the earth exists in God's image: male and female, young and old, rich and poor, Pharaoh and slave.

Thus, all humanity points back to the true King, Yahweh, the Creator of heaven and earth. Yahweh, the creator God, had authority over the entire world and not merely a particular region. Humanity—in its entirety—is to reflect this good God's presence in his world and constantly affirm his ownership of it. Looking into the mirror reminds us to whom we—and the entire world—belong.

Let us not miss an obvious but remarkable implication: from the beginning God entrusts his work into the hands of people. While humanity was part of the creation itself, God draws near to them and singles them out for the care and nurturing of his world. Humanity was made good and whole, and they were called to respond to their God's gracious invitation to steward his world. Mark Allan Powell captures the surprising nature of this arrangement:

> We own nothing; but manage everything. God trusts us in a way that we are reluctant to trust each other (or ourselves) and places confidence in us beyond anything that our record thus far would seem to warrant.[28]

So man and woman were made in God's image, and our role in the world included nurturing, developing, and protecting the rest of creation. From the beginning God calls his people to participate in his purposes of caring for his world. He invites us to share in his generosity and thus in his work.

God Owns by Giving

God can invite us into this activity because he made this world. He is the potter and we are the clay (Isa. 64:8; Jer. 18:6; Rom. 9:21). We will discuss in chapter 2 how God's lordship — and thus his ownership — has been denied, how sin has shattered the pottery, and how his creation has been pillaged. Nevertheless, there is but one God who made all things, and so all things ultimately point back to his rightful ownership.

What God Creates He Owns

We confess God's work in creation when we say, "God owns everything." The Psalms also repeat this connection:

- Know that the LORD, he is God! It is he who made us, and we are his (Ps. 100:3).
- The earth is the LORD's and the fullness thereof, the world and all who dwell therein, for he has founded it upon the seas and established it upon the waters (Ps. 24:1–2).
- The heavens are yours; the earth also is yours; the world and all that is in it, you have founded them. The north and the south, you have created them (Ps. 89:11–12).

When Old Testament writers spoke about creation, they did not merely refer to the origin of the universe. They knew about this origin in the distant past because they knew this God in their present, and therefore they passionately called God's people to live before this loving Lord as his faithful stewards. Nothing, however insignificant, could be credited to God's creatures without also seeing it as the work of the giving God.[29]

Of course, most of us have an easier time believing that God created the universe in the past than that he has provided us with everything we have in the present. This is especially true when we think of personal paychecks and college diplomas, which God tends to give us after periods of hard work and personal exertion. The Bible teaches that it is never easier to forget about God than after he has richly blessed us. Affluence can produce a spiritual amnesia.[30] While our society teaches us to keep careful catalogues of all our accomplishments, the Bible reminds us that everything on our personal résumé belongs to God, for the power of productivity itself comes from him:

> You may say to yourself, "My power and the strength of my hands have produced this wealth for me." But remember the LORD your God, for it is he who gives you the ability to produce wealth. (Deut. 8:17–18; cf. 1 Cor. 4:7 NIV)

All of creation points back to the one true Lord and Giver of life.

The Dynamic Nature of God's Ownership

The Scriptures present the movement of divine giving and receiving as a cycle: everything comes from God, is sustained through him, and will be given back to him. Few passages in Scripture provide a more breathtaking introduction to the subject of God's ownership than Romans 11:36:

> For from him and through him and to him are all things. To him be glory forever. Amen.

These simple words of praise give an all-encompassing view of the world and its purpose. *All things* come *from* God, are sustained *through* him, and will eventually flow *back to* him as the ultimate Owner of everything. Nothing is excluded.

And yet, the way in which God owns everything is somewhat surprising. Romans 11:36 indicates God's ownership is much more *dynamic* than we might expect. While we often associate the idea of "ownership" with locks and keys, safe deposit boxes, bank accounts, and home security systems, God's ownership is fundamentally different. Unlike us, God does not own by keeping, but by giving.[31] His lordship and ownership is expressed in a life-giving cycle that moves from him, through him, and to him in a beautiful threefold movement that warrants closer attention.[32] This dynamic nature of divine ownership illuminates the relationship between "giving" and "getting."

One mistaken idea is that God simply "gives" out of a calculated desire to "get." In other words, God creates everything merely because he has needs that he wants fulfilled. As we have already shown, this does not reflect the biblical vision of the triune God.

A second mistake argues that God gives without any apparent purpose or goal, with no thought of the gift's reception, use, or concern for return. This comes perhaps from an underlying fear that if God has any expectation of return from his gifts, then their graciousness is lost and his giving seems to merely be a divine economic exchange. While such fears have some legitimacy, the Bible does describe and even expects some sort of genuine response to God's gifts. "We are *not*," as Yale scholar Miroslav Volf has said, "the final destinations in the flow of God's gifts. Rather, we find ourselves midstream, so to speak. The gifts flow into us, and they flow from us."[33] In the end all things return "to God." As the early church father Irenaeus (c. 130–202) perceived in the second century, for God to give all things necessarily requires that he be the ultimate Owner of everything:

> For how could there be any *pleroma* [fullness] or principle, or power, or any other God, since it behooves God, as the fullness of all things, to contain and envelop all things, and to be contained and limited by none. For if there is anything beyond Him He is not the fullness of all things, nor does He contain all things.[34]

Ultimately, the comprehensive fullness of God's giving and receiving, as presented in the Scriptures, overcomes all of our fears. Since God did not create to satisfy any inadequacy or need of his own, but out of the fullness of his delight and love, this delight and love flow to the creatures as generosity and back to God as thanksgiving and praise. Creation reflects and therefore shares in — or "beholds" — God's great glory.[35] Our good has by his hand become a means of God's ultimate glory, intrinsically connected (cf. Ezek. 36:22–27).

The nature of this connection is a key to a healthy view of God and ourselves. As God's giving does not impoverish but enriches him, so we, as we offer back to God the gifts he has given and sanctified in us, are enriched in his glory and are satisfied in and through him.[36] Below we will unpack the cycle of "from him, through him, and to him" in more detail to show the relationship between God's giving and his owning.

From Him

We have already explored God's act of creation as the ultimate source of all our good, so here we simply mention a few more texts proclaiming that all things are *from* God.

- Behold, to the LORD your God belong heaven and the heaven of heavens, the earth with all that is in it (Deut. 10:14).
- You are the LORD, you alone. You have made heaven, the heaven of heavens, with all their host, the earth and all that is on it, the seas and all that is in them; and you preserve all of them; and the host of heaven worships you (Neh. 9:6).
- Who has first given to me [God], that I should repay him? Whatever is under the whole heaven is mine (Job 41:11).
- The heavens are yours; the earth also is yours; the world and all that is in it, you have founded them (Ps. 89:11)

Clearly the idea of God as Originator and Owner was understood from the earliest times in the Hebrew Scriptures and that idea is not lost with the formation of the New Testament. Only now the connection is directly linked to the Lord Jesus, the Christ: "yet for us there is but one God, the Father, from whom are all things and for whom we exist; and one Lord, Jesus Christ, through whom are all things, and through whom we exist" (1 Cor. 8:6). The triune God shows himself as the One from whom everything comes and through whom everything is sustained.

Through Him

To say that all things are *through* God affirms that God is constantly orchestrating and upholding every infinitesimal detail that swirls around us. From planetary orbits to electrons encircling the nucleus of an atom, he not only sustains but also guides, directs, and rules the entire created world. This shows how different God's ownership is from ours. We easily forget or neglect our possessions; God never does (Heb. 1:3; Col. 1:17). Botanists, for example, suspect that the oldest living redwoods in California are somewhere between two and three thousand years old—God has been sustaining them ever since they were saplings, since the age of the Parthenon.[37]

Previous generations called this "providence." God did not make the world "very good" to abandon it. He never abandons his creation, as if God wound creation up like a clock and then walked away never to interfere again. Although Bette Midler's lyrics proclaiming "God is watching us ... from a distance" may move us, this distance does not provide much comfort and hope.[38] The God who creates is also the God who sustains. A merely sympathetic God who is distant, not acting, helping, or promising a future, is not a God worthy of our worship and trust. And that is not the Sustainer God proclaimed in Scripture who says to the waves, "Thus far shall you come, and no farther" (Job 38:11). If God's caretaking activity ever ceased, even for a moment, the universe would instantly collapse. But Yahweh's presence is evidenced by his continued care of creation, often represented in agricultural images:

> You [God] care for the land and water it;
>   you enrich it abundantly.
> The streams of God are filled with water
>   to provide the people with grain,
>   for so you have ordained it.
> You drench its furrows
>   and level its ridges;
> you soften it with showers
>   and bless its crops. (Ps. 65:9 – 10 NIV)

Why is it that rather than embracing God as the owner and caretaker of this world, we pit science against theology? We become confused, believing that once we understand the way things tend to work, we can do away with what is then deemed "mythology." Yet is not the God who is the Creator also the Sustainer of this world, ensuring the very repeatability and structure of the universe that scientific observation is completely dependent upon? Science is a beautiful thing, and ethical scientific endeavors actually display God's glorious governance rather than diminish it.[39]

God's providential care also calls for our care of his creation: "He makes grass grow for the cattle, and plants for man to cultivate" (Ps. 104:14 NIV). John Chrysostom, the famed fourth-century preacher, captured the universal nature of God's provision:

> God generously gives all things that are much more necessary than money, such as air, water, fire, the sun—all such things. It is surely not true to say that the rich person enjoys the sun's rays more than the poor person does. It is not correct to say that the rich person takes in a more abundant supply of air than the poor person does. No, all [these] things lie at the equal and common disposition of all.[40]

Sadly, as we will discover in a later chapter, human actions have affected how the poor and rich enjoy the air.[41] However, the aim of creation was that our activity would reflect and be a means of God's governing. God gives us all our gifts that we might freely give. As Paul told the congregation at Corinth, "You will be made rich in every way so that you can be generous on every occasion" (2 Cor. 9:11 NIV).

Behind the call for human effort, however, is always God's lordship and ownership over it all. This is the Lord's land, his animals, his earth. So even when the droughts come, we look to the Creator for renewal. Because the loving Lord of the universe has promised to maintain the ebb and flow of all things through himself, we may trust him in the midst of uncertainty (Hab. 3:17–19).

The life-giving nature of God's ownership should dispel any fear or suspicion we may have about belonging to God. But it doesn't. Why? God's ownership is inseparable from his sustaining providence. To be owned by God does not mean that we are imprisoned and forgotten about; rather, it means we are loved, that we live and move and have our being through him (Acts 17:28).

To Him

Zechariah was one of many prophets who, like Paul, spoke of God's ownership not only in terms of the *beginning*, but also in terms of the *end*. He spoke of a day when all the world's wealth would come rushing back to God as the absolute Owner of everything (Zech. 14:1–21; cf. Rev. 21:24–26). "On that day," wrote Zechariah, "HOLY TO THE LORD will be inscribed on the bells on horses, and the cooking pots in LORD's house will be like the sacred bowls in front of the alter. Every pot in Jerusalem and Judah will be holy to the LORD Almighty" (Zech. 14:20–21 NIV). In the end, just as in the beginning, every element of creation will reflect God's ownership.

Much earlier in Israel's history the same words, "HOLY TO THE LORD," were engraved on the gold plate that the high priest wore as a sign of being exclusively dedicated to God (Ex. 28:36). By saying that the same sacred words would be inscribed on ordinary objects like pots and pans, Zechariah revealed just how far the redemptive reach of God's ownership will ultimately stretch: to every nook and cranny of creation.

But the greatest significance of the words "all things … to him" in Romans 11:36 lies in the fact that Paul wrote them as an outburst of praise. He had just spent over ten chapters outlining the good news of faith in the Lord Jesus Christ, who has brought justification and hope. Paul was this excited because he saw the glory of redemption, which we will explore in later chapters. The beginning of the biblical narrative stresses God's ownership of all things. The end of the story also highlights the role of the Master to whom all things are returned. But how this occurs is surprising. By saying that all things are "to him," Paul reminds us that God's ownership is not "a thing of the past," but of the future as well.

Conclusion

When we speak of God's ownership, some people may think that this is just putting a religious spin on the need to donate money. The recognition of God's ownership and Christian stewardship has fallen on hard times. As Randy Alcorn puts it, "To many it is no longer relevant to the day in which we live. To some it's just a religious cliché used to make fund-raising sound spiritual. It conjures up images of large red thermometers on church platforms, measuring how far we are from paying off the mortgage."[42] But the gospel itself shouts to us of God's lordship over all that we are and have. Why does it do that?

This is not about raising money to build a bigger sanctuary, a hospital, or art gallery; it is about knowing and obeying the God we worship. It is about understanding who He is and who we are. Only by affirming that Yahweh is the God of creation, with everything flowing from him, through him, and to him, can we rightly relate to this God.

Of course, the strikingly beautiful idea that all things flow back to God leads us to ask about the fallenness of the world we live in. Does He even want any of this back and are we the ones to give it? Our blessed state of belonging has become a cursed condition of bondage. To answer these questions we must now turn from the fullness and glory of creation to the utter brokenness caused by our sin.

Jesus answered them, "Truly, truly, I say to you, everyone who commits sin is a slave to sin."

John 8:34

[Sin] is not the beginning, but it is a turning-away from the beginning, the abandonment of the origin, the break with that which God had given and established.

Emil Brunner[1]

Just as a physician might say that there very likely is not one single living human being who is completely healthy, so anyone who really knows mankind might say that there is not one single living human being who does not despair a little, who does not secretly harbor an unrest, an inner strife, a disharmony, an anxiety about himself, so that, just as the physician speaks of going around with an illness in the body, he walks around with a sickness, carries around a sickness of the spirit that signals its presence at rare intervals in and through an anxiety he cannot explain.

Søren Kierkegaard[2]

"I Me Mine"

George Harrison, of The Beatles[3]

O greedy men, what will satisfy you, if God Himself will not?

Augustine[4]

chapter two

Everything Appears Lost

The Great Tragedy

Imagine the world, utterly new: God's gladness glistening on the wet garden. Far-flung forests, drenched with dew and pools of light, begin to bud, swell, and sway for the first time. Living creatures freely move on the land and in the sea, birds fly above the earth and across the expanse of the heavens. A bright river flowing out of Eden splashes its way through the rich forest floor and divides into four separate headwaters that spill into lands where gold, bdellium, and onyx are found. Imagine all this brand new bounty, fruit and flowers unfurling.

It's important to imagine because *this* was the perfect environment Genesis portrays in which the human race first began to doubt God's generosity. A talking snake mysteriously appears and starts asking questions: "Did God really say, 'You must not eat from any tree in the garden'?" (Gen. 3:1 NIV). Of course, the truth was just the opposite. Only a few verses earlier we learn of how God blessed Adam and Eve by giving them every plant and tree bearing fruit with just one exception (Gen. 1:29; 2:16 – 17). But Satan succeeds in his attempt to make the Creator sound like a close-fisted curmudgeon. As Bruce Waltke describes it, Satan distorts the perspective of our first parents by emphasizing God's one *prohibition*, not his *provision*:

> Adam and Eve are surrounded by wonderful trees and provisions in the garden, including the tree of life, but all Eve can see is the one

tree of which they cannot partake. Once Satan can get our eyes on what we cannot do, we are sure to do it.[5]

This garden is Paradise: if humanity fails in this ideal setting, then there is no hope for humanity to keep faith anywhere else.... In contrast to much sociological thinking, namely, that the way to improve humans is to improve their environment, humanity at its best rebels in the perfect environment. Sodom and Gomorrah, where humanity sunk to the lowest levels of violence and sex, was at the time like the "garden of the LORD" (Gen. 13:10). Our modern world is no better.[6]

Sin: Turning and Taking

What actually happened is fairly simple. Adam and Even decided to *turn* from him to whom they belonged and to *take* what had not been given.[7] They had walked with God in the cool of the day; they had known his gentle presence, his manifold blessing, his profound generosity. In fact, he had offered them everything in the garden but the fruit of the tree of the knowledge of good and evil (Gen. 2:16–17). Everything else is theirs to enjoy.

There was no shortage of fruit to be eaten, no hunger pains were felt. They had broad freedom under God's care — Adam and Eve were to enjoy God's creation and live in harmony with it. But God had given them a clear warning — to eat from this tree would bring catastrophic consequences. Don't miss the irony here: Adam and Eve lost everything precisely by reaching out and taking something that was not theirs. They expected to be filled, but in reality they were emptied.[8] Thus, as the Creator of humanity, God's command to them was not arbitrary or cruel, but wise and gracious.

Think, for example, how scientists remind us that life on this planet is held in delicate balance: if the earth were only a bit closer to the sun, relatively speaking, our planet would be incapable of life. We do not question such observations. But God's moral laws of creation should be taken just as seriously. When parents tell a child not to touch the electric socket, they are doing it not because they are creating arbitrary rules or because they simply love to limit their child, but because they desire to protect the child. Similarly, only God could rightly handle the tree of the knowledge of good and evil, but in any hands besides his it would be deadly.

Remember King David in the story of the ewe lamb (2 Sam. 12:1–7). He had every good thing, yet he turned from this to take by force what God had not given. The fall that happened in the garden at the beginning repeats over and over and is with us to this day.

Rejecting Yahweh's generosity, we cultivate a suspicion that God is holding out on us. Rather than rest in the security of God's peace, we risk and lose everything to try to become our own masters. We take what is not given. Succumbing to the seduction of the serpent, Adam and Eve steal and eat the fruit, and we all live with the consequences (Gen. 3:1–7). The problem involves not just what they take but whom they betray.

Adam and Eve did not appreciate that God's warning was genuine—he had their welfare in mind and wisely told them the truth about it. Eating the forbidden fruit, they rejected God's lordship, calling into question his character and snubbing his provision. Surprising as it may seem—surprising because we are not familiar with a holy God whose Word can always be trusted—this one act of disobedience led to the start of sin, pain, and death (Gen. 3:8–24).

One person's actions can transform the world—in this case the transformation produced destruction.[9] As Paul concludes, "it was through one individual that sin entered the world, and through sin, death; and in this way death passed through to the whole human race, inasmuch as everyone sinned" (Rom. 5:12).[10]

But sin was not merely the problem of our first parents, for it is our problem. Having eaten from the tree of knowing good and evil, humanity lost its innocence before God, before one another, and before the rest of creation. The garden was lost, along with our place of peace within it. We all now participate in this most basic sin, whether we want to admit it or not. As John R. Schneider says, "we all [now] have this desire somewhere within ourselves to be ridiculously tiny versions of God, answerable to none but ourselves."[11]

Shalom Compromised

G. K. Chesterton memorably argued that the idea of original sin is the one Christian doctrine for which we have undeniable empirical evidence.[12] Simply turning on the evening news or picking up the morning paper reminds us that this is far from a perfect world we are living in. Our world does not seem to reflect peace in any meaningful sense. We can try to ignore and deny the reality of our sin and its consequences, but at some point it comes crashing in from the outside and pouring out from the inside.

George Buttrick tells the story of a lecturer who spoke to a gathering of businessmen and displayed a large piece of white paper on which was a small black blot. "He asked what they saw. All answered, 'A blot.'" Of course, Buttrick admitted. "The test was unfair: it invited the wrong answer. Nevertheless," he pointed out, "there is an ingratitude in human nature by which we notice the black disfigurement and ignore the widespread mercy."[13]

We are broken and we live in a broken world. Shalom was the peace of God ruling the world he had created. So when sin entered the world, shalom was lost. This beautiful Hebrew word (*šālôm*) carries with it the idea of peace, not only as the absence of hostility, but of wholeness and harmony: in the shalom of Eden, people were made to live well with one another, with the earth, and under Yahweh.[14] This was an environment for total flourishing in every direction: here God was exalted, creation was enjoyed, and relationships were pleasurable. Neal Plantinga comments:

> But once we possess the concept of shalom, we are in position to enlarge and specify [the nature] of sin. God is, after all, not arbitrarily offended. God hates sin not just because it violates his law but, more substantively, because it violates shalom, because it breaks the peace, because it interferes with the way things are supposed to be. (Indeed, that is why God has laws against a good deal of sin.) God is for shalom and therefore against sin. In fact, we may safely describe evil as any spoiling of shalom, whether physically (e.g., by disease), morally, spiritually, or otherwise.[15]

From this height humanity fell, and we cannot help but grieve. No person alive today escapes the ravages of this plummet from wholeness to brokenness, from flourishing to fear, from peace to division.

Personal, social, and cosmic peace is elusive. There seems to be disharmony between people and the environment, oppression of citizens by governments, disunity among families and races, and fear etched onto so many faces. When examining the statistics and reports of the pain in this world, they can make us legitimately wonder about God, this universe, and our place in it.

Let us consider a few facts about the state of the world. The evidence about hunger, abuse, addiction, racism, and general injustice is disturbing, but undeniable. All of the following points do not necessarily directly relate to personal sin, but they all do clearly display the fallenness of our world.

- US children born poor have a 50 percent chance of staying poor and almost a two-thirds chance of remaining so if they are African American.[16]
- Addiction is one of the United States' biggest public health problems, costing $524 billion (including lost wages and costs to the public health care and criminal justice systems) each year.

The majority of the estimated twenty million alcoholics and drug addicts in America (and millions more compulsive gamblers, over-eaters, and sex addicts, if you accept an expanded understanding of addiction) never get help.[17]

- Nearly 8 percent of Americans are compulsive shoppers, carrying an average of $23,000 in debt (not including home mortgages).[18]
- Today 30.5 percent of the American public are obese.[19]
- Every day 24,000 people die from hunger and hunger-related causes throughout the world. Of those, 18,000 are children. One person dies of hunger every 3.6 seconds. That is more than 16 people each minute, or 1,000 each hour, which translates into 8,760,000 every single year. One in six people on the planet is hungry.
- World population is not the reason for starvation, contrary to what some might believe. Nearly one billion of the planet's six billion people are undernourished because of food-distribution problems, natural disasters, government policies, civil unrest, inequitable trade policies, lack of knowledge, and greed.[20]
- In 1994, in about 100 days, almost 1,000,000 people were murdered in the Rwandan genocide. Other genocides have occurred throughout history, and they continue even to this day.[21]

But statistics like this can be abstract. So just think about times in your life when you have known isolation, rejection, hurt, neglect, or abuse. Each of us has known and witnessed great sadness, and this is not just some statistic from a newspaper, but a reality in our lives. Loved ones we know live every day with the scars of their past, and those scars reflect the brokenness of this fallen world. Although we can still see signs of the goodness of creation around us, it is no longer merely "good." As Blaise Pascal once observed, "What can be seen on earth indicates neither total absence, nor the manifest presence of divinity, but the presence of a hidden God. Everything bears this stamp."[22] Something profound has been lost, and our vision has become clouded so that God's goodness is easily forgotten.

From Celebration to Grief, from Love to Fear

Although praise and celebration marked the creation, the fall into sin put a new song into the air. Rachel's haunting song of weeping for her children echoes the mourning song of creation as it experiences the fall (Jer. 31:15). Laughter has given way to lament.

Before the fall human labor was a blessing, but now it is a burden. Soil grows hard, animals become resistant, bodies move toward decay. Whereas originally everything made was good, now even the best things appear tainted.

Nudity represented our primitive parents' former freedom; with the fall they covered themselves, demonstrating their new awareness of the shame and guilt that stole over them. By rejecting God's lordship, Adam and Eve began to know a painful vulnerability, the fear of exposure, and the sting of violence. The changes were swift and pronounced: from truth to accusation, from harmony to fracture. Although creation was made in God's overflowing love, rebellion against the Creator plunged humanity into an ever-growing desire for mastery and a fear of the other.

By taking what God had forbidden (because it was deadly), our parents changed human nature and the world.

From Belonging to Bondage

At the mention of "sin," people often have one of two responses: either they quickly agree that they are not perfect, that they occasionally do "bad" things, and thus trivialize the idea of sin; or they think of sin only as the heinous actions that get newspaper headlines and exclude themselves from its grasp. Maybe we think of sin as an impolite word, a brief loss of temper, or the telling of a half-truth. But sin is much more extensive and deep than we care to admit.

Above all, sin is a form of bondage, a relentless grip that holds us under its power (Rom. 6:16). Al Wolters has an interesting way of reminding us of this reality:

> This link between "evil" and "enslavement" is very foreign to the modern mind because of our pride in human autonomy. Yet this association is obvious in the Scriptures and was accepted without question by Christians for many centuries. A curious and instructive relic of this earlier easy identification of evil and bondage is preserved in the Italian language. The common Italian word for "bad" or "evil" is *cattivo*, which is the direct descendent of the Latin *captivas* (*diaboli*), "captive (to the devil)."[23]

This derivation reflects a genuine understanding of the Bible's teaching that all sin is a form of spiritual slavery. Further, the effects of sin not only bind and enslave people, but all of creation as well.

Personal Bondage

At its most basic level the Bible teaches that bondage to sin is deeply personal. It is not only a cosmic or social reality that exists "out there," but also an inward imprisonment. As Jesus declares, "everyone who commits sin is a slave to sin" (John 8:34). German theologian Wolfhart Pannenberg explored the implications of this text in a way that might surprise our democratic ears:

> There is no natural freedom [according to the Bible], and making choices does not yet guarantee our freedom. In John 8, we have this conversation between Jesus and his Jewish partners who are proud of being freeborn and not slaves. Jesus tells them, "If you sin, you are a slave. You will be free when the Son makes you free."

Pannenberg goes on to explain:

> Christian proclamation should have criticized the Western ideology of freedom by telling the public that *having choices doesn't mean freedom*. The alcohol-addicted person or the drug-addicted person is also making choices. The problem is that he or she always makes the same choice—to take the drug or drink the bottle—again and again. *Having choices doesn't yet guarantee freedom.*[24]

Even though we don't sense that our freedom has been compromised, Jesus said that it has. Under sin's dominion this virus affects everything we do. In fact, it affects every aspect of who we are.

In the early church, St. Augustine spoke of sin as that which bends or curves us toward the ground, making us more like the beasts and less like the God whom we were to image. He speculated that we were created to have our heads and hearts raised toward Yahweh, and that sin is that which turns our gaze from him. Martin Luther picked up this imagery in the Reformation, arguing that sin actually bends or curves us upon ourselves (*homo incurvatus in se*). We were designed to embrace God and others, but instead we are now consumed with ourselves. Luther's protégé Philip Melanchthon described sin as the painful reality that the human heart turned in upon itself.[25]

These authors are all saying that the clearest result of human sin is the brokenness of the human heart. While humanity was once inclined toward the Creator, basking in his love and presence as they communed with him, now fallen people run from him and attempt to live apart from the Lord, away from the giver of all good gifts, the enabler, the source of light and life. The result is slavery, not freedom.

Sin affects us all, without exception. Anyone who has read William Golding's *Lord of the Flies* is familiar with the idea that even children will turn an island paradise into a land of chaos and fear. But this is not true just of boys left without parents. Even the most well-intentioned person or the self-controlled and responsible model citizen cannot escape the ravages of sin's grip.

Here we should clear up some common confusion about the nature of sin in people. When theologians speak of the "total depravity" of human nature, they certainly do *not* mean that a person is as bad as he or she can be. It is not that we do "terrible" things at every opportunity, but that the original harmony among God, humanity, and the earth no longer stands. Of course we might be much worse, as individuals and as a group.

"Total depravity" means that every aspect of our human person (our totality), including our mind, will, affections, and even our bodies, has been affected by the fall. This ruptures our relationship to God and others: we do not think as we ought, feel as we should, will as we might. Sin has distorted our judgments, twisted our affections, and confused our volitions, even damaging our physical bodies. We often wish to deny sin in ourselves, but every day we face the consequences of it, from the aches we feel in our joints to the frustrations we undergo with our teenagers to the jealousy that provokes us to undermine others. Anyone truly close to us, who knows us with our guard down, can testify to our brokenness. There is a sickness in our soul, and this sickness points back to our fall from belonging to bondage.

Social Bondage

Sin has compromised our shalom, as evidenced by the rampant injustice, anguish, greed, and sorrow that permeates our world. Many of these problems are bigger than merely private sins. Sometimes theologians speak about "structural sin," that is, sin that affects whole institutions and communities. For example, certain economic arrangements promote unjustified wealth for one group at the expense of another; this appears "reasonable" to those it benefits. Unfortunately, it is normally the global poor or those without a voice who suffer most under such arrangements. "Personal evil can be simultaneously strengthened and disguised by social relationships."[26] When everyone around us believes and lives as we do, we may be blind to our participation in (or suffering under) structural sin, but it is real nonetheless.

We often live in blissful ignorance or in denial of such structures. Ron Sider's assessment appears accurate:

> Christians frequently restrict ethics to a narrow class of "personal" sins. In a study of over fifteen hundred ministers, researchers discovered that theologically conservative pastors spoke out on sins such as drug abuse and sexual misconduct, but failed to preach about the sins of institutionalized racism and unjust economic structures that destroy just as many people.... In the twentieth century, evangelicals have become imbalanced in their stand against sin, expressing concern and moral outrage about individual sinful acts while ignoring, perhaps even participating in, evil social structures. But the Bible condemns both.[27]

Even if we do not directly participate in such structural sins, they nevertheless affect the world in which we live, and therefore we may not ignore it.

There is, perhaps, no more graphic example of structural sin and the bondage it promotes within human society than outright slavery itself. Not only is human slavery an evil of the past, it haunts our present as well. In fact, according to the U.S. Department of State, human trafficking is the third largest criminal enterprise in the world.[28] Sex trafficking in particular has become a booming global industry that enslaves thousands of women and children every year.

The International Justice Mission (IJM) tells the story of a fourteen-year-old girl named Panida from northern Thailand. After her father died and her mother contracted AIDS, Panida was tricked into accepting a well-paying job offer from a man who promised her a few months of work. But, as IJM tells the story:

> The man's intentions were never to give her a job. He instead took Panida through a border checkpoint into Malaysia, where he sold her to a local brothel owner. The brothel owner told Panida that he had paid an enormous sum for her, and that she must reimburse him by selling her body to the brothel's many customers. She was told that she would have to service five to 10 customers a night and that if she failed to meet her quota or refused customers, she would be beaten and abused.[29]

Panida was miraculously rescued through the efforts of IJM on the very night she was supposed to be raped for the first time. But tragically, thousands of women and children remain in this brutal form of bondage all around the world today.[30] We may wish to ignore such stories, but our neglect does not make them go away.

Relational Bondage

Sin affects every aspect of our society, our politics, and our homes. No human relationship is free from this corrosive power. Sin manifests itself in even the best of our associations. For this reason we intimately know disappointment, frustration, and struggle. Spouses manipulate each other; employers take unfair advantage of their employees; local sheriffs are caught laundering money; pastors are guilty of misusing their positions to prey on the vulnerable. Genuine friends can silently hope that their closest relations don't prosper beyond them.

Even joyful grandparents can distort their grandchildren's ability to love them as they spoil the children in order to receive a desired response. Exploring the complications of human relationships distorted by sin, Miroslav Volf has observed, "A man may shower a woman with gifts, but he may be doing it so that he can ingratiate himself to her, enjoy her, keep her, or even worse, so that he can display her as a trophy."[31]

Behind some of the most apparently loving relationships there lurks the threat of domination. This is because the desire to captivate and control others belongs to the essence of our fallen condition. It also helps explain the common human experience of fear and anxiety about our relationships. Not far under the surface, many of us face troubling questions about our place in this world. Are we genuinely loved? Are we truly secure with one another? "We all desire to be desired by the one we desire."[32] But we wonder how vulnerable we can be without facing rejection.

We need to be overwhelmed by the depth and passion of God's love, of his gift, of our belonging to him, before we can become freed to live in this broken world as agents of his grace and mercy. But his loving gift changes not merely us as individuals: it also invites us to seek changes for the world. Divine grace will move us from the individual to the relational, and then it will move us to address the social and structural bondage around us. This means we will ultimately become concerned not merely with our own sins, but with structural sin, with injustice and violence, with hunger and exploitation.

Creation's Bondage

When the Bible speaks about sin's intrusion into this world, it also describes the effects on the entire cosmos. Nothing in creation has gone untouched by the fall. Because of humanity's organic and representative relationship to the rest of creation, our plunge into sin has affected the entire world. From the cancer cells that infest our bodies to the giant tsunamis that strike unsuspecting coastal villages, the entire physical creation is now said to "groan" under this "bondage to decay" (Rom. 8:20–22).

Now, instead of enriching our worship of God, the world is abused, broken, and subject to "futility." If you could somehow hear the metal on the airplanes rushing toward the World Trade Center on 9/11, I believe you would hear it crying out, "Don't make me do this; I wasn't made for this." If we could hear the paper used in the pages of demeaning pornography, we would hear them crying out, "Please don't make me do this; I wasn't created for this." Creation feels the weight of sin, even when we do not.

In our fallen state, even beauty and delight are frequently discovered next to disturbance. A scientist once told his friend, artist Makoto Fujimura, that the autumn leaves are most beautiful on the trees by the roadside because they happen to be distressed by the salt and pollution. Upon reflection, Fujimura observes, "Every beauty suffers,"

> Every sunset is a reminder of the impending death of Nature herself. The minerals I use [to paint with] must be pulverized to bring out their beauty. The Japanese were right in associating beauty with death.[33]

Great artists can help us see this tension in the world. Not only can they confront us with the glories of creation, they can also show us the brokenness of it all: light alongside darkness, magnificence next to degradation, hope not so far from despair. The whole of creation, according to Scripture, is currently in "bondage to corruption" (Rom. 8:21). Thankfully, this groaning will not be the final word for the creation, and God will turn its mourning into singing. The trees and rocks will cry out, they will sing to God's praise, and this breathless heaving will not last forever. "He has torn us to pieces" says the prophet Hosea, "but he will heal us; he has injured us but he will bind up our wounds" (Hos 6:1 NIV).

Possessed by Our Possessions: A Sign of Bondage?

Of all the different examples of our lack of self-mastery, the love of money is perhaps the most powerful. Jesus himself even suggested that money is God's only real rival for our trust. "No one can serve two masters. . . . You cannot serve both God and Money" (Matt. 6:24 NIV). And the apostle Paul said that "people who want to get rich fall into temptation and a trap and into many foolish and harmful desires that plunge men into ruin and destruction" (1 Tim. 6:9 NIV).

The Bible abounds with stories that tell of the "ruin and destruction" that come as a result of the love of money. Most of us are familiar, for example, with the ancient cities of Sodom and Gomorrah, whose infamous wickedness led to fiery destruction. But how well do we remember exactly what sin roused God to rain down fire and brimstone? Often, Sodom and Gomorrah have been associated with all kinds of sexual perversion, of which they were certainly guilty (cf. Jude 7), but according to the prophet Ezekiel, this was not their primary problem. "Behold," the prophet says, "this was the guilt of your sister Sodom: she and her daughters had pride, excess of food, and prosperous ease, but did not aid the poor and needy" (Ezek. 16:49; cf. Isa. 1:10–17; Amos 4:11).

Or consider the "ruin and destruction" that came upon Achan and his entire household when he stole some of the consecrated spoils after the battle of Jericho (Josh. 7:1–26). Disaster fell on the house of King Ahab and Queen Jezebel not long after they conspired to steal Naboth's ancestral property (1 Kings 21:19). And notice how Ahab's life is described: "There was none who sold himself to do what was evil in the sight of the LORD like Ahab" (1 Kings 21:25; cf. v. 21). He was in bondage. Similarly, all the treasures and and even some of the children of Israel's royal family were carted off to Babylon because of King Hezekiah's pride in his possessions (Isa. 39:1–8).[34] And we cannot forget the story of Judas himself, who committed suicide after betraying Jesus for thirty pieces of silver (Matt. 26:14–16; 27:3–5).

Money has a peculiar power that can profoundly capture us, taking on a quasi-divine status and creating a sort of bondage. Saint Ambrose recognized this danger when he wrote, "Therefore possessions are so called that we may possess them, not they possess us. Why do you regard the master as a slave? Why do you invert the order?"[35]

The Old Testament has much to teach us about what it means to be locked into this insatiable love of money. "Whoever loves money never has money enough; whoever loves wealth is never satisfied with his income" (Eccl. 5:10 NIV). Luxuries have a strange way of becoming necessities. Our appetites expand as we grow increasingly accustomed to our own affluence. When was the last time our personal resources grew while our spending diminished? When we make more, we buy more—we "need" more.

We are consumed by our consumerism and possessed by our possessions. Our eyes and ears are held captive to a constant onslaught of advertising that fuels our passion to possess more and more things we don't really need so that we can impress more and more people we don't even like.[36] What is this if not a sign of bondage?

The Dawning of Darkness: Sin, Death, and the Devil

As I noted in chapter 1, the Heidelberg Catechism begins by proclaiming that our only comfort in life and in death is that we "belong—body and soul, in life and death—not to myself but to my faithful Savior Jesus Christ." What I haven't yet mentioned, however, is that as the answer proceeds it declares what "cost" God had to pay so that we may now "belong" to him. Only by the "cost" of Jesus' "own blood has [he] fully paid for all my sins and has completely *freed me from the dominion of the devil.*"[37] The second part of this book will speak of this hope of redemption, but for now it is important to acknowledge what that expectation includes. Humanity needs to be "freed ... from the dominion of the devil." This may sound medieval to some of us, but the Scriptures show us that we live in a fallen world, in a demonic darkness (Eph. 6:12).

Acknowledging the Power of Darkness

We can't really believe in a personal devil or demons anymore, can we? New Testament scholar Rudolf Bultmann (1884–1976) once claimed that since we live in an age with light bulbs, electricity, and the like, we simply cannot be expected to believe in things like Satan.[38]

I have grown suspicious of this kind of argument, believing it tells us more about Bultmann's modernist commitments than it does about the actual world in which we live. How could Bultmann make such a conclusion in the face of Hitler's atrocities, which slaughtered millions of Jews? Is it really so hard to believe in demonic forces when one looks at the endless wars that plague the world? What about the destructive racism that not only divides people by the color of their skin but by the identity of their tribe?

While the power of Satan may be hard for Bultmann to admit in the wake of twentieth-century modernity, it seems easily recognized by millions of people living in poverty, oppression, addiction, and fear. How often do we hear stories about "demonic activity" from people who live in Africa, Asia, the Middle East, and South America? Yet we in the West struggle to understand their experiences, their stories.[39] Is it really just a change in geography that makes people open to the idea of a demonic realm? Could the truth be that our denial of satanic activity says more about our spiritual state than about the actual nature of things?

Although almost half of all professing Christians in America today deny Satan's existence, the Bible teaches that there is an evil one who acts as the "god of this world" (2 Cor. 4:4), the "ruler of this world" (John 16:11), and "the prince of the power of the air" (Eph. 2:2).[40] His is a kingdom of darkness, so much identified with sin that we are even told that those who sin "belong" to him (John 8:44–47; 1 John 3:12). Like an invading army that uproots entire populations and carries them off into captivity, the enslaving effects of sin and Satan have attempted to rob God of the paradise he created (cf. Ps. 47:1–9; 83:18; Dan. 4:25–26; 5:21).[41]

Belonging to the Dark Side?

As important as it is to be mindful of the many different forms of bondage that have come as a result of the fall, we should not lose sight of how the Bible includes them all under what it calls the "domain of darkness" (Col. 1:13).[42] "For we do not wrestle," Paul says, "against flesh and blood, but against the rulers, against the authorities, against the cosmic powers over this present darkness, against the spiritual forces of evil in the heavenly places" (Eph. 6:12). This is a menacing matrix of evil that the New Testament presents as a kind of spiritual empire led by Satan. Scripture often portrays this activity in terms of darkness and blindness, from which we need deliverance (cf. Isa. 42:7; Luke 22:53; Acts 26:18;).

One of the reasons we have such a hard time embracing God's ownership as good news is that we don't understand the alternative. We may even think that resisting God's rule will make us *free*. But the story of humanity's turning from God shows that the only alternative to belonging to God is slavery to sin, death, and the devil. As much as the evil one would like for us to think otherwise, belonging to ourselves is not an option.[43] We will always belong to somebody. The only question is whom? Scripture reveals that freedom from God is enslavement to sin. The moment we threw off the cords of God's love was the instant in which the chains of Satan's dark kingdom snapped shut around our neck and ankles.

Conclusion: How Can God Get It All Back?

The good creation has fallen: it has turned on the Creator and rejected his lordship. We have moved from belonging to bondage. The claim that "God owns everything" has come under attack, been compromised, or contested, inasmuch as God's earthly kingdom has been supplanted and usurped. God's freely made world has been lost, plundered, and ransacked. Rather than worship Yahweh as the creator King, the world has found itself under a new diabolical prince who enslaves, terrorizes, confuses, and destroys.

While the Bible links creation's bondage to God's greater plan of redemption (Rom. 11:32), the Scriptures acknowledge that things are not as they're supposed to be. Something has gone wrong. Something precious has been lost (cf. Luke 13:34–35; John 8:47). For unlike God's heavenly throne room, where his holiness and glory are so overwhelming that creatures there honor him freely and without reserve, his earthly dominion is full of pretenders to his throne who plunder his possessions. He will redeem and reclaim his land, his creation, his people, but he will do it in a way that none would expect from a great King and Master.

We will begin to see in the next chapter that the story of God's life-giving ownership of creation, which began with the words "Let there be light ..." (Gen. 1:3), does not end with the dominion of darkness (Isa. 9:2, 4, 6–7; 42:7; Matt. 4:16). God, being rich in mercy, was unwilling to leave his creation in bondage and has reasserted his claim to creation in the person of Jesus Christ, "whom he appointed the heir of all things" (Heb. 1:2), though not in the way that we might think. If we are to recognize how God reclaims what was lost, we must turn our attention to exploring what the kingdom of God—and the King—is all about.

Make a joyful noise before the King, the LORD!
Let the sea roar, and all that fills it;
   the world and those who dwell in it!
Let the rivers clap their hands;
   let the hills sing for joy together
before the LORD, for he comes
   to judge the earth.
He will judge the world with righteousness,
   and the peoples with equity.

Psalm 98:6b – 9

For the LORD is our judge,
   the LORD is our lawgiver,
the LORD is our king;
   it is he who will save us.

Isaiah 33:22 NIV

There could never have been a stage of Israel's history when the kingdom of God was looked for apart from the coming of Yahweh.

George R. Beasley-Murray[1]

Modern scholarship is quite unanimous in the opinion that the Kingdom of God was the central message of Jesus.

George Eldon Ladd[2]

chapter three

The Coming
of the King

Recognizing the Messiah?

Early on in all four Gospels we read about a dusty prophet who not only ate locusts and honey but also baptized a young Jewish carpenter.[3] At first, John seemed hesitant to baptize Jesus, recognizing Jesus as his superior. John is such a fascinating figure. Even at this early date he proclaimed that this Nazarene is the "Lamb of God, who takes away the sin of the world!" (John 1:29).

Yet as the years passed, John appeared as a mixture of confusion and hope in regard to Jesus. During Herod's reign, the tetrarch imprisoned John because the prophet spoke out against aspects of the ruling family's immoral conduct (Matt. 14:3–4). While in prison John kept hearing reports about Jesus, and with the incoming news John's confusion and curiosity seemed to grow. Jesus was not acting as he expected the Messiah King to act.

This traveling preacher was not exactly the revolutionary force that some expected. Why wasn't Jesus encouraging a military uprising against the foreign presence that was occupying the holy land? Where was the Messiah's violent judgment that had been expected (cf. Ps. 2:6–12)? Where was the ax, the fire, and the winnowing fork John forewarned about (Matt. 3:10–12)? Yet John also knew that Jesus was working in some remarkable ways.

John finally sent his own disciples to ask Jesus this great resounding question: "Are you the one who is to come, or shall we look for another?"

(Matt. 11:3). In other words, John wanted to know if Jesus was really the Messiah, the King for whom he had prepared the way.

As was Jesus' common custom, he did not directly answer questions about his identity. In response to John's question if Jesus was "the one," Jesus gave what might appear to be a strange answer.

> Go and tell John what you hear and see: the blind receive their sight and the lame walk, lepers are cleansed and the deaf hear, and the dead are raised up, and the poor have good news preached to them. (Matt. 11:4–5).

In this response, Jesus was drawing from a few key passages of Isaiah, and thus he was linking his own identity with the ancient promises of God. Isaiah spoke of a day when the deaf would hear and the blind see (Isa. 29:18; 32:3–4), when the dead would live (26:19), and when "the eyes of the blind shall be opened, and the ears of the deaf unstopped; then shall the lame man leap like a deer, and the tongue of the mute sing for joy" (35:5–6). Similarly, Isaiah 61:1 is a messianic reference that identifies this coming one with the promise of good news brought to the poor. Consequently, Jesus' reply to John's question was an answer filled with depth, depth rooted in the Old Testament.

What might be missed from Jesus' careful answer to John, however, is that many of these references to the prophecy of Isaiah are located *directly in contexts in which warnings are also found*. In other words, the verses Jesus alluded to in Isaiah are often right next to God's promises to deal with iniquity, to bring punishment and "terrible recompense" on this coming "day of vengeance" (cf. Isa. 29:20; 34:4; 61:2). Such woeful judgments parallel what John had clearly expected as he preached next to the river Jordan, and thus the apparent lack of judgment on the part of Jesus understandably confused this prophet.

Jesus' response was subtle and yet fascinating. Through his answer Jesus indicated to John that he was indeed the Messiah and that John was not wrong to look to Isaiah for this confirmation. However, Jesus also pointed out that John's messianic expectations had neglected the other side of the promises, missing the "more positive expectation of restoration, good news and new life" that God would bring with the Messiah.[4]

What Is the Kingdom of God?

From the outset of his ministry, Jesus appears proclaiming, "The time is fulfilled, and the kingdom of God is at hand; repent and believe in the gospel" (Mark 1:15). But to appreciate the significance of this message and Jesus' relation to the kingdom of God, we must survey some terrain. Starting in the Old Testament and moving into Jesus' words and actions in the Gospels, we can begin to understand just how important and expansive this idea of the kingdom is and why it serves as necessary background for all else we will say in this book.

Old Testament Background

Although the exact words "kingdom of God" are not found in the Old Testament, the universal assumption is that Yahweh is the sovereign King who will "reign forever and ever" (Ex. 15:18). As the Creator, he ultimately rules over the whole world and all nations (Ps. 96:10; 97:1; 99:1). Since Yahweh dwelt among Israel in particular (cf. Deut. 33:5), they had a king among them (Num. 23:21), a king "who rides through the heavens to your help, through the skies in his majesty" (Deut. 33:26; cf. Ps. 93:1). This is no passive Lord.

Throughout the songs of Israel we hear this royal echo again and again. "The LORD, the Most High, is to be feared, a great king over all the earth" (Ps. 47:2), since "the LORD is king forever and ever" and his enthronement has no end (Ps. 10:16; 29:10b). Leading the worshipers of Israel, the sons of Korah would sing out to the "LORD of hosts, my King and my God" (Ps. 84:3). Although there were countless kings and competing territorial "gods," Israel affirmed Yahweh as "a great God, and a great King above all gods" (Ps. 95:3); the joyful noise from the trumpets declared the one true King, who is the Lord (Ps. 98:6).

With this background we can understand that Israel's problem in the early days before the monarchy was not that it had desired a "king," but that it wanted a "king like the other nations" (1 Sam. 8:5, 20; cf. 12:12). In this request Israel was denying Yahweh as their true and only Lord (8:7; 10:19). Yahweh had already included the promise to give a king in the most ancient of blessings (Gen. 17:16; 35:11; cf. 49:8–12), but one who would serve under his sovereignty.[5] In humility this king was to care for and protect his people (Ps. 72), memorizing God's law as he recognized that even he remained under the true King's rightful reign (Deut. 17:14–15, 18–20).

By way of contrast, when Israel demanded a king for themselves—"like the other nations"—Samuel warned of the tyranny such a rebellious request would bring by saying, "This is what the king who will reign over you will do: He will *take* your sons ... He will *take* your daughters ... He will *take* the best of your fields and vineyards ... and you yourselves will be his slaves" (1 Sam 8:11–17 NIV, emphasis added). Consequently the people would suffer through excessive taxes, the unending quest for military strength, and the danger of growing arrogance (Deut. 17:16–17, 20). Yet God, while remaining King of kings, could give Israel a good and faithful king as a *gift*, as he does with David. As M. J. Selman points out, "If God has a kingdom to give, then he too must have a kingship of his own, and one that is of a higher order."[6]

Thus, the assumption throughout the Old Testament was that Yahweh is the true King above all who are given authority to rule, and yet it was clear that (1) the world did not display a peaceful kingdom, and (2) his chosen people Israel had not lived faithfully under his rule.

So there is a tension within the Hebrew Scriptures: God is King, yet it seems hard to recognize his kingdom on earth as it is in heaven. Psalm 24 in its own way captures this apparent tension. "The earth is the LORD's and the fullness thereof, the world and those who dwell therein, for he has founded it upon the seas and established it upon the rivers" (vv. 1–2). This is *his* world. And yet, "Who shall ascend the hill of the LORD? And who shall stand in his holy place?" (v. 3).

The kingly line of Israel had proven unfaithful, as had God's chosen people. They had brought idolatry instead of equity, domination instead of deliverance, and God rejected their worship because of it (Isa. 1:10–17; 58). They did not have "clean hands" or a "pure heart"; but the promise remained that the one who had these would "receive blessing from the LORD and righteousness from the God of his salvation" (Ps. 24:4–5). Finally the psalm concludes with a mixture of expectation and confidence:

> Lift up your heads, O gates!
>> And be lifted up, O ancient doors,
>> that the King of glory may come in.
> Who is this King of glory?
>> The LORD, strong and mighty,
>> the LORD, mighty in battle!
> Lift up your heads, O gates!
>> And lift them up, O ancient doors,
>> that the King of glory may come in.
> Who is this King of glory?
>> The LORD of hosts,
>> he is the King of glory! (Ps. 24:7–10)

Who is the King of glory? What would it mean for him to rend the skies and come near? What would it look like for him to usher in his kingdom in the midst of the chaos, the fears, and the division of this present world? The songs in the book of Psalms that celebrate the king are like "royal robes," says Bruce Waltke. They are like the robes "with which Israel drapes each successive son of David at his coronation." But none of Israel's kings has shoulders broad enough to wear them. "The Psalter's giant robes hang loosely" until—in the fullness of time—King Jesus comes. "Here was a son of David with shoulders broad enough to wear the Psalter's magnificent robes."[7]

Such is the message we hear coming from John the Baptist, warning that the kingdom was at hand. Judgment loomed no doubt, for none—not even Israel—could escape God's call for justice and Torah obedience. John came warning, preparing the way. Jesus came announcing that it was now time, the judgment, the new ordering of things was here, and God's kingly rule was about to be manifested on earth as in heaven. Central to Jesus' entire life and teaching was the inauguration of his kingdom.

Judgment would come, and it was rightly associated with the Messiah King. But the great surprise would be Jesus' relationship to that judgment, for he would astonish all by being both the Judge and judged (Rom. 3:26). To know how this is possible, we must, like John, come to terms with Jesus' complete identity.

Signs of the Kingdom and the King

The idea that God is King of creation and Israel is not a new, first-century scheme. New Testament scholars almost universally agree that the central message of Jesus was the kingdom of God. So what is the big deal? Answer: "The most distinctive fact in Jesus' proclamation of the Kingdom was its present inbreaking in history in his own person and mission."[8]

Whether people recognized it or not, something new was happening: with the coming of the Son of God people were encountering the kingdom of God because they were encountering the King. Jesus was not starting a new religion: rather, we discover in him that the kingdom he proclaimed and embodied was an extension of Old Testament expectations actualized in and through this particular person. To borrow J. R. R. Tolkien's language in *The Lord of the Rings*, in the Gospels we learn of "the return of the King."

But it took eyes to see and ears to hear for a person to recognize Jesus as King. He did not look or act as worldly kings look and act (Matt. 20:25–28). Thus, throughout the Gospels we frequently discover the King and his kingdom as often both hidden and revealed, both veiled and unveiled. The pressing question arising was not *if* the King and his kingdom had come, but *"Are we worshiping the true King; are we in his kingdom?"*

Throughout the Gospels we discover that Jesus' very words and actions testify to these kingdom realities. To understand the importance of what Jesus said, we must look at what he did. To unpack the significance of Jesus' actions, we must listen to his words.[9] What becomes undeniable in his words and deeds is that he had a unique relationship to the kingdom of God. He came with matchless power and authority over nature, over the demonic, over sickness, and ultimately even over sin and death itself. Once the culmination of all of this became realized through Jesus' resurrection and ascension, the Spirit birthed the church, which then gave witness to the pulsating reality of the kingdom of God among its members.

Sometimes we can miss the obvious when it comes to Jesus. Probably as a combination of two millennia of repeating the stories as well as the lingering influence of "modernist" skeptical assumptions, we find it easy to overlook the significance of much of what is recorded about this man, especially in terms of his "mighty works" or "miracles."[10] These actions testify to his messianic identity and, consequently, to his unique position as the King.

These are the very things that are at the heart of Jesus' answer to John's question about whether he was the expected one. In these signs of the kingdom, we begin to feel the tension between the Lord of creation and a shattered and disturbed world. Just as we explored creation and fall in the previous two chapters, here in Jesus' words and deeds we see him never denying the chaos of this world, but we also see him reexerting God's reign over it in fresh ways. Let us begin with his power and authority over nature.

Nature. God alone created all things, the heavens and earth, and all that is contained therein. He alone is the Lord of nature. Therefore, it is remarkable that during Jesus' life and ministry we find him displaying power over nature in a way reserved for God alone. With Jesus we find a person who can walk on water (Mark 6:48–51), multiply scarce resources by creating food where there was little (Mark 6:35–44; 8:1–9; cf. Ps. 23:1; 72:6; Ezek. 34:25–31), even catching fish that were previously unresponsive (Luke 5:1–11; John 21:1–11). Such stories are well documented throughout the four Gospels. Let us look more closely at one example.

Jesus lies almost lifeless, asleep in the back of the disciples' boat in the midst of a life-threatening storm. Out at sea, losing hope of rescue, the disciples are full of fear and panic, so they hastily wake Jesus: "Save us, Lord; we are perishing" (Matt. 8:25). Remarkably, Jesus rises and, looking out at the violent waters and whipping winds, declares: "Peace! Be still!" (Mark 4:39). Notice, however, that Jesus is not speaking here to the frightened disciples, but to the natural elements that seem out of control. Once he spoke this "rebuke," we read that "the wind ceased, and there was a great calm" (Mark 4:39).

At this point we might assume that those in the boat would be full of celebration and laughter, but instead, we learn that they "were filled with great fear and said to one another, 'Who then is this, that even wind and sea obey him?" (Mark 4:41; cf. Matt. 8:27). This is no party trick; it frightens those present, for it is clear that this man has a power and authority over nature that displays God's majestic power through him, demonstrating the presence of God's sovereign reign.

When the violence of nature was calmed in this manner, it was a taste of the time when the chaotic sea, representing tribulation, death, and darkness, will no longer exist (Rev. 21:1) when the wolf and the lamb will sit together in peace under God's rule (Isa. 11:6; 65:25).[11] Only the King can rule and command his creation like this. As we have seen in the previous chapter, while all of God's creation belongs to the Lord, that relationship has been compromised and called into question, and thus Jesus' actions here must be viewed against that cosmic and historical background. Jesus was reclaiming what belongs to God.

Demonic realm. Stories of Jesus' mighty deeds over nature are almost always found next to the retelling of his clashes with the demonic. As we have already noted, whatever uneasiness we may have today in the Western world with the idea of Satan and a demonic realm, we must be careful that we do not vacate the biblical text of its clear assumptions that such realities exist, bringing violent hostility and pain. Jesus comes and confronts these very powers that oppose the good creator God. Jesus liberates people from being *possessed* by such harmful and controlling powers, freeing them in order that they might belong to God.[12]

Notice, for example, that right after Jesus begins his ministry and calls his first disciples, he encounters "a man with an unclean spirit" (Mark 1:23). Disturbed by this possessive spirit the man cries out, "What have you to do with us, Jesus of Nazareth? Have you come to destroy us? I know who you are—the Holy One of God" (1:24). As he did to the winds and sea, Jesus "rebukes" the spirit, demanding that the spirit free the man from his bondage. After a violent moment the spirit bursts out of the tormented man so that everyone is amazed, looking at one another and asking: "What is this? A new teaching with authority! He commands even the unclean spirits, and they obey him" (1:27).

Similarly, right after Jesus' calming of the storm, he heals another man with an unclean spirit. Here was a man so violent he could not be restrained, and his days and nights were filled with the heartbreaking rhythm of walking among the tombs, hurting himself with stones, and crying out in agony (see Mark 5:1–20). Upon seeing Jesus, the spirit (here identified as "Legion," claiming to be "many") recognizes the Nazarene as "the Son of the Most High God." Displaying his awesome authority now not only over nature but over the spiritual realm, Jesus sends the vicious spirits away into a herd of about two thousand pigs, who rush down a steep bank and into the sea. Consequently, the formerly hysterical man is now found "sitting there, clothed and in his right mind" (5:15).

What is the response of the townfolk? They do not rejoice or celebrate the way Jesus has just plundered Satan's dark kingdom, but instead they plead with him to leave! For as it turns out, this formerly contorted man is not the only one who had been "possessed." While he is now restored, standing there in his right mind, the herdmen of the swine show they are more worried about their investment in the pigs they have lost than the man who was saved. They remain possessed by their possessions (Acts 16:16–20).

Those who saw Jesus perform these mighty acts were also frightened because some part of them knew and understood that he did what only one uniquely empowered with God's kingly authority could do. This Spirit-empowered and anointed man was the one whom Satan himself had confronted, but over whom Satan could not gain control (Luke 4:1–12). Jesus' whole ministry unfolds as he displays dominion over the brokenness of this world and the evil powers that seem to control it. Jesus was reclaiming what belongs to God.

Sickness. We find Jesus consistently bringing health where there was sickness, such as to the hemorrhaging woman (Mark 5:25–34), the man with dropsy (Luke 14:1–4), and the ten with leprosy (Luke 17:11–19).[13] Yet these miracles were never merely shows of abstract power, for they always pointed to something—the kingdom that was breaking through, invading and changing the present world. These miracles pointed to the kingdom; ultimately, they pointed to the King.

Throughout the Gospels there is a running irony, especially highlighted in the gospel of John. Those with eyes, ears, and education in the Torah are not the people who tend to see, hear, and rightly understand Jesus as Lord. However, Jesus frees those with obvious disabilities to really see and hear him (e.g., Mark 7:31–37; 8:22–26).

John draws this irony out in detail when he describes the Pharisees pestering the beggar who was born blind in John 9. They keep asking how

Jesus had healed him and wanting more information about the healer's real identity; consequently this poor and uneducated man ends up giving a theological lesson to these teachers of the law—a lesson he seems to enjoy giving. He who was blind sees, and those with sight are clouded in darkness. It is this former blind man—not the religious scholars—who, having experienced Jesus' unique power, makes a remarkable confession: " 'Lord, I believe,' and he worshiped him" (John 9:38). Jesus then gives a cryptic response to the man: "For judgment I came into this world, that those who do not see may see, and those who see may become blind" (9:39). We need to linger a bit to consider the significance of Jesus' comment.

Jesus through his kingdom was turning everything upside down, or better, right side up. He was reversing the order of the fallen world; he was restoring dignity, hope, and the beauty of communion. He was unsettling the structures and values of this world that display a destructive quest for control and power and replacing them with ... himself.

God's judgment is coming, but we discover that it ultimately is placed on Jesus' shoulders for the sake of the world. This self-giving movement will be the great display of his power, of his authority, of his kingship. And it is because of this grace-filled movement that the kingdom will be understood as a gift. Only the poor, the needy, the blind, and the deaf can appreciate the new eyes they receive and the new ears they are given, which allow them in their poverty to embrace the King and enter his kingdom. They are brought into the kingdom not because of what they have, but because they recognize their need and receive the Gift.

Right after Jesus gives sight to a blind beggar named Bartimaeus (Mark 10:46–52), we read about his "triumphal entry" (11:1–11). The lowly spread out their cloaks on the road as Jesus rides by on a donkey, and they shout with kingly expectation, "Hosanna! Blessed is he who comes in the name of the Lord! Blessed is the coming kingdom of our father David! Hosanna in the highest!" (11:9–10).

The King has come. But notice that his kingly arrival into Jerusalem is not accompanied with military might, nor with the praise of the political and religious authorities, nor with the influence that attaches itself to riches. The Son of David rides a borrowed beast, a humble donkey that doesn't even belong to him (Mark 11:1–3). He rides a donkey, a symbol of peace, rather than a decorated horse, a symbol of military power.

Jesus is not a military commander, he is not a Roman official, and he is not an established religious power broker. The reality is that the King has come, and he has come to reveal and establish God's reign and rule over all things. The crowds seem to understand the kingly reference of his ride into Jerusalem, but they still misunderstand the kind of King he is. Here is the God of life "humble and mounted on a donkey" (Zech. 9:9), coming as the Son to begin the reversal of what went wrong with God's creation. Jesus is reclaiming what belongs to God.

Death and sin. What is both wonderful and frightening at the same time is the climax of Jesus' expression of love and lordship over all of this physical pain, demonic rage, and blinding human sin. Jesus shows his ultimate authority and power by facing death and sin head on, for they are the very enemies of humanity. This is anticipated even before Calvary.[14]

Not only could Jesus make the bleeding stop and feeble legs work, he could raise the dead.[15] Lazarus was Jesus' friend, and he deeply loved him. Sadly, Lazarus had grown sick and died; this is a real death, not a hypothetical one, for Lazarus's sister is worried about his decaying body starting to smell (John 11:39). What will Jesus do?

Jesus goes to his friend, now dead, and he goes in power, not in passivity. As Martha comes running to Jesus, she appears a tortured mixture of hope and painful disappointment, for she believed Jesus could have saved her brother if he had arrived earlier, but it was now too late. "Your brother will rise again" is Jesus' response (John 11:23). Then he acts and declares with alarming boldness what should shatter the popular illusion of Jesus as a mere moral teacher or a simple peasant preacher.

Jesus speaks and acts here as King. The King of the creation exerts his power over his fallen world, recapturing what had been taken from him. Jesus weeps before the tomb of Lazarus, for not only does he keenly feel the devastating reality of being faced with human death, but even more, he seems aware of all that this represents—the brokenness, the chaos, the pain, the sin that overshadowed God's good creation. Here is death, the great sign of the terror and consequence of this sin-drenched world. Jesus feels that, and he weeps; he weeps for his friend, he weeps for his world.

John Calvin is right when he comments here that "Christ does not approach the sepulcher as an idle spectator, but as a champion who prepares for a contest ... for the violent tyranny of death, which he had to conquer, is placed before his eyes."[16] Dead Lazarus responds; he rises; he lives. Jesus the King is ready for battle. We begin to see that Jesus has power even over death, representing his great power over sin itself. In coming chapters we will see more fully how God overcomes the realities of sin that not only condemn us, but also pollute us. For now, we should not miss that by facing death and sin, Jesus is reclaiming what belongs to God.

The poor. Before we leave our discussion of the kingdom of God, we need to take a particular look at Jesus' proclamation to the poor. We remember that Jesus concluded his answer to John's question if Jesus was "the one" by emphasizing that the poor were being evangelized (Matt. 11:5; Luke 7:22: *euangelizontai*). Why is this an important indication of Jesus' identity?

Throughout Jesus' ministry he consistently seemed to show a kind of partiality for the poor. From the beginning of the Gospels, starting with Mary's great song of faith (Luke 1:46–55), we discover Jesus linked with the humble, bringing satisfaction and hope to the poor. Along the same lines we find that the first sermon of Jesus recorded in Luke's gospel describes him standing up in the synagogue, reading from Isaiah 61:1–2:

> The Spirit of the Lord is upon me,
>> because he has anointed me
>>> to proclaim good news to the poor.
> He has sent me to proclaim liberty to the captives
>> and recovering of sight to the blind,
>>> to set at liberty those who are oppressed,
> to proclaim the year of the Lord's favor. (Luke 4:18–19)

After reading this messianic passage and capturing the attention of his hometown audience, Jesus declares, "Today this Scripture has been fulfilled in your hearing" (Luke 4:21). The crowd knows the implications of what he is declaring of himself, for they start to grow restless, arguing that this man from Nazareth, Joseph's son, should not make such claims about himself (4:22). Clearly Jesus is indicating that he is the Messiah, and this is clear enough that some want to kill him for it (4:28–29). For our purposes, we notice again the link between Jesus as Messiah King and the proclamation of good news to the poor. This was crucial to his messianic identity.

God has always been concerned for the poor. He demanded that his kings, who were meant to serve as his representatives, must be just and particularly concerned about the poor (Ps. 72:1–4, 12–14; Prov. 29:14; Isa. 11:4; Jer. 7:5; 22:1–4). When God was not feared, kings were unfaithful in this regard and faced God's severe displeasure (Isa. 1:10–17; 3:14; Jer. 22:1–30). When the nation of Israel failed to care for the poor, God's judgment was penetrating—their sacrifices became offensive to God; he would not listen to their prayers or delight in their appointed feasts (Isa. 1:10–17; 58:1–14).

But God's promise was that one day he would bring "health and heal-ing, and I will heal them and reveal to them abundance of prosperity and security" by restoring the fortunes of Judah and Israel (Jer. 33:6). The point is that there would be a time of restoration, but this restoration could only come from God. This is the God who gathers "the outcasts of Israel," "heals the brokenhearted," and "binds up their wounds" (Ps. 147:2–3).

Psalm 146 provides a model for the expectation shared among God's people who had suffered so much, including poverty, exile, and humilia-tion. Believers were warned about putting their trust in princes who could not bring salvation; instead, they should put their hope in God, who made all of creation, who "executes justice for the oppressed, [and] who gives food to the hungry"(Ps. 146:7). Since this was a song regularly sung and memo-rized by first-century Jews, the concluding stanzas reverberate with Jesus' preaching and ministry, concluding with a focus on the marginalized:

> The LORD sets the prisoners free;
>> the LORD opens the eyes of the blind.
> The LORD lifts up those who are bowed down;
>> the LORD loves the righteous.
> The LORD watches over the sojourners;
>> he upholds the widow and the fatherless,
>> but the way of the wicked he brings to ruin. (Ps. 146:7b–9)

Throughout the Scriptures it is abundantly clear: God opposes the proud but gives grace to the humble (e.g., Ps. 34:18; Prov. 3:34; James 4:6–10). God honors the poor and meek as they put their trust in him despite the pain they experience in this world. He is near them. Those who take the position of genuine humility (whatever their social status), are promised that God intimately hears their prayers (1 Kings 8:48–49; Ps. 51:17; 86:1; Dan. 9:16–23)

Jesus' entire life and ministry embodied the good news to the poor. While often the hard-hearted leaders did not believe, Jesus was well received by the unclean, the disenfranchised, foreigners, the marginalized, women, or children, and these groups often possessed profound faith in Jesus and his Father (Matt. 8:8–10; 9:2, 22, 28–29; 15:28; etc.). While saying that the poor are blessed for theirs is the kingdom of God, Jesus subsequently flipped the coin and offered a "woe" to the rich who find their "consolation" in their wealth rather than in God (Luke 6:20, 24).

Yet this message of good news that Jesus proclaimed to the poor was not restricted to the financially distraught. Even those who have means may be considered "poor" if they truly recognize their great need and dependence on God's grace. In this way, Jesus makes it clear that all sinners are indeed poor—even if not materially so (cf. Luke 6:20/Matt. 5:3).

What is required of all, but often much harder for the wealthy, is to accept one's poverty and reach out to Jesus as the true Lord of all things (Matt. 19:16–30/Luke 18:18–30). But as the example of Zacchaeus makes clear, the good news of Jesus can free a wealthy man from the bondage of earthly treasures as he experiences God's salvation. For, as Jesus says, "With man this is impossible, but not with God; all things are possible with God" (Mark 10:27 NIV). The "Son of Man came to seek and to save the lost" (Luke 19:10), and Jesus' message and actions bring vindication to those who, despite their smallness in the sight of the world, cling to God in faith (Luke 16:25). As he reaches out to the poor, Jesus is reclaiming what belongs to God.

No Longer Doubt the King

This chapter began with John the Baptist sending a question to Jesus, "Are you the one?" I want to conclude by noticing something in Matthew's rendering of this same exchange between Jesus and John. When Matthew retells this episode in his gospel, he does something unusual in his writing—he explicitly refers to Jesus as "the Christ [Messiah]" (Matt. 11:2). In so doing, Matthew is reminding his readers that although John had doubted Jesus' identity in the middle of his ministry, "from Matthew's perspective the time for doubt had passed."[17]

In Jesus' ministry we begin to get a glimpse of the vastness of his kingly authority. Here is one who displayed the signs of ushering in the coming kingdom of God: he healed the blind, cleansed the leapers, raised the dead, and proclaimed the good news to the poor.

Now the truth is clear and must be believed by Matthew's readers—Jesus is the Messiah, the Son of God, as the culmination of his words and works make clear. This is why it makes sense that although John was the greatest of prophets, even the least of those who live in the kingdom of God are greater than John (Matt. 11:11//Luke 7:28; cf. John 5:36). John stood at the hinge of time, on the very edge as the kingdom of God was breaking in. He prepared the way, and just before his beheading he began to realize that the kingdom of God was coming in a way that defied all expectations.

What Went Wrong?

Nathan was a prophet, and he confronted the great king David about his complete moral failure in forcing Bathsheba into adultery with him, having her husband Uriah murdered, and wrongfully using Joab to accomplish this. David was drawn in by the story of the ewe lamb and ended up pronouncing proper judgment upon himself.

He rightly acknowledged that the penalty must be severe but did not realize until the last moment that he had sentenced the king, and so himself, to death. Like Adam and Eve before him, David took what was not given and the results were calamitous.

This world, God's world, is a mess. Every day the fall darkens everything. God gave his creation everything it needed, but it chose to take the one thing that was not given. One would think that in order to fix this God should take something back. He doesn't. Instead, he gives even more away. In fact, he gives everything away.

part two

God Reclaims All by Giving All: Son, Spirit, and Kingdom

The Vineyard Owner
How Will God Get Back What Was Lost?

"HEAR ANOTHER PARABLE. There was a master of a house who planted a vineyard and put a fence around it and dug a winepress in it and built a tower and leased it to tenants, and went into another country. When the season for fruit drew near, he sent his servants to the tenants to get his fruit. And the tenants took his servants and beat one, killed another, and stoned another. Again he sent other servants, more than the first. And they did the same to them. Finally he sent his son to them, saying, 'They will respect my son.' But when the tenants saw the son, they said to themselves, 'This is the heir. Come, let us kill him and have his inheritance.' And they took him and threw him out of the vineyard and killed him. When therefore the owner of the vineyard comes, what will he do to those tenants?" They said to him, "He will put those wretches to a miserable death and let out the vineyard to other tenants who will give him the fruits in their seasons."

Jesus said to them, "Have you never read in the Scriptures:

" 'The stone that the builders rejected
   has become the cornerstone;
this was the Lord's doing,
   and it is marvelous in our eyes'?

Therefore I tell you, the kingdom of God will be taken away from you and given to a people producing its fruits. And the one who falls on this stone will be broken to pieces; and when it falls on anyone, it will crush him."

Matthew 21:33–44

And this is the testimony: God has given us eternal life, and this life is in his Son.

1 John 5:11 NIV

Rings and jewels are not gifts, but apologies for gifts. The only gift is a portion of thyself. Thou must bleed for me.

Ralph Waldo Emerson[1]

But there is a great difference between Adam's sin and God's gracious gift. For the sin of this one man, Adam, brought death to many. But even greater is God's wonderful grace and his gift of forgiveness to many through this other man, Jesus Christ.

Romans 5:15 NLT

He who did not spare his own Son but gave him up for us all, how will he not also with him graciously give us all things?

Romans 8:32

God stretched out His hands on the Cross, that He might embrace the ends of the world; for this Golgotha is the very center of the earth.

Cyril of Jerusalem, A.D. 347[2]

Save me, for I am yours.

Psalm 119:94 NIV

chapter four

The Gift of the Son

Render to Caesar . . .

In an effort to trap Jesus and draw him into political turmoil, the Pharisees sent some of their disciples to question him. Knowing that people often lower their guard in the face of flattery, they approached Jesus with a compliment and then a question:

> "Teacher, we know that you are true and teach the way of God truthfully, and you do not care about anyone's opinion, for you are not swayed by appearances. Tell us, then, what you think. Is it lawful to pay taxes to Caesar, or not?" (Matt. 22:16b–17).

But Jesus saw right through them. "Why put me to the test, you hypocrites? Show me the coin for the tax" (Matt. 22:18b–19a). They then brought him a denarius, a coin representing the common laborer's payment for a full day's work. Jesus took the coin and held it up for all to inspect. "Whose likeness and inscription is this?" Since an image of the Roman ruler, the emperor himself, was emblazoned on all of the state coins, they quickly responded: "Caesar's." Jesus replied: "Therefore render to Caesar the things that are Caesar's, and to God the things that are God's." Jesus' enemies marveled at his answer and left (vv. 21–22). But a question lingers: What is it that is so strange, so provocative about his answer?

While this passage has often been used as a proof text for paying taxes and honoring the civil government, this is far from what Jesus was actually emphasizing. He wasn't simply talking about taxes, and his answer extends well beyond politics. What he was claiming is revolutionary.

On the coin was the image of Caesar. And the language Jesus used here for "image" is *eikōn*, from which we get the English word "icon." In a word, Jesus was able to take us back to the garden, back to the beginning, back to Adam and Eve. The denarius coin might have been made in the emperor's image. But Adam and Eve were "minted" in God's image and likeness—all human beings (including Caesar) have been made as icons of God, imaging the Creator and serving as his representatives in the world.[3]

It is as if Jesus were standing by a lake or mirror, and as he pointed to the people's reflection he declared, "Render to Caesar the things that are Caesar's, and to God the things that are God's." Caesar may seem as if he demands a lot with his taxes, but Jesus' reply powerfully points us back to the Creator himself, from whom all things have come. Jesus makes it clear that God is not merely interested in our wallets, he wants all of us because he is the Creator of all. Since we are made in God's image—since we are imprinted with the image of God—we should render *everything* we have, our very selves, to him.

But who has given everything to God? Who has lived a life poured out for others with a pure heart, upheld justice and righteousness, avoided sin completely, both publicly and privately? Who has loved God with their whole heart, soul, strength, and mind? Who has consistently loved neighbor as oneself? We owe what we cannot pay, discarding what we should love and diminishing what we should exalt. Thus, we find ourselves left with the age-old question posed by Jesus himself when he asked, "What shall a man give in return for his soul?" (Matt. 16:26).

Our problem is *not* that we have neglected and offended Caesar; our problem is that we have neglected and offended the Creator. We have not "rendered to God" what is his due. Instead, we have rejected his love, his gifts, his calling. We have not rebelled against Caesar—we have rebelled against God!

Thus, we find a theme or a question running throughout the Bible as a whole that asks: Insofar as God's possessions have been plundered as a result of humanity's fall in sin and bondage, how is God going to get everything back? How is humanity to be forgiven their debts and be restored to all the blessings of belonging? In short, how is God going to reclaim *full* ownership over everything?

Here we encounter the unspoken paradox of Jesus' encounter with the Pharisees. For only Jesus is able "to render to God the things that are

God's." Only he can give what is required in exchange for our lives. Thus, as he offers himself, he offers himself as a substitute for us, in our place. The paradox of Jesus' response here is that we owe everything to God but we cannot give it, so God himself will give what he demands. This will be God's great gift to the world: himself.

God's Great Gift to the World

In the most familiar verse in the entire Bible, we read a sentence that is now so common we can miss the dramatic nature of what is said. In this verse we discover something radical about who God is and how he works. Here we face the nature of God's plan to restore his fallen world, to bring it back into his warm embrace, and to free it from the powers of sin, death, and the devil. But what we discover in this verse is that the way God brings redemption is, at its most basic level, by giving a gift, the Gift. Listen afresh to John 3:16:

> For God so loved the world, that he gave his only Son, that whoever believes in him should not perish but have eternal life.

Here at last we discover the grand contradiction that God reclaims everything by giving everything away. Rather than tearing his possessions from his enemies' hands, he bestows even more on us so that we might not "perish." But to fully appreciate the radical nature of God's act of love, we must first remind ourselves of what is meant by this reference to "the world."

Who Is the "World"?

We must keep in mind that in John's writings "world" (*kosmos*) is not normally a reference to this planet or creation in general, although there is no doubt God loves everything he has made. But according to John the "world" represents people *in their fierce opposition and hostility to God*. Elsewhere John describes the "world" as those who "hate" Christ (John 7:7). If the world hates you, Jesus says, remember that they "hated me first" (John 15:18). In other words, the world represents us in our rebellion against God, a revolt going all the way back to humanity's original fall from God in the garden.

Given the nature of what the "world" represents, it makes sense that elsewhere in the New Testament believers are warned not to "love the world" (1 John 2:15). We cannot love enmity with God. Similarly, Christians are to make sure we are *not* "conformed to this world" (Rom. 12:2). We are not to be like the world *in its opposition to God*. Nevertheless, hatred for people, even in their rebellion against God, is not what we discover modeled in the gospel. God's people are consistently called to love even our enemies (Matt. 5:44; Luke 6:27 – 36).

Rather than becoming like the world in its opposition to God, believers are called to imitate God's love for the rebellious world, a love that seeks to draw people back to a loving communion with the Creator. Thus, in 1 John 2:15 we are told not to love the world, but John goes on to explain this "love" is characterized by a selfish desire for "the things in the world," such as "pride in possessions" (1 John 2:15 – 16). And that means it is a twisted love, focused on self rather than the other. But this is not how God loves the world in John 3:16, where God *gives*. The kind of love that must be rejected is the *exact opposite* of God's love for the world: God's love gives, a worldly love takes.

The Son Is Given

When we read that God "so [*houtōs*] loved the world, that he gave his only Son," the point is essentially the *manner* and the *intensity* of God's love for the world. He loved us *this much* and in *this way*.[4] The emphasis is therefore on the exceedingly great means by which God has brought about our salvation.

In Genesis 22 we read a troubling story, in which God tests his servant Abraham by calling him to offer his son as a sacrifice.[5] God commands Abraham to give up his only son Isaac, whom he loves. But just as the agonizing event is about to be completed, we hear a voice from heaven: "Do not lay your hand on the boy or do anything to him" (Gen. 22:12). Abraham notices a ram in a nearby thicket and Isaac is spared. We can finally breathe again.

We are then taken back to the earlier words of faith that Abraham spoke to Isaac before they arrived at the site of the sacrifice — maybe with great trepidation in his voice — as he promised his son, "God will provide for himself the lamb for a burnt offering, my son" (Gen. 22:8). And now we understand, but we lose our breath again. The ram in the thicket ultimately pointed forward to the true Lamb, the full and final offering. Yet here we realize that there is no substitute for the gift of God's Son. This is important because the New Testament consistently interprets both God's love and Jesus' death in terms of this sacrificial gift that is given.[6] This is how God loves: *he gives*.[7] And what does he give? Himself.

Out of his love for a broken and defiant world, God gives. He gives this gift. It's a little strange. Don't we normally give gifts to celebrate an achievement or to mark a joyous occasion, such as a birthday, anniversary, graduation, or something along those lines? Occasionally we give a gift after a misdeed, as when a man sends flowers to a woman as a peace offering for some failing on his part.

But here, the innocent and offended party is the one who gives the gift: God has done nothing wrong, nor have we achieved anything worth celebrating. God looks at his rebellious creation, defined by its resistance to him, and what does he do? He gives a gift, *the Gift.*

A Gift, Like a Jewel

Historically, Christian theologians have long recognized that while there is but one gift of the Son, this gift and the atonement it accomplishes is like a multifaceted jewel. Thoughtful Bible readers will notice, for example, that what Jesus accomplished by giving himself up "for us" on the cross is described in an extraordinary variety of different ways, using different language, imagery, and metaphors. In fact, biblically speaking, we can talk about the gift of the Son with different imagery:

- Reconciliation (Rom. 5:10; 11:15; 2 Cor. 5:18–21, etc.)
- Sacrifice (Matt. 26:28; 1 Cor. 5:7; 6:20; 7:23; Eph. 5:2; 1 Peter 1:18–19; Heb. 7:27; 9:14, 26: 10:12; Rev. 5:9)
- Redemption (purchase) (Matt. 20:28; Acts 20:28; Rom. 3:24; 1 Cor. 1:30; Gal. 3:13; Eph. 1:14; 1 Tim. 2:6; Titus 2:14; Heb. 9:12, 15; 1 Peter 1:18–19; Rev. 5:9)
- Justification (law court) (Isa. 53:11–12; Rom. 3:24; 8:1; Gal. 3:13; 2 Cor. 5:21; Heb. 9:28; 1 Peter 2:24)
- Propitiation—turning away God's wrath (Rom. 3:25; Heb. 2:17; 1 John 2:2; 4:10)
- Christus Victor—Christ portrayed as a great victor over the enemies of God (1 Cor. 15:54–57; Gal. 1:4; Col. 1:13; 2:15; Heb. 2:10).

To summarize, then, the gift of the Son is like a multifaceted jewel. Turn over this gift, as it is revealed in the pages of the Bible, and you will find that it is much like turning over a loose diamond in your hand. No sooner will you see light shine from one angle than a flash will illumine the next.

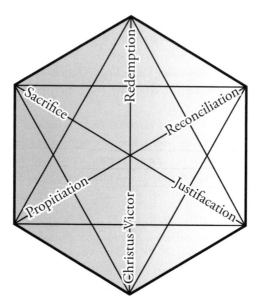

The Multi-Faceted Gift of the Son[8]

The various planes of the image display the superabundant, saving significance of a single gift. For, as Kevin Vanhoozer has rightly said, "the atonement ultimately concerns God's self-giving."[9] To receive this one gift of God in his Son is, therefore, to receive a gift of infinite blessing and benefit. Many other aspects of the atonement could be listed, but the illustration helps make clear just how exceedingly precious the gift really is — accomplishing "such a great salvation." Unfortunately, it is not possible to explore every surface here. For now, we simply turn to look at one plane more closely — the idea of purchase or "redemption."

Redeemed by God

The gift of Christ as our Redeemer makes sense of the apparent contradiction that God takes everything back by giving everything away. Paradoxical as it may seem, this is essentially the story of redemption — *God reclaims ownership by paying an exorbitant price for what was already his.*

Recognizing Who Was on the Cross

Out of his love for the world the Father sends the Son by the Spirit to become one with us. The Son of God — God himself — becomes a man.

He does not cease to be what he was, but he becomes what he was not. The God who made everything somehow inhabits his creation and as a man becomes a creature. Fourth-century author Chromatius, commenting on how a few mysterious "wise men" (magi) recognized and worshiped this child from the beginning, lays out the paradox:

> A boy he is, but it is God who is adored. How inexpressible is the mystery of his divine honor! The invisible and eternal nature did not hesitate to take on the weaknesses of the flesh on our behalf. The Son of God, who is God of the universe, is born a human being in the flesh. He permits himself to be placed in a manger, and the heavens are within the manger. He is kept in a cradle, a cradle that the world cannot hold. He is heard in the voice of a crying infant.[10]

There is no stronger affirmation of God's love for fallen humanity than his willingness to become human. Yet Christians do not believe that we merely had a visitation from the gods, but that in Jesus of Nazareth we encounter the true and living God, and he looks back at us through human eyes. And this man, who is none other than God himself, comes with the most scandalous mission—he comes to suffer and die!

Melito of Sardis preached one of the earliest Christian sermons we have recorded outside of the Bible. In this Passover sermon Melito considers the gravity of the idea that Jesus, the Son of God, suffers and dies on the cross. Imagine hearing Melito passionately proclaim these words in the early second century. He asks his congregation who it was that died on the cross:

> Who was it? It is a heavy thing to say, and a most fearful thing to refrain from saying. But listen, as you tremble in the face of him on whose account the earth trembled. He who hung the earth in place is hanged. He who fixed the heavens in place is fixed in place.... Though the people did not tremble, the earth trembled. Though the people were not afraid, the heavens were afraid.[11]

Christians proclaim the unthinkable. We believe that God became a man, the man Jesus Christ. God, who cannot suffer and die, becomes a man so that he can do the incomprehensible: the God-man dies.[12] In his Son Jesus Christ, the God of life and holiness faces the reality of death and sin. What kind of God are we talking about here? He becomes a man not merely so that we might better understand his teachings, but that he might bring reconciliation. He dies that he might overcome sin and death.

Why the Cross Is Necessary

Jesus the Son of God did not merely live in this fallen world in order to show solidarity with us, but he was willing to suffer and face death so that we might experience true healing and life.

> For while we were still weak, at the right time Christ died for the ungodly. For one will scarcely die for a righeous person — though perhaps for a good person one would dare even to die — but God shows his love for us in that while we were still sinners, Christ died for us. (Rom. 5:6 – 8)

He was willing to exchange his own life for ours.

But why was the cross necessary in the first place? Two words are the basis of any full response: *holy love*. A different way of putting it would be *holy generosity*. Although we cannot explore this fully here, a few points are necessary.

God in his righteous love and generosity could not simply turn a blind eye to sin without compromising his character. In fact, we make a great mistake — though understandable — when we pit God's love against God's justice. In much of Western culture, including in the church, we seem to value the idea of love far more than justice, probably because we are often able to take a great deal of justice and the rule of law for granted. That is, until we are treated unfairly by the police or corruption infiltrates our courts. But if you consider another culture or a minority group that commonly experiences the cruel effects of injustice, you will find people longing for justice (e.g., atrocities of Nazi Germany, the massacre of Tiananmen Square, rape of women and children, the genocide in Rwanda, etc).

In Scripture, we find that God is both loving and just. Neither attribute of God may be compromised, for God's is a holy love and a wise justice. Sin evokes God's just wrath, and the real nightmare would be if it didn't. The light of his character cannot cease to pierce the darkness anymore than the sun can cease to shine.

Nineteenth-century author and famed hymnist Horatius Bonar explained the fundamental importance of this point when he asked:

> Which is the more unchangeable and irreversible, the vow of pity or the oath of justice? Law and love must be *reconciled*.... The one cannot give way to the other. Both must stand, else the pillars of the universe will be shaken.[13]

God cannot look at wickedness and call it good.[14] To do so would compromise his identity. God cannot be unloving; neither can he be unjust. He cannot deny himself.

Scottish theologian P. T. Forsyth (1848–1921) had been trained in and was initially sympathetic with the leading theology of his day, which had rejected the classic confession of divine wrath against sin. He had been taught that Jesus' cross was a powerful moral example for us, but it meant nothing in terms of dealing with human sin against a holy God and his good creation. To say the cross dealt with divine justice and wrath was to make God sound angry and unloving. Since Jesus represents God's love, clearly we cannot speak of God's wrath, can we?

Forsyth came to reject that view. While it sounded appealing on the surface, he was convinced that by neglecting the reality of divine justice, we undermine God's love, not enhance it. "Do not think of God's judgment," Forsyth wrote, "as an arbitrary infliction, but as the necessary reaction to sin in a holy God. There alone do we have the divine necessity of the cross in a sinful world—the moral necessity of judgment."[15] You cannot compromise God's justice while commending his love, for the true value of God's love can only be understood *in relation* to his justice. And this relationship between God's love and justice is essentially embodied in the cross. In Christ crucified we perfectly encounter God's holy love, his holy generosity.

Our plunge into death is overcome only by the life of God in Jesus Christ. By the life, death, and resurrection of Jesus, God overcomes the darkness of sin, maintains his justice, and expresses his love. This takes us to the heart of the gospel.

Purchased by Christ

John Stott reminds us that to speak of Christ's death for others must be understood against this backdrop of divine giving: "On the human level, Judas gave [Jesus] up to the priests, who gave him up to Pilate, who gave him up to the soldiers, who crucified him. But on the divine level, the Father gave him up, and he gave himself up, to die for us."[16] This "giving up" is what is at the heart of redemption.

The concept of redemption is rooted in the ancient practice of reclaiming slaves, prisoners, exiles, and property upon the payment of a sum. Biblically, the idea of "redemption" (*lytroō*) comes from the word family for "ransom" (*lytron*). Leon Morris makes the compelling case that the language of payment is undeniable in reference to the biblical notion for how God secures our release.[17]

As difficult as it might be for our modern sensibilities, the idea of God purchasing us by and through the gift of Jesus is hard to avoid when reading the New Testament. A few examples will suffice. The new hymn to be sung by the heavenly community before the Lamb emphasizes this language of redemption:

> Worthy are you to take the scroll
> and to open its seals,
> for you were slain, and with your blood
> you ransomed people for God
> from every tribe and language and people and nation. (Rev. 5:9)

Likewise Paul reminds believers that "you were bought with a price" (1 Cor. 6:20). In fact, Scripture does not shy away from the idea that by Christ's death he has ransomed us for God (Matt. 20:28; 1 Tim. 2:6; 1 Peter 1:18–21). Jesus makes this utterly clear when he shows the focus of his mission: "For even the Son of Man came not to be served but to serve, and to give his life as a ransom for many" (Mark 10:45). He willingly exchanged his life for ours. There is no getting away from the fact that redemption language and imagery are prominent in Scripture and early Christian writings.[18]

Yet for us today, the idea of being "purchased" doesn't make a lot of sense. We are happy to receive, but we don't want to be bought.[19] How can we speak of being redeemed for a "price" and not end up reducing the gospel to a mere business transaction? And who is being paid, anyhow? Understandably, the whole thing simply rubs us the wrong way. Yet might there be some forgotten truths within these biblical images that we need to reconsider?

In the New Testament, Christ's redeeming work often points toward two foundational promises. First, Jesus offered himself up for us to rescue us from bondage to sin, death, and the devil. Second, as Redeemer, the Son purchased us for God and brought us back into the security of all that is *his own.*

The Gift of Belonging to God

All of God's gifts to us in the gospel are gifts of belonging—gifts we receive and experience in terms of belonging to God. God's grace does not primarily consist in any *thing* we can hold in our hands, but in whose hands we are held. While we experience God's grace in countless ways, we should keep in mind that his grace is grounded upon our belonging to God. Accordingly we pray "save me," with the psalmist, for "I am yours" (Ps. 119:94).

The dynamics of this relationship of belonging extend beyond anything we might possibly "possess." God's grace is not something we take hold of. Grace takes hold of us. As Paul says in Romans 14:7–9:

> For none of us lives to himself alone and none of us dies to himself alone. For if we live, we live to the Lord; and if we die, we die to the Lord. So, whether we live or die, we belong to the Lord.
>
> For this very reason, Christ died and returned to life so that he might be the Lord of both the dead and the living.

Jesus died and was raised so that we might belong to him. As long as we remain outside of Christ, all the benefits of what he has suffered are of no value to us.[20] But those who are "in Christ" by his Spirit find their identity in belonging to God. "Or do you not know that your body is a temple of the Holy Spirit within you, whom you have from God? You are not your own" (1 Cor. 6:19).

Paradoxically, it is only in belonging to the Lord who bought us that we can possess anything ourselves. As Paul says in 1 Corinthians 3:21–23: "All things are yours ... and you are Christ's, and Christ is God's."[21] Notice the connections here: because we belong to Christ, and Christ is God's, everything changes. We belong to the Creator of the universe, and thus we belong to the one who provides in all ways. Belonging to God "in Christ" is the key that gives us access to all that is his. "So let no one boast in men. For all things are yours, whether Paul or Apollos or Cephas [ministers of the gospel] or the world or life or death or the present or the future—all are yours" because you belong to Christ (1 Cor. 3:21–22). The redeemed belong to Christ because he offered himself in our place.

Becoming God's Slaves

Once redeemed by God we are no longer described as slaves to sin, but surprisingly we are still described as "slaves." Paul concludes that "having been set free from sin, [we] have become slaves of righteousness" (Rom. 6:18–19). Later he describes believers as "slaves of God" (6:22). By itself, the illustration of slavery is an inadequate representation of what it means to belong to God. In fact, Paul himself seems to recognize this when he admits that he put this "in human terms" (6:19). This is why the Bible uses such a vast array of imagery to get at this single point, like multiple facets on a diamonds reveal its full brilliance. While slavery is a good image in the sense that it suggests God's full lordship and our complete submission, it is also undesirable and problematic because of the harshness it suggests.

While the language of "slavery" simply sounds offensive to us, we must remember that it is because we think of it in terms of evil masters who abuse power and position. "In one sense a slave is not free," writes biblical scholar Anthony Thiselton, "but in another sense the slave who has been granted privileges can enjoy all the resources of his master's property and all the protection of his master's care."[22] This is part of the historical context. Let's be clear: no fallen person could ever be a "good" slave owner—there can be no defense, for example, for the heinous history of American slavery or contemporary forms of slavery today, with all of their evils. Yet, we learn that being slaves of God is the very way we discover genuine life and freedom (Ps. 119:32, 45). Martin Luther understood this when he remarked:

> God "seizes us for his booty, by his Spirit he makes us his slaves and captives—which is not bondage but royal freedom—that we willingly may choose and do what he chooses."[23]

While we might struggle to make sense of the language of slavery used by Paul and then Luther, it is probably because we have a distorted view of God and what it means to "belong to him."

The Lost Son

Consider the simple force with which Jesus' parable of the prodigal (Luke 15:11–32) illustrates the truth that God's grace does not consist in anything we can hold in our hands but in whose hands we are held. Jesus said,

> There was a man who had two sons. The younger one said to his father, "Father, give me my share of the estate." So he divided his property between them.
>
> Not long after that, the younger son got together all he had, set off for a distant country and there squandered his wealth in wild living. After he had spent everything, there was a severe famine in that whole country, and he began to be in need. So he went and hired himself out to a citizen of that country, who sent him to his fields to feed pigs. He longed to fill his stomach with the pods that the pigs were eating, but no one gave him anything.
>
> When he came to his senses, he said, "How many of my father's hired men have food to spare, and here I am starving to death! I will set out and go back to my father and say to him: Father, I have sinned against heaven and against you. I am no longer worthy to

be called your son; make me like one of your hired men." So he got up and went to his father. (Luke 15:11–20 NIV)

The crucial moment in the story comes when Jesus says that the young man "came to his senses" (Luke 15:17). Coming to his senses was not so much about his realizing the challenges of serving as a pig-hand, but instead he realized his desperate need for reconciliation and belonging. That was the moment when he finally understood that what he needed was not found in the father's belongings but in belonging to the father.

At the end of the parable, Jesus drives the same point home again when the father finds his older son angry and upset outside the house because of the party thrown in celebration of the lost son's return.

> "Look! All these years I've been slaving for you and never disobeyed your orders. Yet you never gave me even a young goat so I could celebrate with my friends. But when this son of yours who has squandered your property with prostitutes comes home, you kill the fattened calf for him!"
>
> "My son," the father said, "you are always with me, and everything I have is yours. But we had to celebrate and be glad, because this brother of yours was dead and is alive again; he was lost and is found." (Luke 15:29–32 NIV)

The root of the problem was the same for both brothers. Both elevated the gift above the Giver. Both thought that what they needed consisted of possessing their father's belongings rather than belonging to their father. What the younger son learned, however, was that if God's grace were to be found in the things we hold in our hands—our inheritance, our possessions, our children, our reputation, our house, our career, our spouse, or even our life—grace could be lost. When famine hits, when trouble strikes, we are in danger of losing it ten thousand times a day![24] But because God's gift to us consists of an unbreakable bond of belonging to him through redemption in Jesus Christ, we rest secure in the knowledge that he watches over us as his own (John 10:11–13; cf. 6:37–39). Just like a young child who has nothing, lacks nothing, because his father has everything, we enjoy the sheer abundance of belonging to God.

Whenever we look to something beyond this relationship of belonging for joy or consolation, the problem is not that we want too much, but too little. Our deepest feelings of despair and dissatisfaction do not ultimately spring from a lack of possessions or belongings but from a failure to recognize whose child we are. Comfort comes when we, like the prodigal son, come to our senses and realize for the first time that to belong to the Father is to experience far greater wealth than our own individual portion of the inheritance could ever provide.

Conclusion

"I'm going all in." This is an expression taken from gambling and Hollywood films. It conjures images of the gambler's face chiseled with both resolve and fear as he pushes a pile of poker chips to the center of a green table. The stakes are high and clear. He's all in. When Christ held up the denarius in Matthew 22:15–22 and ends with the proclamation, "Render to Caesar the things that are Caesar's, and to God the things that are God's," he was "going all in." There was no possibility of keeping one chip back. And this is the paradox. By going all in to God we risk everything and nothing at all.

we risk everything and nothing at all.

... but the righteous shall live by his faith.

Habakkuk 2:4

The cross is Christ's loving gift of himself for "me," for us, for all. His death for sins was not anything other than an act of love, a voluntary gift of the self.

Michael J. Gorman[1]

For by grace you have been saved through faith. And this is not your own doing; it is the gift of God.

Ephesians 2:8

God does not believe for us, or in us; we believe. Yet, it is only by God's grace that we believe. His gift is simultaneously our act.

Sinclair Ferguson[2]

He is the true bread of life. He is not only the giver but the gift itself, for whose sake all earthly gifts exist.

Dietrich Bonhoeffer[3]

chapter five

Believing the Gift

The Challenge of Faith: Believing the Gift

He came at night, presumably so that no one would see him. His stealthy actions point to a risk. He was risking his public persona, his social capital. And for what? So that this teacher of the Jews, this Pharisee, could talk privately with a carpenter's son of questionable paternity (cf. John 8:48b). Jesus tells his late night visitor that he must be "born again." He must believe.

Has it ever occurred to you what a strange thing faith is? Reflecting on the mystery of faith, Walter Marshall (1628–1680) once observed:

> Men naturally esteem, that [faith] is too small and slight a thing to produce so great effects: as Naaman thought washing in the Jordan, too small a matter for the cure of his leprosy [2 Kings 5:1–14]. They contemn the true means of entering in at the straight gate, because they seem too easy for such purpose; and in this way they make the entrance not only difficult, but impossible to themselves.[4]

There surely must be more to accepting the Gift than just "faith." Well, yes and no. Yes, there is more to it than we might imagine; but no, it really is that simple. John 3:16 states that "whoever believes in him should not perish but have eternal life"; in other words, this trust is the difference between eternal life and death. We need to be careful, though, because sometimes we reduce faith to mere intellectual assent that God exists. Christians often call people to believe in God, but what does that mean? In John 3 Jesus is having a conversation with Nicodemus, calling him to be "born again," because that is the only way Nicodemus can see the "kingdom of God" (3:3). God is bringing new life to those who are "perishing," but faith is the necessary instrument by which this new life is received.

Nicodemus was "a man of the Pharisees" and "the teacher of Israel" (John 3:1, 10). So Jesus cannot merely have been calling this man to acknowledge the existence of a Deity. Nicodemus already did that. His position demonstrated that he was deeply religious and believed there was a God, namely, the God who had called Israel to be his people. This was not merely a generic deity or vague "higher power" that Nicodemus was willing to affirm, for surely he thought he was affirming the God of his fathers, the God of Abraham, Isaac, and Jacob.

Yet there is a tension here. Jesus in this passage is not merely telling Nicodemus to give intellectual assent to the existence of the supernatural, the power of positive thinking, or even the God of Israel. He is calling Nicodemus to *receive God's gift, Jesus himself, and to trust him over everything else.* This may sound easy, but it is not. To accept the gift means we must admit some challenging truths about ourselves and about God.

Confessing Truths about Ourselves

Faith in Jesus requires us to admit that we need to be rescued. We are headed for death because we have turned from the Lifegiver to whom we belong. Jesus calls us to admit that our lives are desperate (cf. Rev. 3:17–18). Everything on the surface may appear good: we may be publicly respected citizens, genuinely loving toward our families and friends, maybe even good at our jobs or role in society. But Jesus challenges us to be completely honest with ourselves and with God. We may actually be living in profound darkness and be blind to our own struggles—to the shiver, the ache, and the hardness of our hearts. But Jesus reveals "that hideous strength" of our sin and the brokenness of this world.[5] We see the emptiness of our self-absorption, and we know that we have run from God. We have betrayed our Creator and Lord. Not feeling this to be true is no protection from the fact that it is true.

Amid a violent conflict between former friends, one might shout at the other in anger, "You are dead to me; you no longer exist." Families sometimes go through such agonizing times that they disown one another, denying each other's existence. That is what we have done with God. We have lived in denial, not simply of his existence but of his rightful place as our Lord, our Creator, and our King. Therefore, to believe in Christ is to admit that we have rejected God and lived in denial of his presence and lordship.

Confessing Truths about God

Jesus also shows us, however, that this God is not what we might expect. In John 3 he tells Nicodemus that God's own Son, his gift of love to the world, is the "lifted-up" Son of Man (John 3:14). Jesus here anticipates his crucifixion, so he calls us to trust him to give us life even though he dies — or, rather, because he dies. Incredible! The event that should shape our understanding of who this God is and what he is like is the death of the Son on a cross. In his unity with God, Jesus shows us that the cross stands at the center of God's identity. God has come among us in order to die in our place. What kind of God are we dealing with? Saint Augustine explains:

> The Lord Jesus Christ, the God-man, is both a manifestation of divine love in us and an example of human humility among us, so that our great pride might be healed by an even greater contrary medicine. For a proud man is a great misery; but a humble God is a great mercy.[6]

God rescues his lost world, not by coming with military weaponry, not by seizing political control, not by taking over the academy and teaching everyone the truth. This God, who created everything, instead comes as a babe, lives a human life, spends much of his time among the poor, the disenfranchised, the confused, and then suffers and dies. "The magnitude of the love is matched by the magnitude of the gift.... God loved all there was, and gave all he had."[7] But how shall we react to this? The apostle Paul directly responds to this in Romans 8:31–32:

> What then shall we say to these things? If God is for us, who can be against us? He who did not spare his own Son but gave him up for us all, how will he not also with him graciously give us all things?

For those who embrace this Gift of God, everything changes. Now there is nothing that can separate us from the love of God that is in Christ Jesus our Lord (Rom. 8:38–39).

Take Heart: The Courage of Faith

Faith takes courage. Trusting is not easy. The difficulties of faith arise not only from our stubbornness, but also from our wounds. We have lived; we have dreamed; we have risked our hearts, trusting in someone or something that later failed us. Sometimes this is not a simple disappointment but a crushing encounter with the chaos and pain of this world. We have been hurt, and the call to trust is not asking a small thing of us: it asks for everything.

One day Jesus returned to Capernaum, where much of his Galilean ministry was based (Matt. 9:1–8//Mark 2:1–12//Luke 5:17–26). Upon hearing about his arrival, some men brought a paralytic to him. Mark and Luke give us more detail than Matthew, revealing this to be no small task. Jesus was preaching in a house, and there was no room left inside. So in order to get to Jesus, the four men carrying the paralytic lifted the man onto the roof, removed part of the tiles (Luke 5:19), and then lowered him before Jesus and the crowd in the house.

Who were these men who brought the paralytic? Were they his friends? Or were they simply village residents who had been moved by scenes of power and grace from earlier episodes of Jesus' ministry? Whatever their story, we know that they carried this vulnerable person to Jesus with great expectation. But this was no quick venture—they were carrying dead weight, and by the time they finally arrived, the house was packed and they couldn't get in. Bringing this paralytic to Jesus clearly cost these men; they expended great personal energy and social capital and probably incurred financial consequences by dismantling someone's roof. They wanted to get the man to Jesus so much that they took these remarkable measures. They believed Jesus could bring healing. While we are quick to imagine an air of excitement and anticipation as this scene unfolds, we should also see signs of tension.

And how did the paralytic feel about all of this? Since we know the end of the story, we often assume that he was excited, feeling mostly joy and anticipation. But is that the case? He had just been dragged to this house and then awkwardly lowered through a roof. Everything stopped. All eyes were on him. As a paralytic, he had experienced the public gaze before, but now he felt the stares of all those eyes even more keenly as he was lowered into tight quarters.

Again, he was acutely aware of his paralysis. He was different, an outsider. Had this man never had his hopes raised in the past? Have there never been times when he thought he might get better, only to have those hopes dashed (cf. John 5:7)? Being lowered before Jesus and the crowd, was the paralytic nervous, excited, hopeful, or pessimistic? Or were all of these emotions bouncing around within him, creating a bundle of contradictions not easily untangled? Would this "work"? How would Jesus respond? What would happen?

What is the first thing Jesus noticed? All three Gospels that record this event report the same thing: "Jesus *saw their* faith" (Matt. 9:2; Mark 2:5; Luke 5:20).[8] Jesus paid attention first not to the paralytic, but to those who have brought the wounded man to him. Apparently their actions, their posture, and their presence made this faith obvious. Everyone there observed Jesus looking at them, and it somehow became clear that "he saw their faith." These men knew that Jesus could heal and restore, and so they brought the needy man who could not bring himself.

Yet the Gospels do not record Jesus speaking any words directly to these four men. Instead, having acknowledged their faith, his gaze turned to the disabled man on the mat. Jesus declared: "Take courage" (NASB), or as many translate it, "Take heart."[9] "Take heart, my son; your sins are forgiven" (Matt. 9:2). When Jesus fixed his eyes on the paralytic, what did he see? Surprisingly, he didn't focus on the man's obvious physical aliments. Rather, Jesus' eyes penetrated to a greater level of suffering—the pain of a crushed heart, a broken spirit, a defeated soul. He saw a man in need of freedom. He saw a man in need of forgiveness.

When I was in high school, a friend of mine, Jesse, was in a terrible car accident after a party, and his leg had to be amputated.[10] He was in the prime of his life: athletic, able, and promising. Now his leg was gone. Different people respond differently after going through something like that, but Jesse plunged into anger and depression. His despair grew, the darkness hovered, the misery was palpable and bitter. It was painful to see and almost unbearable to be around. Jesse was angry, not just mad at himself, not just disappointed with people who had let him down, but Jesse was furious with God.

Might the paralytic not have been angry with God? It is hard enough to have a severe disability in the twenty-first century, but imagine living with those limitations and challenges in the ancient Near Eastern world. The sense of shame and underlying suspicion that surrounded such situations (cf. John 9:2) would have been almost unbearable. Such brokenness was associated with the lack of wholeness and thus reminds us of the breaking of shalom, which is why, for example, someone with such conditions could not be a priest (cf. Lev. 21:16–24).[11] This man had suffered tremendous physical and emotional pain. Can you blame him if he felt abandoned by the Creator and even angry with him? When Jesus looked at this paralytic, he saw sickness, but not merely of the body. This man needed to be liberated—not merely from his lifeless limbs, but from his suffocating sin. He needed grace. He desperately needed divine love.

Jesus told him to "take heart ... your sins are forgiven." Why "take heart"? I think Jesus was telling the paralytic that his ultimate issue was with God. This man would need courage to be reconciled with the sovereign Lord. But Jesus called him to that very task, to take heart, and to trust that his sins were forgiven. Jesus declared it to be so. And when he spoke, Jesus did not sound angry with the paralytic; his words reverberated with compassion. Employing the language of *family*, Jesus addressed him as "my son" (Matt. 9:2//Mark 2:5).[12] Calling him "my son" was another call to courage. By using that language Jesus said, "You belong to me; take heart."

Later in Matthew 9 Jesus also addressed a despairing woman with familial language. The woman had covertly touched his garment to be healed of the constant flow of blood she had had for twelve years (Matt. 9:20–23// Mark 5: 24–34//Luke 8:43–48). She reached out, hoping to be healed, but also hoping not to be noticed. Again, how often had her hopes been dashed? Because of her continual bleeding (most likely menstrual), she was considered "unclean." This meant that she was not allowed to partake in public worship, and anyone who touched her would be "unclean" (Lev. 15:19–33).

She was desperate. Mark tells us that she had "suffered much under many physicians, and had spent all that she had, and was no better but rather grew worse" (Mark 5:26). At the very least it was a risk for her to believe, but she longed to be whole. So, having heard about Jesus, she approached him, hoping, risking her heart by believing that this man could save her from her pain. Clearly she expected to receive something.

Attempting to just tap him secretly, she approached Jesus from behind; she extended her hand and touched the fringe of his garment. Only two people in this large crowd knew. Jesus perceived "that power had gone out from him," and he turned to see who had touched him (Mark 5:30). Sounding a bit frustrated with Jesus, the disciples observe that clearly Jesus had been "touched" by countless people since he was in the middle of a vast multitude. But Jesus kept scanning. What was he waiting to see? What would identify the person? Apparently faith.

> And when the woman saw that she was not hidden, she came trembling, and falling down before him declared in the presence of all the people why she had touched him, and how she had been immediately healed. And he said to her, "Daughter, your faith has made you well; go in peace." (Luke 8:47–48)

Matthew tells us that the first thing Jesus said to her was, "Take heart, daughter" (Matt. 9:22). He did not judge her for unorthodox superstition. He was not angry that she had touched him even though he knew that in the eyes of the crowd it would make him ritually unclean. Instead, Jesus responded to her as he responded to the paralytic, with compassion, power, and the ability to heal both body and soul. Jesus cared for the whole person, and he treated them as family.

Parents, seeing the suffering of a child, know that they would do anything to relieve the child's pain, for in seeing the child, the parent suffers. A parent desires the child's wholeness and healing. When Jesus turned to the paralytic and the hemorrhaging woman with "my son," "my daughter," he was saying, "Your pain is my pain; your suffering is my suffering. You are not an outcast, but a son; you are a daughter of the King." Jesus saw the man and the woman before him as wounded souls, paralyzed by sin, fear, and pain, as well as with physical infirmity. "Take heart, my son; your sins are forgiven." "Take heart, daughter; your faith has made you well."

This Jewish rabbi removed the distance between these two people and God. How? An exchange took place, vividly displayed in his encounter with the bleeding woman. As "power went out" from Jesus to her, not only was she healed, but he would now be considered "unclean." He took on her shame and her forsakenness and wiped out her uncleanness with the purpose of giving her fullness of life. Seeing healing through his touch in a similar instance, Matthew concludes: "He took our illnesses and bore our diseases" (Matt. 8:17, echoing Isa. 53:4).

Jesus brings back shalom. His healing powers in these scenes consistently point to an even greater power, his power over sin itself. In the house with the paralytic, Jesus upsets the crowds by demonstrating just how near God has come. When Jesus announces to the paralytic that his sins are forgiven, the man hears the voice of God bringing hope and promise to his despairing soul. Jesus is not merely proclaiming a generic or past forgiveness, but his speaking accomplishes the forgiveness because of his divine authority to forgive—the paralytic's sins are being forgiven in and through Jesus. "He is blaspheming!" remark the scribes in the crowd: "Who can forgive sins but God alone?" (Mark 2:6–7). The scribes are right to say that only God can forgive sins, and the gospel writers do not dispute this point. But Jesus here displays his oneness with God as his Son. Affirming their rightness and wrongness, Jesus answers the scribes:

Why do you question these things in your hearts? Which is easier, to say to the paralytic, "Your sins are forgiven," or to say, "Rise, take up your bed and walk"? But that you may know that the Son of Man has authority on earth to forgive sins" —he said to the paralytic— "I say to you, rise, pick up your bed, and go home." (Mark 2:8b–11)

Jesus comes, he intimately connects himself with the sinner ("my son," "my daughter"), and he brings the healing of God. The scribes, of course, fail to understand the nature of Jesus' unity with God. The disciples have the same problem. For example, during the last Passover supper as Jesus celebrates just before his crucifixion, Philip memorably requests, "Lord, show us the Father, and it is enough for us" (John 14:8). Jesus sounds almost bewildered in his response:

Have I been with you so long, and you still do not know me, Philip? Whoever has seen me has seen the Father. How can you say, "Show us the Father"? Do you not believe that I am in the Father and the Father is in me? The words that I say to you I do not speak on my own authority, but the Father who dwells in me does his works. Believe me that I am in the Father and the Father is in me, or else believe on account of the works themselves. (John 14: 9–11)

Jesus looks at the paralytic and the hemorrhaging woman and he expresses the compassion of the Father (cf. John 10:14–18). The Creator has come. The Son of God, in the power of the Spirit, comes to heal, restore, and recreate. Jesus displays the very love of the Father, for he and the Father are one (10:29–30). Jesus approaches the wounded, the sinner, the broken, not as a dispassionate scientist, but with the heart of the one true Father from whom all other fathers derive their compassion.

We try to clean ourselves up, to make ourselves acceptable to God and each other. Paths of self-improvement become our obsession. It takes genuine courage to follow a different path, to admit our need and receive God's love, the gift of the cross. Jesus says, "Those who are well have no need of a physician, but those who are sick. I have not come to call the righteous but sinners to repentance" (Luke 5:31–32). He comes for us, not because we are worthy, but because we are not. And our sickness is fundamentally our sin, which is manifested in countless symptoms. Saint Augustine commented, "Christ does love sinners, but in the same way as the doctor loves a sick person: to kill the fever and save the person. So the Lord did not come to call the just, but sinners, in order to justify the godless."[13] Later he adds,

Don't be afraid for your past wickedness, however frightful, however unbelievable the things you have perhaps committed. They are grave diseases, but the doctor has mastered them. So don't worry about past sins; in one moment of the sacrament they will be forgiven, and absolutely all of them will be totally forgiven.[14]

In speaking of the sacrament, Augustine refers to baptism; but in the text Jesus speaks not about baptism but about faith. He calls people to trust him and so to receive the forgiveness, joy, and freedom that come when one is reconciled with the Creator. Baptism testifies to this promise. In his embrace we are forgiven.

Believing Is Receiving: Faith as a Gift

As paradoxical as it may appear, the Bible treats faith as a gift. There are at least three dynamics to consider here.

First, faith often comes to us through the community of faith. It comes from other people, from parents and other believers. We need to be reminded of this, especially those of us so deeply shaped by American individualism. When the four men brought the paralytic to Jesus, he saw their faith. The normal means through which God extends the gift of his grace and love is his people, his church. We will talk much more about this in the final two chapters of this book.

Christians sometimes refer to "the faith," which is embodied by the people of God.[15] We do not each invent a "faith," but we join the communion of saints, the living faith (Heb. 11). This is the life-giving faith entered into and shared by God's people throughout the ages (see, e.g., Rom. 4 – 5; Gal. 3:7 – 14). God unites his people to himself and to each other by his Spirit through faith; this is a faith given, received, and then given to others. Entering this movement of divine generosity lies at the heart of properly understood evangelism. But we offer only that which has been given to us, not something we conjure up ourselves.[16]

Second, faith itself is a gift from God. The German New Testament scholar Udo Schnelle, having examined the idea of faith in the apostle Paul's writings, concludes unambiguously, "Faith does not rest on human decision but is a gift of God's grace."[17] For Paul, belief in Christ is a "privilege" (Phil. 1:29); a "fruit of the Spirit" and evidence of the Spirit's generous presence (cf. 1 Cor. 12:3, 9; Gal. 5:22 – 23). This reflects other passages of Scripture as well.[18] God's Spirit enlivens our hearts, grants faith and repentance, gives us ears to hear, eyes to see, wills to respond, and hearts to embrace the Truth (e.g., John 1:17; Acts 11:16 – 18; 16:14; Eph. 2:1, 4 – 10).

In Ephesians 2:8 the point is made abundantly clear: "For by grace you have been saved through faith. And this is not your own doing; it is the gift of God." Schnelle concludes, "Faith, like love, cannot be commanded, but only received, experienced, and lived out. Faith opens up a new relationship to God, a relationship human beings can only gratefully receive."[19] And yet, biblically, we also find that faith and love are both given *and* commanded. To understand this dynamic, we turn to our next point.

Third, while this faith is given, it is still something we do: it is our faith, our response.[20] This is a paradox we should not too quickly try to eliminate. Søren Kierkegaard, the nineteenth-century Danish Christian philosopher, toys with this paradox regarding love, but I think it equally applies to faith. The sacred Scriptures strangely *command* us to "love God and neighbor," and yet, how can one be commanded to love? You can command someone to pick up sticks, to drink milk, to sing and dance. But command to love?[21]

The same question applies to faith, which is commanded, and yet, in some sense, seems impossible apart from divine provision. At one point the prophet Ezekiel declares God's expectation of his audience: "Cast away from you all the transgressions that you have committed, and *make yourselves a new heart and a new spirit*! Why will you die, O house of Israel?" (Ezek. 18:31, emphasis added). He calls for an active response from his listeners—they are to believe and respond to Yahweh.

Yet we find that Ezekiel elsewhere, without apparently sensing any tension, describes how such a new heart and spirit comes about. God, by his Spirit, will "give them one heart, and a new spirit I [the Lord] will put within them. I will remove the heart of stone from their flesh and give them a heart of flesh, that they may walk in my statues and keep my rules and obey them. And they shall be my people, and I will be their God" (Ezek. 11:19–20; echoed in 36:26). This "heart of flesh" is the heart of living faith, of a loving relationship with the Creator. We are commanded to have new hearts, and yet only God can give them to us. Faith, therefore, is more complicated than we often admit. It is somehow understood as both an amazing gift and a costly demand.

I think Steve Brown captures this dynamic when he says, "You can't love until you have been loved, and then you can only love to the degree to which you have been loved."[22] Love, like faith, is not something we invent, but something we experience and then respond to. Genuine love is something that is simultaneously received and given. Along the same lines, faith in God is both received and practiced. It is both a gift of God and also our response to God's grace and mercy.

God commands us to exercise faith (and love). And yet the Scriptures show that faith and love are first given and received.[23] But the nature of the gift does not nullify our responsibility to believe or to love. Faith and love are simply set against the larger canvas of God's lavish provision.[24] Although we may try to flatten out this paradox, the Bible never does. Paul senses no tension when he declares, "Work out your own salvation with fear and trembling, for it is God who works in you, both to will and to work for his good pleasure" (Phil. 2:12b–13). There is human responsibility here, and there is divine mercy. We work, not in order to secure salvation, but since "God works in us" we are able to work. It is our work. It is God's work.

But this is not a matter of dividing up the pie 50/50 or with some other percentage. Rather, we recognize that even as we work, we do so *only as a result of God's preexistent work and good pleasure.* "I am sure of this," Paul affirms, "that he who began a good work in you will bring it to completion at the day of Jesus Christ" (Phil. 1:6). And to the Colossians he writes, "For this I toil, struggling with all his energy that he powerfully works within me" (Col. 1:29). We are called to believe, to struggle, and to fight the fight of faith; and yet we are encouraged to know that as demanding as that can feel, we are ultimately empowered "with all *his* energy" as he works in us by his Spirit.

In this belief—which cannot be understood apart from God's provision—we become captured by the wonder of God's grace, and we discover the joy of being used by God as vehicles of his great generosity to the world. We begin to follow and imitate him who is "the founder and perfecter of our faith" (Heb. 12:2). We begin to love the world as he does. We have to believe, which means we have to receive. And when we do, we enter the movement of divine generosity.

Trusting the Gift Changes Us

Believing in the Gift, we live out of God's generosity toward us. Out of his radical love for us, we can love others, even our enemies. As recipients of God's great treasure, we become people who give our treasures, including our time and talents, for the sake of the world. We emulate God's extravagant love for the world, following the path of his Son, the path of the cross. As those who have been forgiven, we forgive. As people who have experienced new life, we take the side of life, justice, and peace rather than that of death, abuse, and chaos.

But this kind of belief is hard. Plenty of evidence from the history of the church and our own lives shows how far short we fall of this transformative faith. Again, we need to confess hard truths about ourselves. Believers still sin—the struggle remains. But we are not just talking about intellectual assent. Faith is more than cognitive agreement with factual data, or with persuasive philosophical arguments or "proofs" for the existence of God.[25] Our active faith humbles us and trusts the radical humility of God. Such faith requires everything we are, all our trust, all our hope, all our life.

You may remember the adventures of Indiana Jones in *The Last Crusade.* In the final scenes of the movie Indiana has to get through a series of traps and challenges on his way to the chamber of the Holy Grail. The final challenge is a great chasm that looks bottomless and impassable. But Indiana has his father's research notebook that tells him that he must step out in faith. It's a tense moment where he closes his eyes, sticks out his foot, and steps forward into the abyss. Just when you think he will tumble to certain death, his foot hits solid ground, and he finds himself on an invisible rock bridge, allowing a safe crossing.

Indiana had to trust in the work of his father (as do we), and he had to believe. It wasn't easy. It took everything he had to step out like that. But the chasm between God and us was overcome when God crossed, when he came. Jesus Christ is God with us (Matt. 1:23), one with us—coming to us and then taking us back to God. He is the bridge, the way, the life. Jesus is God's great Gift to the world, and he calls us to embrace him.

Reconsidering Nicodemus

We have already observed that John 3:16 is one of those passages we are so familiar with that, ironically, we can miss its message. Having heard the words a thousand times, we may still find ourselves asking, *Have I ever really heard the message?*

We must reconsider the story of Nicodemus one last time. For in John's gospel, this man provides us with one of the clearest portraits of someone truly transformed by the message in the most famous verse in the Bible.

Nicodemus's story begins in darkness. The evangelist John records that Nicodemus came to Jesus "by night" (John 3:2). This is a provocative detail, since John's gospel repeatedly contrasts goodness and evil by way of light and darkness.[26] On the occasion of Nicodemus's first encounter with Jesus, he arrives as a *shady* character. He comes in the darkness; he seems to represent blindness and the struggle to believe. But Nicodemus will appear again at the end of John's gospel, and in a very different light.

We don't always get to see the end of the story for people described in the Bible. But in this case we do. Nicodemus's last appearance in the gospel of John describes a man engaged in one of the most beautiful acts of generosity recorded in Scripture. Jesus has been crucified and all of his friends have fled. Nothing is clear at this point. But Nicodemus and Joseph of Arimethea, at great personal risk, seek to care for the body of their crucified Lord. As John describes the scene:

> Nicodemus also, who earlier had come to Jesus by night, came bringing a mixture of myrrh and aloes, about seventy-five pounds in weight. So they took the body of Jesus and bound it in linen cloths with the spices. (John 19:39–40)

In other words, Nicodemus had received God's gift, and he was transformed by it. The first man ever to hear the message of John 3:16 eventually understood it and experienced the transforming power of the gospel. We see it in the seventy-five pounds of spices, which amounted to "extravagance in the extreme" for a Jewish burial.[27] We see it in the risk Nicodemus took by identifying himself with his crucified Lord, because his crucified Lord had identified with him. Nicodemus believed in the gift of Jesus, and from his fullness Nicodemus received "grace upon grace" (John 1:16).[28]

The greatest risk of faith is that it might not be true. That calls for courage. To truly believe Jesus and believe it matters; to believe that we will be saved. Nicodemus believed, and yet look at the Lord he believed in — he was dead! Greater than even his errand in the night, Nicodemus now appears in a far darker place; he is called to believe even as he is bearing the dead body of Jesus, and he does. The gift of faith shines in the darkness, even before Easter morning. And yet this Messiah is not overcome by death, but he overcomes it. He rises, he lives, and we now live in him by faith. Take courage, the object of your faith is true. In him we are healed; in him we are forgiven.

How great a God is He who gives God!

Augustine[1]

Now we have received not the spirit of the world, but the Spirit who is from God, that we might understand the things freely given us by God.

1 Corinthians 2:12

And I believe in the Holy Spirit, the Lord and Giver of Life, who proceeds from the Father [and the Son], who with the Father and the Son together is worshiped and glorified.

Niceno-Constantinopolitan Creed, 381 AD.

Father and Son are, each in his own way, the givers, and the Spirit is the Gift that they give. Father and Son are God as giver, the Holy Spirit is God as Gift.

Thomas Smail[2]

And when you pour yourself out over us, you are not drawn down to us but draw us up to yourself: you are not scattered away, but you gather us together.

Augustine[3]

chapter six

The Gift of the Spirit

God Keeps Giving

They were spent. The disciples had followed Jesus the Messiah, putting their hope in him, only to see him die a bloody death. Then, in just a matter of days, as they faced the darkness of disillusionment, they encounter the resurrected Jesus, alive! Touch, see, and believe. Jesus was now recognized as the crucified and resurrected Lord, the Son given from the Father for the sake of the world. But what does this mean? Surely now Jesus will stay with them!

With the resurrection the disciples, though tired and confused, have Jesus with them again. A new age was dawning where the risen Messiah would, by his glorious presence, change the world. This must be the end.

But before long the resurrected Jesus tells the disciples it is time for him to go. He will now return to his Father. Can you imagine the disciples looking at one another, wondering what this all means? Doesn't it seem like God gives a gift, only to take it away the moment people begin to realize its value and significance? How can Jesus' ascension be good for the disciples? How can his "departing" be good for the world?

Jesus anticipated just how difficult his departure would be for the disciples and tried to prepare them for it. This is why he spent so much time during the last supper focusing on the future. In a room full of people who had sacrificed much to follow him, Jesus reveals that he will be going away, but he gives them this encouragement: "Let not your hearts be troubled" (John 14:1). Urging them to believe in God and trust in him despite what is about to occur — the late night arrest and bloody crucifixion — Jesus holds out the promise of resurrection. There will be much to fear, but they should turn to God.

During the last supper Jesus tells the disciples, "I will not leave you as orphans; I will come to you" (John 14:18). When children lose both parents, they lose the comfort of belonging and are left vulnerable and alone. Knowing that the disciples have this growing fear of abandonment, Jesus promises not to desert them. Paradoxically, he will continue to give, even as he is taken away. Unimaginable as it may seem, Jesus tells the disciples that it is to their "advantage" for him to go away; "for if I do not go away, the Helper will not come to you. But if I go, I will send him to you" (John 16:7). Elsewhere the New Testament tells us that God was pleased to have "all [his] fullness" dwell in Jesus (Col. 1:19), who is the "radiance of the glory of God" (Heb. 1:3). But according to Jesus, we are to consider ourselves even more blessed than his disciples were when he was physically with them. How is this possible? Who is this Helper? How can it be to our advantage for Jesus to leave?

"The Gift of God"

When God gives, he gives nothing short of himself. As the one who alone is called "the gift of God" (John 4:10; Acts 2:38; 8:20; 10:45; 11:17; Eph. 4:7; Heb. 6:4), the Spirit is given by *all three* persons of the Trinity, not only proceeding to us from the Father and the Son (John 14:26; 15:26; 16:7), but also freely giving himself and distributing his gifts as he wills (Heb. 2:4).[4] When the Father gave the Son, this was not his final gift. In his triune generosity, God continues to give in ways that his disciples could not have asked or imagined. Encountering the resurrected Jesus confirmed the reality of God's presence *with* the disciples through the Son. Receiving "the gift of God" meant the Father, Son, and Holy Spirit — the triune God — now abides *within* all who believe.[5] By the Spirit, God gives himself in such a way that he is not only with us, but in us.

Can God Really Be Given?

In seventeenth-century England John Biddle created great controversy because of his rationalistic readings of Scripture. One of Biddle's claims was that the Spirit spoken of in the Bible cannot logically be God. His argument was simple: "He that is the gift of God, is not God." Later he expanded his point. "He that is not the giver of all things, is not God. He that is the gift of God, is not the giver of all things."[6] Therefore, since the Spirit is "given" by God, he cannot be God himself — the Giver of all things.

Although we reject Biddle's rationalism, we should note that he wrestled with what we far too glibly accept. This man was dumbfounded by what we take for granted — the deep paradox and seeming impossibility that the Almighty God himself could be given.

Nevertheless, the Holy Spirit we receive is God himself — a person of the Trinity. The Spirit is no mere wind or breath, but biblically he is a person, since he comforts (e.g., John 14:16 – 18); he can be grieved (Eph. 4:30) and sinned against (Matt. 12:31 – 32); he teaches (Luke 12:11 – 12; John 15:26), speaks and reveals (Acts 6:10; 13:2; 2 Peter 1:21), and gives gifts as he wishes (Rom. 12 – 3 – 8; 1 Cor. 12:7, 11); and he intercedes for us (Rom. 8:26).

Furthermore, throughout Scripture the Spirit is recognized as having divine identity: to lie to the Spirit is to lie to God (Acts 5:3 – 4), he possesses the divine attributes (e.g., Ps. 139:7; 1 Cor. 2:10; Heb. 9:14), he participates in divine works as only God can (e.g., Gen. 1:2; Job 26:13; 33:4; Ps. 33:6; 1 Cor. 6:11; 12:4), and he receives divine honors. Christians are baptized not only in the name of the Father and the Son, but also in the name of the Holy Spirit (Matt. 28:19; cf. 1 Cor. 12:13; 2 Cor. 13:14; 1 Peter 1:1 – 2). There is only one God, and that God reveals himself as eternally the Father, Son, and Holy Spirit. Therefore, worship and glory are rightly directed toward the Spirit of God.

Not surprisingly, St. Augustine anticipated Biddle's type of argument against the Spirit's divinity by concluding, "He is given as God's gift in such a way that as God he also gives himself. You can scarcely say he is not his own master," since this is the one who blows where he wishes (John 3:8) and gives as he wills (1 Cor. 12:11).[7] Augustine's point is that the Spirit's own self-giving is a proof of his divinity (cf. Phil. 2:5 – 11), not of his inferiority to God. While the Spirit is sent, he also comes. So, there is never any division or disunity in the one true God who eternally exists as Father, Son, and Spirit. What we discover here is the pattern of divine movement and grace. The Spirit, who is given by the Father and the Son, freely comes even as he is sent, and in this freedom he remains eternally understood as the Gift of God, and as the eternal gift he draws people into God's triune life.

The German philosopher Immanuel Kant once claimed that "the doctrine of the Trinity, taken literally, has no practical relevance at all."[8] But the divine movement of God's generosity is Trinitarian: it proceeds from the Father, through the Son, and it is completed by the work of the Spirit.[9]

And, as we will increasingly discover in later chapters, truly Christian generosity is Trinitarian: it flows from and reflects the triune life of God. This theme takes us to the heart of biblical generosity, since every true act of Christian charity is ultimately an overflow of God's life and love poured into our hearts by the Holy Spirit.

The Spirit as Both Holy and Given

Here we discover a powerful paradox about the Spirit: not only is he described as "the gift of God," but he is also called *holy*. There are nearly one hundred verses in the New Testament where he is named the "*Holy Spirit*," his most common biblical title.[10] While such familiar names for the Spirit are often taken for granted, the combination of these two ways of describing the Spirit—as being *holy* and yet also *given*—is really striking. The reason is that the concept of *holiness* involves the idea of being *separated for special use and possession by God*. The "holy bread" used in the Old Testament tabernacle, for example, was called "holy" because it was not for "common" consumption (1 Sam. 21:4). Only the priests of God were authorized to eat it because it was set apart for God, and they could only eat it in a holy place (Lev. 24:9). Thus, to be holy conveys the essential idea of absolute *dedication* and *belonging* to God.[11]

Nevertheless, the Holy Spirit who belongs to God, who is set apart as God, is the same "Spirit of Glory" who "rests" upon us (1 Peter 4:14) and is "given" to us (2 Cor. 1:22)! From long ago God promised to put his Spirit "within" his people, bringing new life by his holy habitation (Ezek. 36:27; 37:14; John 3:5–8). And that is exactly what we discover after Pentecost, as God "fills" his people (Acts 2:4). He freely gives to all peoples without reservation—man and woman, slave and free, Jew and Gentile (Joel 2:28–32; Acts 2:17–21). He who is and remains "other" than his creation nevertheless draws near, is present, and sanctifies us. In this movement God gives that which would otherwise remain infinitely *other* than anything we could acquire for ourselves: the Holy Spirit of God himself.

An outworking of receiving this holy gift is that it sets us apart *for God* and *for neighbor*. In this way we find that we are "other," set apart from the world that hoards rather than gives. We are set apart in order to positively pour ourselves out for the world in the love of Christ and the power of his Spirit. Thus, when we use the word "separate" to convey the idea of holiness, we should think of being "separated *to*" God and love for others rather than just "separated *from*."[12]

In receiving this gift we once again discover that all of God's gifts are gifts of belonging—gifts we receive and experience in terms of belonging. Like the gift of redemption discussed in chapter 4, the gift of the Holy Spirit does not primarily consist in anything we can hold in our hands, but in whose hands we are held. To receive this gift is, as Dietrich Bonhoeffer once said, to be "torn from the clutches of the world," set apart as a saint, a holy one of God (cf. Rom. 1:6–7)[13]—set apart to be avenues of God's grace, drawing others into God's life and love.

God in Us

As a father of two young children I have a nightly ritual. Every evening before I go to sleep, I walk upstairs, check on my son and daughter, cover them if needed, and kiss their heads. I do this because I love them and there is something strangely sacred in those moments. With this in mind, I found it fascinating to read about Origen (185–254), who became one of the leading early church fathers. As a young boy he quickly became known for his deep spirituality; one retelling of his youth describes his father standing over his sleeping son, and then kissing his breast with a sense of reverence, knowing that the Spirit of God dwelt within this boy.[14] Origen's father profoundly sensed what we easily forget—the strangeness, wonder, power, and joy of receiving God's Spirit. The Christian claim to receive the Spirit, to have God "in" us, is a mind-boggling claim.

Roman Catholic theologian Yves Congar, in his massive and important study on the Spirit, makes this startling assertion: "God gives himself to us, in such a way that, although it is purely through grace and we hardly dare to confess it, we really possess him."[15] We believe that God has given his Holy Spirit to dwell not merely throughout the world, but particularly in his children.

Similarly, St. Augustine once proclaimed in a sermon: "The heart of the believer is not too small for him, though the temple of Solomon was."[16] Then he asked: What would you do if a patron, someone with great wealth and power, said to you that they were going to move into your home. How would you respond? Given that most of our houses would be too small and broken down for such a distinguished guest, we would likely be terrified, wishing that it wouldn't actually happen, since we would not have the resources to adequately deal with his coming. Yet Augustine concluded, "Don't be afraid of your God's arrival, don't be afraid of your God's feelings. He doesn't squeeze you out when he comes; on the contrary, he will give you more room by coming." Finally he mused, "But why were you trying to make plenty of room for him? Let the lodger himself make more room: For the love of Christ has been spread out in our hearts—not our own doing though, but—through the Holy Spirit who has been given to us (Rom. 5:5)."

As Jesus ascends, the Spirit descends; the Spirit of God is the presence of God. Without reservation the New Testament assumes that where the Spirit is, there is Christ, and encounter with the Spirit of God is encounter with Yahweh. There is one true God, who in his mysterious reality is three persons, each distinct from the other and yet existing in unbreakable unity and perfect oneness. This is why the apostle Paul can fluidly move between the Spirit, Christ, and the Father in Romans 8:9–11:

> You, however, are not in the flesh but in the Spirit, if in fact the Spirit of God dwells in you. Anyone who does not have the Spirit of Christ does not belong to him. But if Christ is in you, although the body is dead because of sin, the Spirit is life because of righteousness. If the Spirit of him who raised Jesus from the dead dwells in you, he who raised Christ Jesus from the dead will also give life to your mortal bodies through his Spirit who dwells in you.

Notice that Paul uses the phrases "the Spirit of God" and "the Spirit of Christ" interchangeably. And this Spirit raised Jesus from the dead—thus distinguishing the Spirit from Jesus, even as he links them together. In other words, where the Spirit dwells, there is the wholeness of God. In this way, the biblical claim should stop us in our tracks, for none other than the triune God, the Holy God, makes his abode in us by his Spirit. But does this matter? What changes when we receive God as this indwelling Spirit?

The Gift of the Future

There is a lot that becoming a Christian does not change. If the new believer was struggling financially before conversion, their financial woes are not instantly taken away. Those previously divorced do not wake to find themselves happily married. If they were living under an oppressive government, they are not straightaway ushered into a land of liberty. On the surface of things, nothing changes for the person who becomes a Christian.

Yet everything changes at conversion. George Eldon Ladd once made the observation that "the gift of the Spirit is the gift of the Age to Come."[17] But what does that mean? Those who encounter God's Spirit are given a taste of a future reality, a future world, a future life. "The drought of the Spirit had ended," says New Testament scholar James Dunn. "The longed for and expected new age had begun" with the outpouring of God's Spirit.[18] Those who receive the Spirit find themselves in "the time between the times," where the ends of the ages overlap (cf. 1 Cor. 10:11). We have one foot in the present and one foot in the future—a tension that produces great joy and suffering, great blessing and conflict. This is what we mean by "eschatology," the study of the "last things," not just in the sense of the abrupt end of the world, but also the ushering in of God's kingdom.

This gift of the future is so rich and complex as to defy neat definition. That's why the New Testament writers rely so heavily on metaphors to portray the Spirit's eschatological significance. We have already mentioned several of these key images throughout this chapter, but now we turn to four in particular: the Spirit as *guarantee, firstfruits, seal,* and *water.* Each of these images provides us with a window into the "already" and the "not-yet" of God's generosity.

Spirit as Guarantee

The language of the Spirit as a *guarantee* or *down payment* primarily comes from the world of commerce. Such down payments in the marketplace mean that a sum of money is paid toward a house or some other purchase to *guarantee* the final payoff. In other words, a part of what will ultimately be given is paid ahead of time as a promise that the last installment will be made. But unlike some down payments in our day and age, such guarantees in Paul's world could not be returned.[19] God has given such a down payment to us in the Holy Spirit (2 Cor. 1:22; 5:5; Eph. 1:13–14).

Some years ago my wife, Tabitha, and I visited Morocco, and while exploring the city of Tangier with a local, we passed numerous shops with window displays that caught our attention. In some of these displays we noticed magnificent belts made of precious metals that were roughly the size of a championship-boxing belt. When we asked our guide about them, he explained that this custom was built on ancient tradition. These were promissory gifts—examples of what is called a *mahr,* an advance gift from men to their prospective wives, giving the women financial security. Apparently these belts were worth a large amount of money, and this was both a guarantee of marriage as well as a form of life insurance should anything happen to the man. Yet at that time, our guide explained, people were delaying marriage because they could not afford the ceremony and expected bridal gifts.

But what man cannot afford or fully understand, God gives. Not merely a jewel or a sum of money, God gives his own Spirit, his own self, as down payment of what is to come (Eph. 1:13–14). Our present circumstances are thus secure as we go into the future because we have received the Spirit.

Spirit as Firstfruits

Another metaphor that casts light on both the present and the future of God's generosity is the idea of the *firstfruits* of the Spirit, which Paul speaks of in Romans 8:23:

> And not only the creation, but we ourselves, who have the firstfruits of the Spirit, groan inwardly as we wait eagerly for adoption as sons.

In the Old Testament the firstfruits offering was not only the *beginning* but also the *best* part of the whole harvest. As a gift that represented the totality, it was both the *first* and the *finest* portion of everything the Promised Land produced.[20] Accordingly, when Paul tells us that God has given *us* the firstfruits of the Spirit, he is saying that we have received not only the beginning, but also a taste of the best part of the fullness God has planned for the future.

This language shifts the picture from God as recipient to God as giver. Israel's understanding of firstfruits was always as *something given to God*. Yet now it is *God who gives to us the firstfruits*. Emphasis here is not on what we give, but on the one whom we receive—the Spirit. God is giving an offering to mere human beings! What had always been expected—namely, offering things to God—is radically reversed. Imagine the shock of the disciples when Christ stooped to the position of the lowliest of servants to wash their feet the night of the last supper. Their astonishment should be matched by ours when we consider that the God of the universe gives offerings to the likes of us and that choice offering is *himself*. The movement of divine generosity consistently shows us God's grace, and those who have now received this gift are freed anew to love the Creator and his creation.

God's new creation began with Jesus' resurrection—which explains why he is called the "firstfruits" from the dead (1 Cor. 15:20, 23)—and continues with his Spirit. God by his Spirit brings new life where he moves, and the evidence of this movement is the fruit he produces, which we will discuss more below. Thus, those who are in Christ and have received the Spirit are now themselves called "the firstfruits," having been saved and sanctified by the Spirit (2 Thess. 2:13; James 1:18; Rev. 14:4). We already have this gift from the future, this "overflow," as Sinclair Ferguson has described it, "from another world."[21] We live out of this new reality even as we confront the clear evidence of our shattered world.

Christian joy and security is not about the absence of pain and sorrow, but about the presence of the Spirit. Our hope is not based on what we see, but on what is not yet visible (Rom. 8:24–25; Heb. 11:1). While circumstances in our lives may make us question God's love and provision, the gift of his Spirit reframes our vision to include the future.[22] While we continue to groan inwardly in anticipation of this future, we have received firstfruits from that future—the Spirit of Christ—who enables us to pray and rejoice in the midst of trouble and scarcity, fear and grief.

Spirit as Seal

One of the primary reasons we can know that we belong to God is that God has given his Spirit as the *seal of* his ownership (2 Cor. 1:22; Eph. 1:13; 4:30). Since the Spirit is active rather than unmoving, this very action assures us that we have been marked out as special possessions of God. As a seal, the Spirit serves as a mark of ownership as well as a means of preventing tampering. We are securely God's, sealed by his Spirit. But how do we experience this assurance?

John Chrysostom (347–407) long ago argued that when Paul claims we receive the Spirit both as a guarantee and a seal, this functions as an "especial forecast." We are confident not merely that God has imagined our future, but that it will become reality, even as it is experienced through time. "You see how, in process of time, He makes them [believers] objects of wonder."[23] What this seal, this gift, marks is our belonging to God, and this relationship becomes more and more evident as God draws us ever more into his life and love. The seal is not earned but given, again reflecting the dynamic pattern of God's ownership.

The Bible speaks of many different ways in which believers belong to the Lord. His people are called "a holy nation" and "a people belonging to God" (Ex. 19:6; 1 Peter 2:9), his "treasured possession" (Ex. 19:5; Deut. 7:6; 14:2; 26:18) that he has purchased and thus possesses (1 Cor. 6:20; 7:23; Rev. 5:9; cf. Hos. 3:2). His people are his "portion" or "inheritance" (Deut. 4:20; 9:26, 29; 32:9; Ps. 33:12; Zech. 2:12; Eph. 1:18), "the sheep of his pasture" (Ps. 100:3; John 10:11–12), and even the "apple of his eye" (Deut. 32:10; Ps. 17:8; Zech. 2:8).

But the Lord did not give us his seal because we were naturally pure or desirable. He sealed us to *make* us holy. People may look at us in our present struggles and see our sin, but God promises that when the future comes in its fullness, no one will question to whom we belong. As the book of Revelation describes the heavenly vision, one image frequently used is that the saints are those who have God's name written on their foreheads (Rev. 7:3; 9:4; 14:1; 22:4). Rather than take this image in a crudely literal way, we can see the point: in glory there will be no doubt to whom God's people belong. Just as a husband and wife wear wedding bands as a sign and seal of their marriage, so God gives us his Spirit to mark us as his, as if God's own name were tattooed on our foreheads.

Spirit as Water

The prophet Joel, based on God's promise, said that in the "last days" God's Spirit would come in powerful and fresh ways (Joel 2:28–32), and that this event would change the world (Acts 2:4, 17). Poured out from heaven, the Spirit transforms deserts into orchards (Isa. 32:15). Like "water on the thirsty land, and streams on the dry ground," the Spirit brings his blessing to all who will experience him (Isa. 44:3). For with this outpouring God declares, "I will not hide my face anymore from them, when I will pour out my Spirit upon the house of Israel" (Ezek. 39:29).

Israel's identity expands as God's Spirit is poured out at Pentecost. His redemptive presence explodes old ethnic boundaries, coming not simply to Jews but also to Gentiles, to men and women, young and old, free person and slave (Joel 2:28; Acts 2:17–18; 10:45). We often miss how socially and politically shattering this was in the ancient world. Reversing the curse of the tower of Babel (Gen. 11:1–9), the Spirit overcomes the language barriers that divide people (Acts 2:7–12), giving us a taste of a future when peoples from all tribes, languages, and nations will worship Christ in harmony (Rev. 5:9; 7:9).

Likened to "springs of living water" that bubble and flow from the earth, the Spirit also is described as cloudbursts and downpours that fall from the sky and bring about new life in the soil. "By his secret watering," Calvin wrote, "the Spirit makes us fruitful to bring forth the buds of righteousness."[24] Isaiah 44:3–5 illustrates the point:

> For I will pour water on the thirsty land,
>   and streams on the dry ground;
> I will pour out my Spirit on your offspring,
>   and my blessing on your descendants.
> They will spring up like grass in a meadow,
>   like poplar trees by flowing streams.
> One will say, "I belong to the Lord";
>   another will call himself by the name of Jacob;

still another will write on his hand, "The LORD's,"
and will take the name Israel." (NIV)

Here again we see how God's blessing primarily consists in belonging to him. While in the West we often take for granted that anytime we turn on the faucet clean water comes out, this is not the case throughout the world, and certainly not in the ancient Near East. Having enough water, and especially clean water, was a crucial issue of life. But against this background, Isaiah reminds us of the cascading waters that not only *create* life but also *consecrate* that life to God.

To experience the Spirit as an abundant supply of nourishing water is to grow up and flourish in the freedom of giving one's self away. For, as we have seen, the one who has drunk of the poured-out Spirit "will write on his hand, 'The LORD's." Once more, the point is not that they are to receive literal tattoos, but they will declare, "I belong to the Lord," and identify themselves with the people of God who have received this life-giving Spirit (cf. Ezek. 36:23–28).

The disciples thought that the coming of the Messiah was the final act of God's giving himself and ushering in his kingdom on earth. While Christ is certainly the central point and person of all history, the coming of the Spirit is another instance where God defies our expectations and overwhelms us with his generosity. So what are we to do now?

It is the Spirit who gives life.

John 6:63

And by this we know that he abides in us, by the Spirit whom he has given us.

1 John 3:24

In love there is no having which does not arise out of surrender. . . . Whoever possesses himself does not love.

Eberhard Jüngel[1]

In claiming us as sons and daughters of God, the Spirit personally possesses us. In providing his gifts for ministry and service the Spirit gives himself to us, is possessed by us.

Edmund P. Clowney[2]

Here we see and are invited to participate in the self-giving of God in love, living in and from this gift, realizing that this, rather than prevailing views of power and success, is what transforms human life, history, the world.

Michael Downey[3]

I began to see that the Holy Spirit never intended that people who had gifts and abilities should bury them in the earth, but rather, he commanded and stirred up such people to the exercise of their gift and sent out to work those who were able and ready.

John Bunyan[4]

chapter seven

Experiencing the Gift

Experiencing the Gift of God's Spirit

Matt and Joan went through a long and strenuous process to adopt their daughter Ghina Kate from Bulgaria. While the adoption became legal and established, Ghina Kate still had to remain in her home country for months until the government officially released her to her new parents. Matt and Joan visited Ghina Kate during this time, joining their daughter in her orphanage, a place she had never left in her eighteen months of life. Although Ghina Kate was truly their daughter "now," she did not yet experience the new life and liberty of being their child until she arrived home with them in the States. Ghina Kate was living in the tension of the now and the not-yet. That is where we live as children of God, waiting to live in the fullness of that reality. Looking back, we now see Ghina Kate's daughterhood as fully realized and secure. But at the time they all had to struggle through the tension of the now and the not-yet.

It is worth mentioning one more aspect of Matt and Joan's adoption. When they finally picked Ghina Kate up to bring her home, Matt and Joan received a new birth certificate that listed Joan as the biological mother. This certificate actually stated that Joan gave birth to Ghina Kate in Sofia, Bulgaria. The government apparently does this so that these new parents have undeniable "parentage" or "ownership" of Ghina Kate—it is as though Joan gave birth to her. Even the Bulgarian government recognizes the need for what is ostensibly a complete engrafting into the new family. It is as if Ghina Kate were born again! By God's Spirit, that is exactly what has happened to us.

We enter the movement of God's generosity when the Spirit of God enters us. So it should come as no surprise that the gift of the Spirit brings about a major turning point in our experience of God's generosity. While every human being has shared the gifts that God gives to all humanity (Matt. 5:44–45), this indwelling by the Spirit is where the movement of divine generosity extends beyond what God has given *to* us and includes what God is now giving *through* us as well. With the gift of the Spirit we have not only been made *recipients* of God's grace, but we are now being transformed as *participants* in the movement of his divine generosity. As Douglas Moo notes, "God's 'giving' to us is not simply a past basis for Christian obedience; it is its continuous source."[5]

The apostle Paul tells us in Romans 5:5 that "God's love has been poured into our hearts through the Holy Spirit who has been given to us." This is key. The Holy Spirit himself has been poured out as a gift, but he also gives gifts of his own, both in and through us. That is to say, he draws people into God's family as adopted children, he fills them, he produces fruit in their lives, and he distributes his own gifts as he wills. Here we will draw particular attention to how adoption, filling, fruit, and spiritual gifts work to bless the community and build others up.

The Spirit of Adoption

Those who have received the gift of the Spirit no longer live as orphans but as co-heirs with Christ, through whom we belong to God as our Father. Of all the ways in which we are said to belong to the Lord, there is no greater blessing than to be his children and to have him as "our Father."[6] Because Christians often take this fundamental privilege to call out to God as Father for granted, we can easily miss how this relationship comes into being.

Rarely does the Old Testament describe God as a Father. When such language or imagery occurs, it portrays him as Father of creation (Deut. 32:6), or occasionally it depicts the king as his representative son (2 Sam. 7:14; Ps. 89:26–29), but most often the imagery is that the nation of Israel was his corporate "son" (Ex. 4:22; Jer. 3:19; 31:9). God is a compassionate Father who cares for his people (Ps. 103:13; Hos. 11:1–4), displaying particular fatherly concern for widows, the fatherless, and the desperate (Ps. 68:4–6).

The practice of referring to God as Father of individual believers really begins in the New Testament. All of the Old Testament references depict the relationship fundamentally from God's perspective, whereas the New Testament shifts the view to that of the Son.[7] Scholars have observed how Jesus uniquely approached God with the distinct intimacy of addressing him as "Abba" (Father), something that simply wasn't done by individuals.[8] In fact, before Jesus, we don't have examples of people personally addressing God as "Abba" in this way. Yet every time Jesus directly speaks to God in the Gospels, he speaks to him as his Father — the only exception is when he cites Psalm 22 ("My God, my God") from the cross. Both within the Gospels and elsewhere in the New Testament, only Jesus speaks of God as "my Father," and he is our Father only because as we are connected to Jesus by his Spirit.[9]

Those who receive the Spirit of God's Son are therefore brought into this intimacy, into this divine life, into God's family.

> But when the fullness of time had come, God sent forth his Son, born of woman, born under the law, to redeem those who were under the law, so that we might receive adoption as sons. And because you are sons, God has sent the Spirit of his Son into our hearts, crying, "Abba! Father!" (Gal. 4:4–6)

Our adoption, our right to be called sons and daughters of God, comes through the Son of God, who became our representative and substitute. Because Jesus had the natural privilege of calling God "Abba! Father" (e.g., Mark 14:36), his connection to us enables us, who receive the Spirit of Christ, to address God similarly in this intimate fashion. "Before we can say Abba, we need to hear the Spirit saying it in our hearts."[10] The indwelling of the Spirit seals our adoption into God's family. As Luke Timothy Johnson notes, "Having been enabled by the gift of God's Spirit to call the source of all being 'Father,' we are able to turn for the first time to other people and say, 'my sister,' 'my brother.'"[11]

This adoption makes us co-heirs with Christ, who is the "heir of all things" (Heb. 1:2), and it assures us that we will enjoy all of the promised inheritance that is to come. As is well documented, adoption in the first century was primarily about choosing an heir who would receive all of the family privileges and carry on the family lineage.[12] There are even examples of adopting adults, since the main goal was choosing an heir. Believers are not "strangers and aliens" but have become "members of the household of God" (Eph. 2:19). Elsewhere Paul declares:

For all who are led by the Spirit of God are children of God. So
you have not received a spirit that makes you fearful slaves. Instead,
you received God's Spirit when he adopted you as his own children.
Now we call him, "Abba, Father." For his Spirit joins with our spirit
to affirm that we are God's children. And since we are his children,
we are his heirs. In fact, together with Christ we are heirs of God's
glory. But if we are to share his glory, we must also share his suffering. (Rom. 8:14–17 NLT)

This passage lays out the rights and responsibilities of adoption. Those
who receive the gift of the Spirit need not be afraid, for we can turn to God
and cry out to him as our caring Father. God is not a boss from whom we
need to hide our shortcomings; he is not an angry judge waiting to impose a
verdict upon us. Matt and Joan and their adopted children understand this
to the core of their beings. God is a loving Father who invites us to rest in
his presence, to soak up his love, to enjoy his kindness. And even when our
hearts condemn us, as they often do, God's own Spirit testifies to us that,
despite our disobedience, we are nonetheless children of our heavenly Father.
We look forward to sharing his glory in the future, and this frees us in the
present to suffer willingly as we extend ourselves to others in Christ's name.

John similarly rejoices over the lavish "kind of love the Father has given
to us, that we should be called children of God; and so we are" (1 John 3:1).
Yet our lives display our failure to experience the Father's love fully. We
often consider ourselves to be lost sheep, inconsistent servants, or forget-
ful children. For that reason John also acknowledges the tension of living
between the times: "Beloved, we are God's children *now*, and *what we will
be* has not yet appeared; but we know that when he appears *we shall be*
like him" (1 John 3:2, italics added). Like Ghina Kate we live between the
times. We are God's children now, but we still long for the true and complete freedom from sin that so easily frustrates our lives and our walking
with our Father. But we are sure of this, that we are in his hand, we are his,
and he will not let us go. Having experienced this love, we now live out of
that love with a freedom to love others.

For John, the sign of the Spirit was the mark of adoption, and the
Spirit's presence brings a profound love and concern for others. God did
not pour out his fatherly love for our self-indulgence, but as an all-sufficient
resource for us to extend to others the grace that God has shown us. And in
that outreach we also experience ever more richly his love for us. "Beloved,
let us love one another, for love is from God, and whoever loves has been
born of God and knows God" (1 John 4:7; cf. 3:16–18). Because we have

freely received the Spirit and have been adopted into God's family, we freely give love to others with the desire that all will come to know God's fatherly love and grace.

Filled by the Spirit

In the New Testament, to receive the gift of the Spirit is to be filled (*plēroō*) with the Spirit and consequently to bear his fruit. As Frederick Dale Bruner once wrote, "Wherever the Holy Spirit comes to a man he comes ... to fill, not only to affect; to dwell, not simply to visit."[13] But Scripture sometimes uses a slightly different word (cf. *pimplēmi*) — though also translated as "filled" in our English Bible — to describe times when individuals and communities experience distinct powers and abilities given by the Spirit for kingdom service.[14] Between these related words we find many of these "fillings" result in the combination of *powerful speech* with *concern for those in need.*[15]

A somewhat common pattern emerges. The Spirit empowers church leaders as they call people to participate in the movement of divine grace by ministering to others. In this way Stephen (Acts 6:5, 10; 7:55), Paul (9:17), and Barnabas (11:22–24) were "filled" with the Spirit as they proclaimed the gospel in his power, and their speech overflowed into radical giving for the sake of those in need.

For example, Acts 4:31 tells us that when the company of believers were filled with the Holy Spirit, they "spoke the word of God boldly" (NIV). But what does this have to do with participating in God's generosity? The next verse shows the connection. Immediately after the disciples were filled by the Spirit and began to speak the word of God, they also began to share their possessions with one another in an extraordinary way (4:32). Acts 4:33–34 continues:

> And with great power the apostles were giving their testimony to the resurrection of the Lord Jesus, and great grace was upon them all. There was not a needy person among them.

The Christians' inspired testimony led to an experience of "great grace," which was ultimately manifested in radical generosity. Christian charity flows from the Spirit-filled proclamation of the gospel (cf. 2 Cor. 8:9; 1 John 3:16–17). Word led to deed.

It makes sense, then, that Barnabas, who is described as "full of the Holy Spirit" (Acts 11:24), "sold a field that belonged to him and brought the money and laid it at the apostles' feet" to be used for the poor (Acts 4:37).[16] As one filled with the Spirit and known as a faithful teacher of the gospel (e.g., 12:25 – 13:7), Barnabas displayed an astonishing generosity from the beginning. By way of contrast, later verses state that Satan filled Ananias and Sapphira (5:3; cf. 13:9 – 10), causing them to withhold money and to lie about what they had done (5:1 – 11). While we may naturally want to qualify the story, noting that Ananias and Sapphira had still given a sizeable amount, the Bible points to a telling contrast: the Holy Spirit creates generosity aimed toward those in need, whereas Satan promotes withholding and manipulation aimed toward self-service. Similarly, Satan fills Judas, who betrays Jesus for thirty pieces of silver.

Yet from a different perspective, another positive connection between being filled with the Spirit and generosity is found in Acts 6:1 – 7. This passage states that a special group of seven men, "full of the Spirit" (6:3), were chosen by the apostles to perform special works of mercy and justice on behalf of the fledgling Christian community. The text specifically focuses on one of these men, Stephen, who is further described as "a man full of faith and of the Holy Spirit" (6:5) and who then becomes the first Christian to give his life as a martyr (6:8 – 7:60).

Strikingly similar connections between being filled with the Spirit, powerful speech, and concern for those in need can be found throughout both the Old and New Testaments. God repeatedly filled the prophets with his Spirit to call his people back to justice and charity. Micah declared, "I am filled with power, with the Spirit of the LORD, and with justice and might, to declare to Jacob his transgression and to Israel his sin" (Mic. 3:8). A few verses later Micah rails against the mercenary motives of Israel's religious leaders who "teach for a price," and false prophets who "practice divination for money" (Mic. 3:11; cf. 1 Tim. 3:3, 8; 2 Tim. 3:2, 4; Titus 1:7).

John the Baptist, whose message of repentance focused almost exclusively on the just use of material possessions (Luke 3:10 – 14), was said to be "filled by the Holy Spirit, even from his mother's womb" (1:15). Similarly, the prophet Isaiah was inspired by the Spirit to call all of God's people to "cry aloud" and to lift their voice "like a trumpet" (Isa. 58:1 – 12) because of the devastating lack of social justice and charity among God's people.

When it came time for Jesus—who was filled with the Spirit beyond measure!—to set his public ministry in motion, he did so by combining words from Isaiah 58 and 61 to form this inaugural proclamation:

> The Spirit of the Lord is upon me,
>   because he has anointed me
>   to proclaim good news to the poor.

He has sent me to proclaim liberty to the captives
   and recovering of sight to the blind,
      to set at liberty those who are oppressed,
to proclaim the year of the Lord's favor. (Luke 4:18 – 19; cf. Isa.
   61:1 – 2; 58:6)

Notice the connections between (1) the work of the Spirit, (2) the proclamation of the Gospel, and (3) God's just and generous purposes. Here again, the text links being filled with the Spirit to speaking boldly and to living as generously toward others as God has been toward us. Such prophetic, Spirit-filled speech is essential if justice and generosity are to flourish in any generation, including our own. Our filling with the Holy Spirit requires that we "cry aloud" when such joy and justice are absent.

Sadly, however, the use of money and material possessions are often dismissed as largely "unspiritual" topics today, or they are considered too personal to be discussed in public, especially from the pulpit. As the research of Princeton sociologist Robert Wuthnow has shown, "The darkest taboo in our culture is not sex or death, but money.... We feel it is inappropriate to burden others with our concerns."[17] In practice, this means we tend to be ignorant of those in our community who are in great need, and this attitude also fosters an unhealthy confusion among us between "needs" and "wants."

Christian Smith, Michael Emerson, and Patricia Snell have come to similar conclusions.[18] They have not only shown that 20 percent of all U.S. Christians give literally *nothing* to church, parachurch, or nonreligious charities (and that the majority give little, just 2.9 percent), but they have also shown that most pastors and religious leaders remain silent about these worrying trends.[19] Why? According to Smith and Emerson, it's because many pastors are understandably nervous to address this imbalance.[20] Our silence about such issues goes against the prophetic movement of the Spirit.

This is another reason we need to be filled with the Holy Spirit, not just in order to do justice and love mercy, but even to start talking about it! We need to speak the Word of God honestly, openly, and boldly to each other and to the world, laying out the implications of the gospel for kingdom living and giving (e.g., 2 Cor. 8:9; 1 John 3:16 – 17). Such conversation and action must not grow out of guilt and fear, but out of the Spirit's life-affirming presence. Fortunately the command to "be filled with the Spirit" in Ephesians 5:18 implies that such filling is accessible to those who ask for it (cf. Luke 11:13), abundantly available to those who believe. As St.

Augustine memorably prayed to God, "Give what you command, and then command whatever you will."[21]

Fruit of the Spirit

In *Pilgrim at Tinker Creek*, Annie Dillard describes the wonder of a fruitful tree: "There is a real power here," Dillard says:

> It is amazing that trees can turn gravel and bitter salts into these soft-lipped lobes, as if I were to bite down on a granite slab and start to swell, bud, and flower.... Water lifting up tree trunks can climb one hundred and fifty feet an hour; in full summer a tree can, and does, heave a ton of water every day. A big elm in a single season might make as many as *six million* leaves, wholly intricate, without budging an inch; *I couldn't produce one*. A tree stands there ... but secretly it seethes; it splits, sucks, and stretches; it heaves up tons and hurls them out in a green, fringed, fling. No person taps this free power; the dynamo in the tulip tree pumps out ever more tulip tree, and it runs on rain and air.[22]

Within the poetic beauty of this passage, Dillard betrays her deep desire to *bear fruit*. It is almost as if she wants to be that tree she sees — like the big elm in springtime producing millions of leaves. But she finds herself unable to produce even one. Unlike the elm and the tulip, she cannot "bite down on granite ... and start to swell, bud, and flower." Yet the promise of God is precisely that those who receive his Spirit become organically connected to the Tree: they are now rooted "in Christ" and bear much fruit. We shall be like trees.

This is the natural and expected outworking of the Spirit's abiding presence: he produces fruit *in* us and *through* us. As Paul teaches in Galatians 5:22–23, "the fruit of the Spirit is love, joy, peace, patience, kindness, goodness, faithfulness, gentleness, self-control." His work is not limited to occasional, even repeated, fillings. It is also a work of slow sustenance, an altogether *organic* process. A healthy tree bears good fruit (Matt. 7:16–18). And while it is beyond our present purpose to try to unpack each of the nine aspects of this fruit here, the *imagery* is deeply significant.

Fruit-bearing is a slow process because it is organic and intricate. We derive life from a source to which we are organically connected. The Spirit unites us to Christ, constituting that organic connection. We are "in Christ" (2 Cor. 5:17; Gal. 3:28; Phil. 3:8–9), and he is in us (Gal. 2:20; Col. 1:27); we abide in him as a branch abides in its vine (John 6:56; 15:4;

1 John 4:13). Our identity, our lives, derive from Christ, to whom we are united by his Spirit. After listing different qualities of the fruit, Paul concludes, "And those who belong to Christ Jesus have crucified the flesh with it passions and desires" (Gal. 5:24).

In truth, we continue to struggle with disordered passions and unhealthy desires. But Paul again fuses the past, present, and future together for those who have received the Spirit: Jesus on the cross put sin to death, and the Spirit connects us to our risen Lord. We "belong to Christ," not so much as property belongs to its owner, but more like the organic connection of fruit and branches belonging to the trunk (cf. Hos. 14:8). Because we are united to him who bore the true fruit of righteousness on a different "tree," the season of harvest has come and the fruit is joyfully expected.

Lest we become discouraged, let us never forget that fruit takes time to grow before it is really ripe. And our fruit can only come from the Lord of the Harvest. As James says as he concludes his epistle,

> Be patient, therefore, beloved, until the coming of the Lord. The farmer waits for the precious crop from the earth, being patient with it until it receives the early and the late rains. You also must be patient. Strengthen your hearts, for the coming of the Lord is near. (James 5:7–8 NRSV)

Let us not be defined by our sin and struggles, but let us delight in the slow developing fruit of God's Spirit in our lives. Let us take confidence in the One who says to us, "O Ephraim ... I am like an evergreen cypress; from me comes your fruit" (Hos. 14:8). For even though the fruit in our lives may be small, the God who gives the fruit will not abandon us, since he who began this work will cause our fruit to be rooted and to ripen in and through his own righteousness.

Finally, we are reminded by the larger context (Gal. 5:13–6:2) that this "fruit" is not merely a privatized matter; this fruit is consistently oriented toward one's neighbor. Whereas the fruit of the Spirit is how one fulfills the "law of Christ" (i.e., loving your neighbor: 5:14; 6:2), the fruit of the sinful nature focuses on self, which consequently tends to undermine one's neighbor. Thus, where the Spirit bears his fruit, there is love and the building up of the community.

Gifts of the Spirit

When Paul speaks of the "spiritual gifts," he emphasizes an underlying goal that must never be compromised: "To each is given the manifestation of the Spirit for *the common good*" (1 Cor. 12:7, italics added). Receiving gifts from the Spirit, we extend our head, heart, and hands to *others*. Thus, whether God's Spirit gives wisdom, knowledge, faith, healing, miracles, prophecy, tongues, or their interpretation, *all* of these gifts exist for the "common good." We may have a variety of gifts, but they all come from the same Spirit.

Sin drives us away from one another, but the Spirit's gifts bring reconciliation and a taste of harmony. "For in one Spirit we were all baptized into one body — Jews or Greeks, slaves or free — and all were made to drink of one Spirit" (1 Cor. 12:13). Thus we should not show favoritism and discrimination in our dealings with one another, since all gifts ultimately come from heaven as a display of divine generosity (cf. James 1:17; 2:1 – 7). Indeed, when the gift of God lands on the scales of human prejudice, they are smashed. Now, with every bias broken, we know that if one suffers, we all suffer, and if one is honored, we are all honored (1 Cor. 12:26).

Entering this stream of God's mercy moves us from self to neighbor. For this reason Paul follows his discussion of "gifts" with an extended commendation of love (1 Cor. 13). Without love — which binds all things together — these gifts get perverted into self-exaltation, and this hurts both others and us. Gifts employed for the concern and nurture of neighbor bring these neighbors before the true Giver of all gifts, who continues to heal and comfort. This is why the sure sign of the Christian is the presence of the Spirit, and the sure sign of the Spirit is ultimately love, and therefore, concern for neighbor (1 John 3:24; 4:7 – 21).

A proper view of gifts from God requires concern for neighbor rather than self. Peter declares:

> As each has received a gift, use it to serve one another, as good stewards of God's varied grace: whoever speaks, as one who speaks oracles of God; whoever serves, as one who serves by the strength that God supplies — in order that in everything God may be glorified through Jesus Christ. (1 Peter 4:10 – 11)

Paul, when listing various spiritual gifts in Romans 12, exhorts the Christians, "Let us use them." These gifts, which include service, mercy ministry, and generosity, are meant for the good of the community, not merely the individual.

James makes a similar point, urging believers to make requests of God while at the same time reminding them why many of their prayers go unanswered. "You do not have, because you do not ask. You ask and do not receive, because you ask wrongly, to spend it on your passions" (James 4:2b–3). What God gives is meant to be spent, so to speak, for the other. Arrogance leads to self-absorption and the destruction of the community, whereas humility and grace build up the common good. Thus, God delights to answer the prayers of the humble, but the arrogant are offensive to him because they put themselves before everyone else (Prov. 16:5; James 4:6–10).

We harm our communities, our world, and ourselves—and indeed, God's own reputation among those who do not know him!—when we reduce the promises of being filled with the Spirit, bearing his fruit, and enjoying his gifts to personal, psychological comfort and peace. Yes, God's Spirit brings a peace that surpasses understanding, and we personally enjoy using the gifts God gives. But the filling, the fruit, and the gifts are dynamic streams of God's own generosity, so that any attempt to use them selfishly goes against their nature. God's Spirit fills his people with compassion and concern for those in greatest need; he grows different kinds of fruit in us, all expressed in love toward the other; and he provides amazing gifts to equip us to pursue the common good. God's Spirit draws us into the life of God and allows us to extend that life and love to others. That is true life, that is freedom, that is a great gift.

The Victorious King
Gives Triumphal Gifts

We are now ready to revisit the ascension of Jesus and the event of Pentecost. This is a movement of Jubilee—a time of triumph, not sorrow. As Jesus ascended, his disciples were not filled with sadness, but with joy, expectation, and hope (Luke 24:52). This would make sense to both a Jewish and Gentile audience.[23]

Three main actions for celebrating a Jewish Jubilee are outlined in the Old Testament: (1) the cancellation of debts, (2) the setting free of prisoners, and (3) and the return of ancestral land (Lev. 25).[24] This was meant to be a restoration and a reminder that everything—people and land—ultimately belongs to God. Jubilee was to occur every fifty years as a taste and anticipation of a future full restoration. While there is some debate as to whether any Jubilees ever happened in Israel's history, the Jubilee motif continued as part of the first-century Jewish mind-set.

For the Gentile audience, similar imagery arose around themes in the "Roman triumph."[25] In this great procession the warrior-champion publicly proclaimed his victory by the two triumphal acts (*actus triumphales*): the enemy was bound to the victor's chariot and led about the capital city, and then the victor distributed gifts, often coins. These coins were frequently minted as "new coins" (*missilia*) that would bear the images of the victory and the new leader.[26] The gifts represented the triumph, and the new emblazoned image on the coin proclaimed the reigning victor.

Jesus' ascension has several parallels to the great triumphal acts and Jubilee. Jesus Christ, the divine Warrior, came as the one filled with the Spirit beyond measure, not only preaching good news to the poor and binding up the broken, but also proclaiming freedom for the captives and releasing the prisoners from darkness as a sign of the year of the Lord's favor (Isa. 61:1–2; Luke 7:21–23). This divine Warrior, the Messiah, rose from the dead in the power of the Spirit, and then he ascended and was seated at God's right hand

> in the heavenly places, far above all rule and authority and power and dominion, and above every name that is named, not only in this age but also in the one to come. And he put all things under his feet and gave him as head over all things to the church, which is his body, the fullness of him who fills all in all. (Eph. 1:20b–22)

His ascension and the pouring out of the Spirit declared the crucified Jesus to be the victorious King, "both Lord and Christ" (Acts 2:36; cf. Rom. 1:4). He has shown his triumph over the enemies of sin, death, and the devil, which plague God's world. Having "disarmed the rulers and authorities" on the cross (Col. 2:15), Jesus' movement through resurrection and then ascension into the heavens is how "God put on public display the reality of that victory over the powers."[27]

As risen King, Jesus likewise demonstrates his manifold treasure and authority to give all great gifts, most especially by giving his Spirit (cf. Eph. 4:7–10).[28] Peter, in his sermon to those gathered on the day of Pentecost, connects Jesus' ascension with the pouring out of his Spirit:

> This Jesus God raised up, and of that we all are witnesses. Being therefore exalted at the right hand of God, and having received from the Father the promise of the Holy Spirit, he has poured out this that you yourselves are seeing and hearing. (Acts 2:32–33)

Those to whom this Gift—the "Spirit of Christ"—is given now bear the very image of the Redeemer, their new King who has set them free. Just as the ancient victor gave out coins bearing his image as gifts to be treasured and spent, we are treasured, and the expectation is that we will be spent in love for Christ and for others. Thus Christians proclaimed that "Jesus was lord, and Caesar was not." N. T. Wright states, "Not only Jesus' resurrection, but also his ascension, carried inescapable political significance."[29] His image is now emblazoned on those who receive his Spirit, for now we belong to him, and he will keep us through his Spirit. We have been returned to our rightful and loving Lord, having been set free from the bondage and debt of sin. "And by this we know that he abides in us, by the Spirit whom he has given us" (1 John 3:24). But what does it mean to receive this triumphal gift given by the King?

Fear not, little flock, for it is your Father's good pleasure to give you the kingdom.

Luke 12:32

Therefore, let us be grateful for receiving a kingdom that cannot be shaken.

Hebrews 12:28

The Kingdom of God is, in fact, a participation in the Holy Spirit.

Simeon the New Theologian[1]

Such is the nature of his rule, that he shares with us all that he has received from the Father.

John Calvin[2]

The kingdom of God is the sum of all spiritual and natural benefits.

Herman Bavinck[3]

Come, you who are blessed by my Father, inherit the kingdom prepared for you from the foundation of the world.

Matthew 25:34

chapter eight

The Gift of the Kingdom

The Kingdom of God Is at Hand

They must be drunk. Heaven's doors had been opened and out came the rushing winds of the Spirit, encircling the house, filling the disciples, and causing a large crowd to gather because of the commotion; there was joy, there was laughter, and there was delight as each heard God's works spoken in their native tongue (Acts 2:1–13). Some responded in wonder, while others stood off and mocked, reducing this scene to the effects of too much wine too early in the day—really early, as it was only 9:00 a.m.

In this scene of surprise, confusion, and power we find Peter. Not long before he had run, he had failed, he had wept. Now, among the crowds he does not flee but he stands and boldly speaks. Peter declares that the time has come; God's Spirit has been poured out because Jesus of Nazareth, who had been crucified, had been raised from the dead, and had recently ascended into heaven. As Peter explains, "God raised [this Jesus] up, loosing the pangs of death, because it was not possible for him to be held by it" (Acts 2:24).

Jesus, who is God's own Son, had come in obscure humility, had lived in faithful constancy, was crucified in shameful poverty; and then what? Jesus did not remain on a cross or in a grave, but, as Peter reiterates, "this Jesus God raised up, and of that we are all witnesses" (Acts 2:32). What happened to Jesus was not a private event but a public reality—he had been crucified under Pontius Pilate, but had subsequently been raised and been seen by many.

But why does this matter? Let us not miss the message of Peter's first sermon: Jesus is King, for "God has made him both Lord and Christ" (Acts

2:36). This was a revolutionary message and far more radical than we tend to realize. Notice that as Peter preaches, he does not ask the gathered crowds to "make Jesus their Lord," nor does he gently encourage them to "accept" him as their Savior. *He is the Lord.* In fact, Peter is incredibly audacious here and concludes by declaring that "this Jesus" is the very one whom "you crucified" (Acts 2:23). Luke tells us that those who heard this "were cut to the heart" (2:37), and they asked Peter and the rest of the disciples what they should do.

"Repent!" That is the first word that comes out of Peter's mouth in response to their question of what they should do. Does that sound familiar?

"Repent" is the first word we hear from Jesus when he began to preach. Matthew quotes Jesus as declaring, "Repent, for the kingdom of heaven is at hand" (Matt. 4:17). In Mark's gospel we likewise overhear a similar message from the mouth of Jesus as he started his ministry: "The time is fulfilled, and the kingdom of God is at hand; repent and believe in the gospel" (Mark 1:15). And in Luke we discover Jesus going from one synagogue to another preaching the "good news of the kingdom of God," since, he explains, "I was sent for this purpose" (Luke 4:43).

Jesus' message was that the kingdom of God was at hand and therefore people should repent. Before Jesus' ministry, this was also the message proclaimed by John the Baptist, who used the same words: "Repent, for the kingdom of heaven is at hand" (Matt. 3:2). Now at Pentecost, after receiving the gift of the Spirit, Peter announces that this kingdom has in fact come and, therefore, all need to "repent."

When we hear the language and call to "repentance," we almost immediately think this means that we need to change our bad habits and clean ourselves up. Walking the streets of Chicago I remember seeing a man holding a sign that read "Repent," and it included a message about the dangers of hell. To many of us, the loud message of repentance represents a call to stop smoking, throw out the pornographic magazines, and discontinue our tendencies to gossip. But is that what John the Baptist, Jesus, and Peter were primarily talking about?

We find continuity between the messages of John the Baptist through Jesus and to the mouth of Peter, because the central message they all proclaimed was the coming of the kingdom. Each spoke from a slightly different vantage point, but in essence the message was the same. The repentance that was needed takes us to the heart of our problem as well as to the heart of the gospel. While we tend to think of repentance as bad news, when rightly understood, it is incredibly good news.

When Peter calls his listeners to "repent," he is calling them to change their whole orientation toward God, as well as how they view themselves and the world.[4] He is telling them that they have a certain expectation about who God is, how he works, and what their place is within his world, and in each of these areas profound change is needed.

Peter, the close companion of Jesus, has been transformed in his own understanding of God, himself, and the world. He, who first confessed Jesus as Messiah and believed this man would conquer as the new King, has recently witnessed his leader die a brutal death. He, who once envisioned himself as loyal and righteous, is now painfully aware of his own sin and weakness through his denial and fear. He, who had assumed Yahweh's concern and love was exclusively for the nation of Israel, now discovers with ever-growing clarity that God is concerned with the renewal of the entire world, including people from all nations. Peter has to repent; he has to change his view of God, of himself, and of the world — and that necessarily entails a kind of disorientation and reorientation that simultaneously shakes up and revitalizes every area of his life.

It is along these lines that we can begin to make sense of the fact that Jesus so commonly holds together not simply repentance and the kingdom, but also a call to belief (Mark 1:15). As the apostle Paul later preached before the Athenian crowd, "the times of ignorance God overlooked, but now he commands all people everywhere to repent," for the risen Christ will judge the world (Acts 17:30 – 31). Later he reiterates that John the Baptizer came with "the baptism of repentance, telling people to believe in the one who was to come after him, that is, Jesus" (19:4). John had called people to be ready to change their perceptions, their expectations, and their lives, and this change would be centered around the coming Messiah King. He is bringing God's kingdom to earth, and all are called to respond to his coming with repentance and faith.

Repentance and faith are, therefore, at the heart of what it means to be a Christian, not because this makes us morally superior, but because it is only by them that we enter the kingdom of God. Those who encounter the kingdom are called to rethink their view of God, themselves, and the world. This brings about a change not simply in their minds, but also in their lives.[5] And yet, even as this change is called for, it is also paradoxically promised as a *gift*.

The Kingdom as Gift

We do not tend to think of the kingdom as gift. We might affirm that the kingdom of God is real, that it is the reign and rule of God, but what does it mean to think of it as something that is *given*? What does Jesus mean when he comforts his disciples with the words: "Fear not, little flock, for it is your Father's good pleasure to *give* you the kingdom" (Luke 12:32, italics added)? In order to understand what Jesus means, we need to look at the context in which Jesus is speaking, and then we need to reenvision this royal gift in light of larger visions and promises connected to the kingdom.

Do Not Be Anxious, the Kingdom Is Given

A voice from the crowd yells out, "Teacher, tell my brother to divide the inheritance with me" (Luke 12:13). Here is a man asking Jesus to solve a domestic dispute. Would Jesus ask for them to act more like good brothers, sharing their toys more fairly and playing nice? No. Instead, Jesus warns that we are all prone to find our security in what we can hold in our hands or claim as our property. Jesus' words are piercing and liberating at the same time: "for one's life does not consist in the abundance of his possessions" (Luke 12:15). Then he goes on to tell a parable. This parable has meaning for all of us, not just for the people in suits who labor on Wall Street.

A rich person who has produced an abundance of crops makes a plan. He decides it will be best to build bigger barns so he can store his windfall. The man says to himself, "Soul, you have ample goods laid up for many years; relax, eat, drink, be merry'" (Luke 12:19). Is there anything wrong with such thinking? Doesn't the story sound like a prudently planned retirement package? Invest your money, save up for the future, develop a nest egg, and then relax and enjoy the ride. I dare say that is not merely the American dream—that is the common Christian dream. "But God said to him, 'Fool!'" (Luke 12:20).

Wait a minute—I thought this was wisdom. What we call wisdom God declares foolish (cf. 1 Cor. 1:18–25). How can that be? First, we must understand that "fool" here has less to do with stupidity and more to do with the Old Testament imagery of rebellion against God.[6] It is the fool who lives as if God doesn't exist, or at least as if all that he has is merely the result of his labor rather than a gift from God (Prov. 18:11).

> One man gives freely, yet grows all the richer;
>   another withholds what he should give, and only suffers want.
> Whoever brings blessing will be enriched;
>   he who waters will himself be watered.
> The people curse him who holds back grain,
>   but a blessing is on the head of him who sells it....
> Whoever trusts in his riches will fall,

but the righteous will flourish like a green leaf. (Prov 11:24–26, 28; cf. 22:9)[7]

The rich man is a "fool," not because he is rich, but because as he expends his unbridled energies trying to secure his own personal peace and prosperity, he becomes blinded to an obvious reality—he is not in control. "This night your soul is required of you," the fool is told, "and the things you have prepared, whose will they be?" (Luke 12:20). Then Jesus delivers the punch line: "So is the one who lays up treasure for himself and is not rich toward God" (12:21; cf. Prov. 23:4–5; Ezek. 28:1–10). Notice the option here: either you are rich in this world and end up with nothing, or you are "rich toward God" and end up with everything. "But Jesus," we naturally respond, "if we don't pinch pennies, if we don't stock up, if we don't look after ourselves, we won't survive." How should we then live?[8]

Jesus' answer is as simple as it is scandalous: live in God's kingdom, not in your own. Do not live according to the prevailing powers and prejudices of the kingdom of this world. *Let the full gift of God's government guide you.* Let me put it differently. Jesus moves immediately from warning us about being possessed by our possessions to encouraging us to take comfort that we belong to God; we are his treasured possessions, and he will never let us go (cf. Ex. 19:5–6; Col. 1:11–14). "Do not be anxious about your life, what you will eat, nor about your body, what you will put on. For life is more than food, and the body more than clothing" (Luke 12:22–23). Jesus lifts his hand, points to the ravens in the sky, and then to the lilies—neither the birds nor the flowers spend their time twisted up with anxiety, since God provides for them. "Of how much more value are you than the birds!" (12:24–27).

Where is Jesus going with all of this bird watching and talk about field flowers, not hoarding, not worrying? Watch his rhetorical move: this is really about the clash of kingdoms.

> Do not seek what you are to eat and what you are to drink, nor be worried. For *all the nations* of the world seek after these things, and your Father knows that you need them. Instead, seek *his kingdom,* and these things will be added to you.
>
> Fear not, little flock, for it is your Father's good pleasure *to give you* the kingdom. (Luke 12:29–32, italics added)

There are only these two options. Either you live under the controlling power and fear of "the nations," or you live under the Father's generous reign and rule. The powers of this world encourage us to grasp and grab. But God's kingdom looks unsettlingly different: *his sovereignty is revealed*

in self-giving. Those who belong to God's kingdom are not to worry. And this lack of worry is established, not by building up a large bank account but by participating in the stream of divine generosity.[9]

Here we run into the paradox of God's kingdom. Right after Jesus tells us the kingdom is a freely given gift, he immediately challenges his flock:

> Sell your possessions, and give to the needy. Provide yourselves with moneybags that do not grow old, with a treasure in the heavens that does not fail, where no thief approaches and no moth destroys. For where your treasure is, there will your heart be also. (Luke 12:33–34).

In God's kingdom, life becomes more secure as we let go, not as we grip tighter. After this Jesus goes on to tell his followers to "stay dressed for action ... be like men who are waiting for their master to come home from the wedding feast" (Luke 12:35–36). Peter eventually interrupts Jesus by asking if this discourse is just for the inner circle or for everyone. Jesus makes it clear that his comments are expansive, not exclusive. They are for all in his kingdom, all who have been entrusted with managing his affairs, as his followers are set "over all his possessions" (12:44).

Notice how disquieting the parable of the talents can be as we encounter just two options for how to live. On the one hand, hoarding or burying what is entrusted to you eventually leads to the reality that even what is given will be taken away. On the other hand, those who "invest" what has been given to them—time, talents, treasures—will receive even greater gifts (Matt. 25:14–30). But this isn't a "health and wealth gospel," because Jesus asks us to "invest" in the needy, seeking returns by fighting injustice and compounding wealth by bringing the words of life to the lost. This is what true repentance and human flourishing look like: *a participation in God's gifts* (cf. Gen. 12:2; Ps. 67:1–2; 2 Cor. 9:11; Eph. 4:28).

No one knows when the Lord will return, but when he does, he expects us to have been faithful with what he has given us (Matt. 25:14–30; 1 Cor. 4:2). But what has been given? He has given us nothing less than his kingdom—both now with its coming and more fully in the future after we have endured the struggles of our days (Rev. 3:21). As his people we faithfully live in his kingdom, and we look forward to its coming fullness as we participate in the movement of God's grace and the outpouring of his generosity. His kingdom is our treasure, our security, and our future inheritance. In God's economy he gives that we might give, and thus we can never forget that what we give has already been given to us.

Therefore, let us be grateful for *receiving* a kingdom that cannot be shaken, and thus let us offer to God acceptable worship, with reverence and awe, for our God is a consuming fire.

... Through him then let us continually offer up a sacrifice of praise to God, that is, the fruit of lips that acknowledge his name. Do not neglect to do good and to *share what you have*, for such sacrifices are pleasing to God. (Heb. 12:28–29; 13:15–16, italics added)

The Kingdom as Eternal Life and Salvation

To appreciate the reality even more fully that the kingdom is a gift, we must make some final connections. Not only does the kingdom point to the reign and rule of God in the New Testament, but it points to the "gift of life and salvation." One point of Jesus' original twist on first-century expectations about the "kingdom of God" is that he uses this phrase to stand "as a comprehensive term for all that the messianic salvation included."[10] Where Matthew, Mark, and Luke tend to speak of the "kingdom of God/heaven," the basic equivalent in John's gospel is the surprising phrase "eternal life."[11]

The only place where the "kingdom of God" is used in John is during Jesus' encounter with Nicodemus. Coming at night this trained Pharisee approaches the itinerant preacher, wondering how he can do these "signs" if God were not with him. Notice Jesus' reply: "Truly, truly, I say to you, unless one is born again he cannot see the kingdom of God" (John 3:3). Nicodemus seems almost distracted, possibly even mocking Jesus by asking how he could reenter his mother's womb just to come out again. But Jesus sticks with the imagery:

That which is born of the flesh is flesh, and that which is born of the Spirit is spirit. Do not marvel that I said to you, "You must be born again." The wind blows where it wishes, and you hear its sound, but you do not know where it comes from or where it goes. So it is with everyone who is born of the Spirit. (John 3:6–8)

There is no question here: the kingdom is a gift of the Spirit. One needs eyes to see and ears to hear the reverberations of the kingdom, and this comes by the life-giving power of the Spirit. As Simeon the New Theologian (949–1022) understood long ago, "The Kingdom of God is, in fact, a participation in the Holy Spirit."[12] Only by God's generosity through his Spirit can one be born again, experiencing the liberty of God's kingdom.

Where the Gospels speak of "kingdom" and "eternal life," scholars observe that the apostle Paul more often employs "salvation" to convey the same basic ideas.

> The concept of the kingdom of God is parallel with the Johannine concept of eternal life and the Pauline concept of salvation. Precisely as those who put their faith in the atoning work of Christ are said to possess eternal life, to be in Christ or to be saved, in spite of the fact that eternal life or salvation are essentially eschatological [future oriented] concepts, so also believers may be said to have entered into the kingdom of God despite the fact that the kingdom of God, like eternal life and salvation, can be properly experienced only at the end of time.[13]

Consequently, we find a peculiar dynamic when it comes to the biblical promise of salvation; it parallels the dynamic of the kingdom that has been inaugurated but is not yet fully realized. Those who repent and believe *have been saved*—past tense (Rom. 8:24; Eph. 2:8–9). Children of God are likewise those who are *being saved*—present reality (1 Cor. 1:18; 15:2; 2 Cor. 2:15). And the saints of God are declared as those who *will be saved*—future promise (Ps. 80:3, 7, 9; Matt. 10:22; 24:13; Mark 13:13; Rom. 5:10). God's merciful salvation—eternal life—is based on God's saving work in the past, God's continuing liberating presence in his people in the present, and God's strong assurance to deliver his people in the future. First and foremost, this is God's grace and his work, not ours. He saves us by giving us new life in his kingdom. "He had descended from above," Dutch theologian Herman Bavinck concluded, "to bestow eternal life, to distribute to his own all the goods of the kingdom."[14]

Given by God out of the abundance of his free grace and mercy, this salvation is always understood as gift. Yet, people are called to believe; they are urged to respond in love-filled obedience as they are expected to actively engage in kingdom work.[15] The "gospel of the kingdom" appears to have "two parts which form an unbreakable unity. The first part is related to the *gift*, the *salvation*, given in the gospel; the other part is related to the *demand*, the *command* in which it is expressed."[16] Contained in the gift of salvation is the command, and likewise, the demands of the kingdom are part of the salvation God provides.

It is a false dichotomy to pit God's gift against human agency—our actions or behavior. We cannot award the kingdom to others since God alone gives it away (Luke 12:32). Yet we genuinely testify to its reality, we *participate* in its vibrancy, we enjoy its rhythms, and in this way we are used by God to expand his kingdom. This was humanity's calling from the beginning (Gen. 1:28), and this is now our calling once again. We are to believe; we are to love; we are to live out of his kingdom, his gift. We do so, not to earn God's love and favor, but because we are liberated by God's love and favor to follow the true King.

In this sense, we are like the armies of Israel who, after the giant Goliath fell dead before David, "surged forward with a shout" (1 Sam. 17:52 NIV). We do not defeat the giant for ourselves, nor do we establish God's kingdom in our power. But having already witnessed the victory, we are called to "surge forward" and join in the fight. As Nicodemus learned, God gives us new life that we might see and live in his kingdom. Thus we "receive" the kingdom like children, joyfully entering into this gift as an unfolding struggle and surprise (Mark 10:15; Luke 18:17).

Because we are given the kingdom, we possess all things in Christ. Because we are given eternal life, we are not bound by the confines of our narrow, short-lived, self-centered lives. Because we are given salvation, we can, by the Spirit, give away the riches of the kingdom, our very selves in truly just and generous ways. We have been given everything in the kingdom, including true freedom, which is another way of saying that we have been restored to truly belonging to our loving Father and Maker. As Martin Luther once brilliantly summarized the Christian paradox:

> A Christian is a perfectly free lord of all, subject to none.
> A Christian is a perfectly dutiful servant of all, subject to all.[17]

We are free and bound to love and serve radically. We are free and bound to pour ourselves out. We are free and bound to give ourselves away. And in so doing we are most like Christ, our Savior and King.

God's Sovereignty Revealed in Self-Giving

What we ultimately discover is that the kingdom of God must be understood in terms of gift because it is ultimately established in the self-giving of God. Because Jesus—the King—has been *given*, his kingdom comes as *gift*. Here we find what Herman Ridderbos has called "the most characteristic and 'revolutionary' reality" that Jesus revealed about the kingdom: "The Son of Man had been invested by God with all power and authority for the revelation of his dominion and was at the same time the one who 'had to' suffer and die. He had come to give himself as a ransom for many."[18] Jesus' message of the kingdom of God is, therefore, the announcement of *God's sovereignty in self-giving*. It is the proclamation—by word and deed—that God's reign has come through the gift of God himself.

Amen Lord

"He judged the cause of <u>the poor and needy;</u> then it
was well. Is not this to know me?" declares the LORD.

Jeremiah 22:16

Blessed are you who are poor, for yours is the kingdom of God.

Luke 6:20

The true interests of a person are at once perfectly
his own and common to the whole Kingdom of God.

Thomas Merton[1]

They are just, therefore, who do not retain anything
for themselves alone, knowing that everything has
been given for all.

Saint Ambrose[2]

Justice without love will never do justice to justice,
nor will "love" without justice ever do justice to love.

Dallas Willard[3]

chapter nine

Living in the Gift

In Native American Cherokee history, the Cherokee tribes had a political system for different challenges faced by their people. Recognizing different personality traits and leadership approaches, the Cherokee had two chiefs: one for peace and one for war. In times of peace, the peace chief ruled. In times of war, the war chief stepped in.

What we find with Christ and his kingdom is that we simultaneously live in a time of both war and peace. We live in both, and Christ alone reigns in both. This is the tension of our lives, and it is the tension of living in God's kingdom in the present.

The King has come, and through the movement of his life, death, resurrection, and ascension, he has begun the renewal of his creation. Now, all who are found in Christ by his Spirit have new life; they are new creatures—though they still live and breathe as before. Serving as a kind of pivot point, Jesus' resurrection makes clear that God's kingdom has come, and the King is now about the business of recreating the world through his life-giving Spirit. The new age has dawned, and the ascended King now rules from the heavens until his return. Cyprian, the third-century bishop of Carthage, concluded that

> Christ Himself ... may be the kingdom of God, whom we day to day desire to come, whose advent we crave to be quickly manifested to us. For since He is Himself the Resurrection, since in Him we rise again, so also the kingdom of God may be understood to be Himself, since in Him we shall reign.[4]

Believers are invited to participate in his heavenly rule as we carry out his commandments by his Spirit. His kingdom is dawning as "heaven" has come bursting through into the present.

Kingdom Inaugurated, but Not Fully Realized

Nevertheless, when we sit down and watch the nightly news, it becomes clear we are not living in heaven. Fear and pain, sickness and death, war and oppression, pettiness and hatred—these are all the absurdities that mark the present world. So what difference did it make to have Jesus come?

"Through Jesus' presence and action," says Pope Benedict XVI, "God has here and now entered actively into history in a wholly new way.... In Jesus, God is now the one who acts and who rules as Lord—rules in a divine way, without worldly power, rules through the love that reaches 'to the end' (John 13:1), to the cross."[5] This is God's kingly rule in Jesus—it is the rule of radical, sacrificial love.

Throughout the writings of the Old Testament and into the Judaism of the first century, there is a common contrast in which two worlds—or more appropriately, two "ages"—are placed against each other.[6] The first "age" is the time in which fallen humanity finds itself living, struggling with its weakness, sin, and the chaos of this world. Here there is no denying the reality of evil, poverty, and death that is so prevalent and unavoidable. But there was another "age" that was longed for, "the age to come," in which God's perfect rule will be actualized; this is the time of resurrection and life, renewal and peace. In the Hebraic background, this "age to come" was not other-worldly, but fundamentally involved a renewal of God's creation, where he purifies, reclaims, and recultivates his earth.[7]

Those who receive God's Spirit and are united to Christ live in the tension of the times—we exist between heaven and earth, so to speak. We pray and act so that God's reign and rule will become more realized in the present world even as it is in heaven.

New Testament scholar Oscar Cullmann memorably argued that the Christian experience is equivalent to living between D-Day (June 6, 1944) and VE-Day (May 7–8, 1945).[8] Once the Allies won the bloody battle of D-Day, there was little doubt that final victory over the German army would eventually be realized. Men and women who remained in the towns and prisons still occupied by the Nazis tell of being able to hear the approaching American troops—they waited expectantly for their final deliverance, but they could not fully enjoy their freedom until the advancement was complete on VE-Day.

Similarly, believers live between D-Day (the cross and resurrection) and VE-Day (the triumphant return of Christ). Our lives must be shaped by the assured knowledge of God's climactic work on the cross, where we hear the earth-shattering words, "It is finished" (John 19:30). But our lives must also be shaped by the final restoration that is still to come. The new beginning is put on public display in the resurrection, which is the start of what is to be fully realized in the future.

The kingdom has come, but it is not yet fully experienced and enjoyed. Carl Braaten captures this tension: "The kingdom of God is both the foundation of the church and the goal of the world. Therefore, we have and we hope; we give thanks and we sigh for more."[9] In the shadow of the cross and resurrection we are confident of God's faithful ongoing renewal in the present and the yet-to-be experienced but certain realities of the future. It is only by God's Spirit that we get a taste of this future reality.

Contrary to pop-Christian fiction like the *Left Behind* series, the New Testament claims that with the coming of the Messiah and his poured out Spirit, the church already finds itself living in the "last days" (Acts 2:16–21; Heb. 1:2–3). "The last days" is not something that Jesus punts into the future, but what he brings as a present reality. The point is that with the coming of the Son and Spirit, we find ourselves in a new age, as we are invited to live in God's kingdom. Living in this time between the times, where God's kingdom is among us but not yet fully realized, God's people become witnesses and agents of his kingdom, and therefore our lives should be governed by the King's values.

Justice and Righteousness: Fundamentals of the Kingdom

What are the governing dynamics of the kingdom? How does God make his judgments and conduct his royal affairs? In short, how does God reign over the universe that belongs to him?

The answer to these questions may be found in what the Bible teaches us about God's "justice and righteousness." These are the key characteristics of his kingdom or, as the Psalms describe them, the "foundation" of God's throne.[10] God's rule as King rests on his justice and righteousness. They are like a great marble slab that lies beneath and supports the place where he reigns. This is why Jesus, after telling his disciples to seek first God's kingdom, quickly added "and his righteousness"; you cannot have one without the other (Matt. 6:33). Elsewhere Jesus included "justice" among what he called the "weightier" or more important matters of the law

(Matt. 23:23). Put simply, "justice" and "righteousness" are indispensible to how God rules over his kingdom.[11]

But what is meant by the words "justice" and "righteousness"? While the answer to this question is rich and complex, for our purposes let us focus our attention on how Scripture consistently identifies *generosity* as the positive characteristic flowing out of justice and righteousness.[12]

> Yes, the LORD will give what is good
>   and our land will yield its increase.
> Righteousness will go before him
>   and make his footsteps a way. (Ps. 85:12–13).
>
> He has scattered abroad his gifts to the poor;
>   his righteousness endures forever. (Ps. 112:9 NIV; cf. 72:6–7; Isa. 45:8)[13]
>
> The wicked borrow but do not repay,
>   but the righteous give generously. (Ps. 37:21 NIV)

Verses like these consistently connect the virtues of justice and righteousness with the idea of generosity. But we see the connection of God's generosity with his exercise of justice and righteousness well beyond places where those particular words are used. For example, when God gave the children of Israel his law for living in the Promised Land, their new life was supposed to be a picture of heaven on earth—a portrait of God's justice and righteousness in tangible terms for the entire world to see (cf. Deut. 26). It was not just an example; it was an invitation.

We find another portrait of justice and righteousness as generosity in the book of Job, which opens with one of the most remarkable descriptions of any human being contained in the Bible: "That man was blameless and upright, one who feared God and turned away from evil" (Job 1:1, 8; 2:3). Similarly, the book of Ezekiel tells us that Job was one of the most righteous men ever to have lived (Ezek. 14:14, 20).

But what was it about Job that made him deserving of such inestimable praise from God? In Job 29:1–25 this man describes, in his own words, what his righteousness actually looked like. Above all, we find that Job's life was characterized by a ceaseless concern for the needs of the poor and oppressed. Job tells us that he rescued the needy and assisted the fatherless (Job 29:12). As one "who comfort[ed] mourners" (29:25), Job gave men reason to bless him with their dying breath and even made the hearts of widows sing for joy (29:13).

According to Job, this is what it meant to "put on righteousness as clothing" and justice as a "robe" (Job 29:14 NIV). Job was like eyes to the blind (29:15) and transportation for the disabled (29:15). He was a father to the poor and an advocate for the stranger (29:16). And finally, Job did not fail to vehemently oppose those who oppressed others, breaking "the fangs of the unrighteous" so that they would drop the victims "from his teeth" (29:17 NIV). Job's life provides us with a full-orbed picture of what generosity that spills over into all of life looks like. His compassion was not limited to check writing; his hospitality was not about social maneuvering. Instead, Job used his resources, time, and energy to pursue the interests of those who were least able to help themselves or repay him for his kindness (cf. Luke 14:12–14; Acts 20:34–35; James 1:27).

We say generosity is the "positive" theme because there are also "negative," even frightening expressions of God's justice and righteousness that must not be overlooked. For example, it is in justice and righteousness that God overcomes those who oppress the poor, the weak, and the marginalized.[14] The Son of God suffered and died in order to preserve God's justice even as he expressed his righteous—or one might say generous—rule. In Christ on the cross, God demonstrated himself to be both the just and the justifier (Rom. 3:26).[15] God does not ignore the injustice of human sin—going back to humanity's fall as expressed by greed—but, as we have seen, he overcomes that fall by his own sovereign self-giving.

Thus, living in God's kingdom means entering the movement of divine generosity. Such living does not ignore injustice and sin, but seeks to right the wrongs of this world through the healing powers and generosity of the gospel.

Following the King, God's people witness to the kingdom in both their words and deeds. Whenever the church chooses between these two, it ends up in trouble, both misunderstanding the King and misrepresenting the kingdom.[16] Having received eyes to see and to experience the reality of the kingdom, the church seeks to imitate the concerns of Jesus' life because we have been liberated by his death. We now seek to fight against the tyrannical powers that create so much pain for humanity. We seek to foster harmony between humanity and nature; we faithfully join in the efforts to promote healing where there is sickness; we fearlessly fight against the demonic powers of oppression and fear that capture so many and wreck so much.

But in all of this, we do it in light of the proclamation of Jesus as Lord, the crucified and risen King who alone has power over death, sin, and the devil. Word and deed always go together in God's kingdom, for here alone is true liberty found and new life enjoyed. This is not merely a "spiritual" life, but a life set free to generously help those in need, and in that, point them to the King.

Kingdom Concerns for the Poor and Oppressed

When the average American hears the word "justice," we typically think of our rights being upheld or fair punishment and procedures followed. For example, we talk about criminals receiving punishment or "justice," or we call a court system or a business transaction "just" because the process used to make the decision or transaction was fair and unbiased. But when the average Old Testament Israelite heard the word "justice," it would have meant much more. To be sure, fair punishment and fair procedures have always been included in the idea of justice (Ex. 23:2–3; Lev. 19:15, 35–36; Prov. 11:1; cf. Amos 8:4–6). But such punitive and procedural justice is not expressive of "justice" in the fullest and most positive sense of the word.[17]

Fundamental to this more expansive biblical portrait of justice is the recognition that God is not blind to the harsh inequalities of our world. Instead, God sees and acts vigorously to *defend* and *restore* those who are weak, poor, and marginalized. As the old pastoral adage says, "God afflicts the comfortable and comforts the afflicted."

Sometimes people have wondered whether this actually means that God himself is biased and unfair. But such conclusions do not follow. In fact, the Bible teaches that it is precisely God's *impartiality* that makes him partial to the poor. It is in *fairness* that God favors the forgotten and receives the rejected. To fail to do so would be unjust. Deuteronomy 10:17–18 makes this point clear:

> The LORD your God is God of gods and Lord of lords, the great, the mighty, and the awesome God, who is not partial and takes no bribe. He executes justice for the fatherless and the widow, and loves the sojourner, giving him food and clothing.

Notice that God's special concern for the disadvantaged is stressed immediately after God's impartiality is affirmed. God's royal *majesty* is seen in his *mercy*. The God of gods—and the King of kings—is the one who feeds the poor, ministers to the prisoner, and brings good news of deliverance. In short, God's justice goes beyond fair procedures and seeks to restore those who have been lost and left out to full participation in the kingdom of God (Ps. 113).

Thus, for God's people ignoring injustice is no better than directly participating in it (cf. Lev. 5:1). When confronted with the realities of injustice, it can be hard to recognize our personal involvement. Yet Scripture views both active oppression and peaceful coexistence with injustice as two sides of the same coin (e.g., Job 31:16–22; 1 John 3:17). To be sure, we do not individually bear the burden of correcting all the world's wrongs, but neither are we to be passive when it is within our power to do good (Isa. 58; James 4:17).

With the coming of the King and his kingdom everything is turned upside down, or better, right side up. "Blessed are you who are poor, for yours is the kingdom of God" (Luke 6:20). This message of Jesus is unpacked by James:

> Has not God chosen those who are poor in the world to be rich in faith and heirs the kingdom, which he has promised those who love him? But you have dishonored the poor man. Are not the rich the ones who oppress you, and the ones who drag you into court? Are they not the ones who blaspheme the honorable name by which you were called? (James 2:5–7)

James, like Jesus, exalts the poor who can be models in their loving dependence on God. And James's warning to the rich likewise echoes Jesus' kingdom concerns. It was Jesus, after all, who made the unsettling statement that "it is easier for a camel to go through the eye of a needle than for a rich person to enter the kingdom of God" (Mark 10:25). It is to our shame when we spend our time trying to figure out how large the "eye of the needle" was (e.g., was it a small entry way into Jerusalem?), rather than rightly hearing the obvious warning of Jesus. While all sinful humanity is actually in great need and dependent on God, those with financial resources and positions of power can fall more easily into the belief that they are the ones who reign and rule rather than King Jesus (Rev. 3:17).

God's generosity, his righteousness, reminds us that his kingdom is always given, never earned. This can be hard for us to hear. We like to think we have what we have earned. We teach our children this. But are we then teaching them the kingdom? All of us in this fallen world begin outside of God's kingdom. We have all, in some way or other, lived the life of the "wicked," whether we engage in prostitution or slander, adultery or greed (1 Cor. 6:9–10). What distinguishes the saint and the sinner, then, is not if they sin, for all have done just that in uncounted ways. But the saint has been forgiven and renewed: "you were washed, you were sanctified," Paul explains, "you were justified in the name of the Lord Jesus Christ and by the Spirit of our God" (1 Cor. 6:11). Thus, as those who have now been justified before the King, we are to reflect the King's justice and generosity.

Bruce Waltke concludes that in the book of Proverbs the concept of righteousness consistently carries with it the idea of extending oneself to one's neighbor, whereas wickedness is a manifestation of self-interest. He coins a proverb himself, which I believe reflects not just the message of the proverbs, but of the Scriptures in general.

> The wicked advantage themselves by disadvantaging others,
> but the righteous disadvantage themselves to advantage others.[18]

Not only in Proverbs, but throughout Scripture this contrast between the "righteous" and the "wicked" is consistent, and the kingdom of Christ simply amplifies what were always God's priorities. Psalm 37 provides an extended comparison between the "righteous" and the "wicked" along these very lines. While many Christians have memorized the encouragement to "delight yourself in the LORD, and he will give you the desires of your heart" (v. 4), we tend to miss the context of those desires. They are to be about giving to those in need! Again, note the contrast. "The wicked borrows but does not pay back, but the righteous is generous and gives" (Ps. 37:21, cf. vv. 25–26). Throughout this psalm we find a long-term perspective upheld; here one looks back and recognizes that all things are ultimately from the Creator, and he looks forward, confident that in the end "the salvation of the righteous is from the LORD; he is their stronghold in the time of trouble" (Ps. 37:39–40). God will bring deliverance from the wicked — the self-absorption of this world — as people find their refuge in him.

Jesus' Sermon on the Mount paints a vivid and radical portrait of kingdom priorities and living, displaying this sacrificial orientation toward one's neighbor. For example, Jesus says what we in ourselves simply cannot hear, believe, or do:

> You have heard that it was said, "An eye for an eye and a tooth for a tooth." But I say to you, Do not resist the one who is evil. But if anyone slaps you on the right cheek, turn to him the other also. And if anyone would sue you and take your tunic, let him have your cloak as well. And if anyone forces you to go one mile, go with him two miles. Give to the one who begs from you, and do not refuse the one who would borrow from you. (Matt. 5:38–42)

Jesus goes so far as to say that we should be willing to comply with unreasonable requests for generosity. Similarly, the apostle Paul praised the example of the Macedonian Christians, who in their "extreme poverty have overflowed in a wealth of generosity on their part" (2 Cor. 8:1–7). And we all know the story of the widow's mites (Mark 12:41–44)—Jesus praised this woman even though her generosity placed her in a condition of continuing financial vulnerability. As we discover in the wisdom of Proverbs, the wicked/evil advantage themselves by disadvantaging others—they steal another person's possessions or injure the innocent. But the righteous respond by willingly disadvantaging themselves, turning the cheek, giving the tunic, walking the extra mile, and freely giving to those in need.

I will never forget years ago when I was a somewhat new Christian sitting in on a high school Sunday school class. The normal teacher was away, so Ed, one of the adult volunteers, read this passage from the Sermon on the Mount and then made a few simple observations. They included things like, "If someone takes your bike, maybe you should let him have it"; "if someone hits your car in rage, maybe you should not require her to fix it." I will never forget how the room exploded, and it was the parents sitting in the class who were so upset. Everyone wanted an asterisk next to what Jesus said, because he clearly couldn't mean what Ed was saying he meant. Whatever one thinks of Ed's interpretation of Scripture, the story illustrates just how nervous we tend to be about disadvantaging ourselves for others. But Jesus makes it clear that this is the way of the kingdom.

Notice also that as Jesus continues his sermon, he nearly equates righteousness with generosity. "Beware of practicing your righteousness before other people in order to be seen by them, for then you will have no reward from your Father who is in heaven" (Matt. 6:1). But what is this practice he is referring to? Giving to those in need (Matt. 6:2).[19] While we rightly hear Jesus calling for authentic concern rather than dangerous showmanship, we should not miss the point that he always assumes we will be helping the needy, though it will be done in wise, even secret ways. Thus, we likewise do not exalt ourselves by praying loudly in public, but seek quiet spaces to cry out the kingdom prayer Jesus taught us:

Our Father in heaven,
>   hallowed be your name.
>   Your kingdom come,
>   your will be done,
>   on earth as it is in heaven.
>   Give us this day our daily bread,

and forgive us our debts,
>as we also have forgiven our debtors.
And lead us not into temptation,
>but deliver us from evil (Matt. 6:9–13)

To forgive others is to recognize how much we have been forgiven. We are delivered from evil—from self-absorption (remember the Proverbs), as we are set free by the King who calls us to order our lives around his kingdom values of grace, generosity, self-control, and love. Thus, we live not under the "master" of money, but under our kingly Master, Christ. Our investments are realigned, for we invest not to establish our own kingdoms, but to pour ourselves into Christ's kingdom (Matt. 6:19–24). John Calvin captures this dynamic when he writes: "Such is the nature of his rule, that he shares with us all that he has received from the Father ... and just as he himself freely lavishes his gifts upon us, so may we, in return, bring forth fruit to his glory."[20]

We conclude this chapter and section 2 of the book by remembering that the fundamental message of the entire New Testament is relatively simple but earth shattering. It takes only three words to say it, but it takes eternity to experience it fully: "Jesus is Lord." Recognizing all that this confession means calls us to repentance and faith. We need to have our views of God, ourselves, and the world reordered and made new. Christ alone becomes our identity, our life, our portion, and our hope. The lines have fallen in pleasant places when we belong to him and his kingdom (Ps. 16:6). We no longer need to be slaves to sin, no longer need to be defined by our struggles, our fears, and our socioeconomic status. We are children of the King, free to love and serve him, securely belonging to him and his kingdom.

Thus, the Christian life is a life ordered by kingdom priorities. Such a life is the life of righteousness, a life of self-giving that extends God's grace to those in need even as it costs us our very selves. In losing ourselves we gain Christ (Phil. 3:8) and all things. Nothing could be better than that.

How Will God Get Back What Was Lost?

We hear dark echoes of our own lives in the parable of the wicked tenants. The Master of the house has created a vineyard with all that was needed to produce a crop. He graciously provides work for the tenants, requiring only that they give him the fruit of his harvest, which was his by right. The Master sends his servants to collect, but the tenants abuse and kill those who would speak truth to them, those who would ask them to fulfill their responsibilities. Finally, they kill the Master's son.

It is a despicable story, and Jesus' listeners pronounce judgment on the wicked tenants, declaring they deserve a "miserable death" (Matt. 21:41).

As with King David in the ewe lamb story, the listeners are simply sentencing themselves to death. It's true; a miserable death is what is required, but that death will fall upon the Master himself. In the story the Master sends his son in ignorance, believing his status will protect him. In reality, the Son of God comes in full knowledge that he is giving himself away to be fully poured out. There is no other way to restore the kingdom. Only by the full and willing sacrifice of God through the Son and sealed by the Spirit can he give everything away to get everything back.

Knowing this weighty truth, how should we live?

We are called to believe, confessing truths about God and about ourselves. We recognize that justice comes as a gift, because it passes over us and falls on Christ. As those soaked in God's forgiveness and grace we find a turning: turning away from sin and turning to generosity, pouring ourselves out even as we are filled by God. This is the path of love and righteousness; this is the vibrancy of living in God's kingdom.

part three

Living in the Gifts: Cross, Resurrection, Church

A Kernel of Wheat
How Then Shall We Live?

JESUS REPLIED, "The hour has come for the Son of Man to be glorified. I tell you the truth, unless a kernel of wheat falls to the ground and dies, it remains only a single seed. But if it dies, it produces many seeds. The man who loves his life will lose it, while the man who hates his life in this world will keep it for eternal life. Whoever serves me must follow me; and where I am, my servant also will be. My Father will honor the one who serves me."

John 12:23–26 NIV

On the bank of some dark river, as we are thrust
backward, onlookers will remark, "They could kill
somebody like that." To which old John might say,
"Good, you're finally catching on."

William Willimon[1]

When Christ calls a man, he bids him come and die.

Dietrich Bonhoeffer[2]

This is how we know what love is: Jesus Christ laid
down life for us. And we ought to lay down our lives
for our brothers. If anyone has material possessions
and sees his brother in need but has no pity on him,
how can the love of God be in him?

1 John 3:16 – 17 NIV

This double kindness is the twofold aspect of Christ:
gift and example.

Martin Luther[3]

For you know the grace of our Lord Jesus Christ,
that though he was rich, yet for your sake he became
poor, so that you by his poverty might become rich.

2 Corinthians 8:9

The self-giving love Christ has for us leads in turn
to the believers' giving themselves for the world in
preaching the gospel, in social action, in peacemak-
ing and through acts of self-giving and self-denial.

Derek Tidball[4]

chapter ten

Following a Crucified Lord

From Receiving to Giving

Having received from God the great gift of himself, we find ourselves in his kingdom, free to live, and as we will learn, free to die. Yet God's generosity does not annihilate our dignity and significance; rather, it liberates our actions as he invites us to participate in the movement of his divine generosity. A personal story from Justin, my research assistant for this book, may help us to better appreciate this gift of participation.

> I remember meeting a homeless woman a few years ago. I was walking down Broad Street in front the library of Chattanooga, Tennessee, when this woman came up to me and began asking for money. Not knowing who she was, I decided not to give her any cash. But when I told her that I'd buy her anything she needed, she took me up on the offer. In fact, she said she needed many things: a coat, some clothes, and shampoo to begin with. Her name was Tammy, and she was living under a bridge.
>
> After helping Tammy that night I didn't hear from her for a few weeks until she called me, right in the middle of church one Sunday morning. She said that she had been raped and needed someone to take her to the hospital. After that, Tammy started coming to church, and our deacons' fund started helping her out.
>
> One of my jobs at church at the time was to fill out these small slips of paper that we gave Tammy and others to exchange for gro-

ceries at the local food bank. The only problem was that Tammy liked to share.

"Don't give this away," I can remember telling her as I would hand her the slip for the food bank. "You need to keep this for yourself. Otherwise you'll run out and have nothing to eat." But after a while Tammy grew tired of being told not to share the food that our church gave her. "I want to give some away too," she replied.

Living under the bridge meant living with other needy people, and so she let me know that it would be unthinkable for her to return there without sharing her groceries. "So, why can't I share some of it?" she asked with an incredulous stare. "Why can't I give some too?"

I found myself taken aback. *Why shouldn't Tammy be allowed to give some of what she'd received? Wasn't that exactly what I was doing?* I paused for a moment. But then I gave her a very pragmatic answer, telling her that our church deacons' fund wasn't set up for that. "We're giving this to *you*," I told Tammy, "not to everyone else you meet." Yet, I recognized the deeper problem: to only receive and never to give is to be belittled — to be humiliated. Over time, I had begun to think of Tammy as a kind of pet project in which I was always the giver and she was always the recipient. Our roles in this relationship were well defined, or so I thought.

But the good news is that God has not only made us to be recipients of his grace but also participants in the movement of his own generosity. Unlike Justin's original advice to Tammy, God does not show us his love and then warn us against sharing it with others. Nor does he give us his grace and then tell us to limit our participation to token tithes and offerings. Drinking in God's love leads to an overflow that sweeps us into the stream of his grace. We have become part of that rushing river, that life-giving water.[5] Indeed, when God shows us his love, he invites us to become *full* participants in his divine generosity. He invites us — even the poorest of us (2 Cor. 8:1–3) — to live lives, however imperfectly, that extend and reflect his own role as Giver.

Imitating God: Image, Imitation, and Imagination

The biblical basis for our *imitation* of God's generosity goes all the way back to the creation of Adam and Eve in the *image* of God. To be human is, at its most basic level, to be *like* God (Gen. 1:26–27; 5:1–3; 9:6; cf. Ps. 8).[6] Men and women are essentially creatures whose whole persons are, in some sense, made to correspond to and reflect the nature of God. What greater privilege could have been given at creation than this initial gift of God-likeness?

> So God created man in his own image,
>> in the image of God he created him;
>> male and female he created them. (Gen. 1:27)

As those who have been uniquely created in the *image* of God, human beings are consequently called to the *imitation* of God. To be sure the task of imitation requires the use of a biblically informed *imagination* because we are also very different from God (cf. Ps. 113:5–6; Isa. 55:9). As we will see later in this chapter, there is both a freedom and a form to this imitation, but we are called to imitate him nonetheless.

The "image" we bear in God's likeness involves the whole person — both *who we are* and *what we do*.[7] That is, it involves both our attributes and our actions — both our *being* and our *behavior*. To be created in the image of God is both an incredible privilege and an amazing responsibility.

While it has often been said that the Bible represents God "anthropomorphically," that is, like a human being, Bruce Waltke argues that it is more accurate to say that human beings are "theomorphic," that is, made like God, so that God can communicate himself to people. "He gave people ears to show that he hears the cry of the afflicted and eyes to show that he sees the plight of the pitiful (Ps. 94:9)."[8]

As we saw in chapter 2, the reason there is so much wrong with the world today is because humanity has failed miserably in this calling to be like God; as a result, God's image has become deeply disfigured and distorted within us. Instead of wanting to be *like* God, we now desire to become God! We twist the original order so that instead of reflecting his character, we attempt to fashion as many little gods after our own image as we can. Instead of seeking first God's kingdom and his righteousness, we seek to establish our own.

Yet, in spite of the catastrophic consequences of our sin, the image of God has not been altogether annihilated (e.g., Gen. 5:1–3; 9:6; Ps. 8). Biblically, our status as image-bearers is never called into question but is always presupposed.[9] Thus, even after the fall God calls his people to follow him by keeping his commandments and shaping their lives around what he values. God tells the Israelites, "You shall be holy, for I the LORD your God am holy" (Lev. 19:2; cf. 11:44–45; 20:7–8; 21:8; Matt. 5:48; 18:32–33; Luke 6:36; 1 Peter 1:16). Such a command assumes humanity's call to image God, to imitate him. Yet as we saw earlier, only the Holy Spirit brings fallen humanity into God's life again, and only by his Spirit can we live in his holiness. So what does this imitation of God look like? *We have to look to the cross.*

The imagery of the cross in the New Testament includes two crucial realities. First, it represents Jesus' death as an effective sacrifice for sin. Second, it calls us to participate in the same pattern of Jesus' self-giving love.[10] As Martin Luther explained,

> Christ is yours, presented to you as a gift. After that it is necessary that you turn this into an example and deal with your neighbor in the very same way, be given to him also as a gift and an example.... This double kindness is the twofold aspect of Christ: *gift and example.*[11]

But far too often this broader message of the cross has been reduced in one direction or the other. Either it has been reduced to an effective sacrifice or as something merely to be imitated. But in contrast to such reductions the Bible teaches that the realities of *amazing gift* and *costly demand* are always held together in powerful tension at the cross. That is to say, we end up missing the greater significance of Jesus' death when either the *gift* or the *demand* of his cross is viewed in isolation from the other. The cross is always *both*—redemptive and exemplary.[12] As John Stott has wisely explained:

> Every Christian is both a Simon of Cyrene and a Barabbas. Like Barabbas we escape the cross, for Christ died, in our place. Like Simon of Cyrene we carry the cross, for he calls us to take it up and follow him.[13]

In other words, Jesus has died to give us life and to show us how to live it. His cross is the *source* of our life and must therefore shape the whole *course* of our life. As Peter summarizes: "Christ also suffered for you, leaving you an example" (1 Peter 2:21).

Having already focused on the first part of this broader message in chapter 4, we must now turn to the second half. As Derek Tidball has said:

> The love of God should never flow into our lives without also flowing through them to others. The cross not only affirms that God loves us, but insists that we must love others in turn. To have received the love of God in our own lives and then to refuse

to share it with others is to turn God's free-flowing grace into a stagnant pool.[14]

As we experience God's love, he also empowers us to participate in the free-flow of his grace, even commanding us to *imitate* the supreme example of his generosity on the cross. Thus, our lives become shaped by a cross that represents both death and life, both poverty and riches, both slavery and freedom. Jesus and his cross become the center, not merely of Christian believing, but also of Christian living. This becomes the key to imaging and imitating God.

Cross-Shaped Living

Understanding the death of Jesus in this way means reexamining our entire lives in light of the amazing gift and costly demand that has been revealed to us in the person and work of Jesus on the cross. That is to say, if you want to know what it means to image God, look to Jesus. While humanity was made in God's image, Jesus himself *is* God's image. To see Jesus—the exact image of God, who bears the very stamp of his nature—is to see what we were always meant to be (Rom. 8:29; cf. 1 Cor. 15:49; 2 Cor. 3:18; Eph. 4:20–24; 1 John 3:2). Christians are those who, by God's Spirit, are being reshaped by this image, now most clearly seen in his Son. His life is defined by his self-giving, and that must define our lives as well.[15]

A Person, Not a Percentage

So what does God call us to give? Finances often reveal a great deal about us and our hearts. We've all heard that to see what someone values, you should look no further than their credit card statement. This bears the ring of truth. As Jesus unabashedly reminds us: "No one can serve two masters, for either he will hate the one and love the other, or he will be devoted to the one and despise the other. You cannot serve God and money" (Matt. 6:24). So we naturally ask ourselves, "What is the Bible's basic standard for Christian generosity? Does giving 'ten percent'—or a tithe—provide the norm for generous living?" Although that sometimes has become the assumption among many Christians today, this answer easily misses the point. Conformity to Christ is our destiny as disciples. Thus, the biblical standard for giving calls our attention to focus on a *person*, not just a *percentage* of our income.

Contrary to popular opinion, the "tithe" or 10 percent giving was *never* the starting place for faithful giving—even in Old Testament times.[16] The

Jews understood the law as calling for somewhere between two and four different "tithes," adding up to approximately 23.3 percent of a family's income.[17] In addition to this, the law called for an array of other obligatory sacrifices and freewill offerings as well (e.g., Lev. 1–7). It included a host of different laws about gleaning, the sabbatical year of release, Jubilee, as well as a whole kaleidoscope of other warnings and economic stipulations that further codified God's concern for the poor.[18]

Taken together, this impressive system of generosity and justice was given to Israel as a way for them to gratefully extend and reflect God's compassionate character. Thus, emphasizing a 10 percent tithe as the basic gauge for giving can prove problematic as it can ironically end up distracting from God's purpose in making us more like him.

There are, of course, important principles we learn from the Old Testament tithes.[19] For example, asking questions like "Who tithed?" in the Old Testament can be illuminating. While we tend to think of the tithe as a "one-size-fits-all" standard of giving, in the Old Testament only those who owned property in the Promised Land actually tithed. Since Old Testament Israel was an agricultural economy, the tithe applied only to crops and livestock (Lev. 27:30–32; Deut. 14:22; 26:1–2; cf. Matt. 23:23), not to all income in any time and place.[20] People who did not own *land* in Israel could not produce their own crops and livestock from which the tithe was supposed to come and, therefore, were not expected to give in the form of a tithe. They were, however, called to give in other ways (e.g., Lev. 1–7).

Thus, the fact that landless Israelites would not have tithed is instructive for us today, reminding us that the Bible identifies no "one-size-fits-all" gift that fulfills all of our financial responsibilities before God. Overemphasizing the tithe above everything else the Bible says about generosity can lead wealthy Christians (including most Americans) into a false sense of self-righteousness; it can also burden those who are truly poor with inappropriate feelings of guilt. By way of contrast, the New Testament praises people who *cheerfully and voluntarily* express love for God and neighbor by giving at great cost to themselves (Mark 12:33–44; 2 Cor. 8:1–7). In this way they pattern themselves after Christ: "For you know the grace of our Lord Jesus Christ, that though he was rich, yet for your sake he became poor, so that you by his poverty might become rich" (2 Cor. 8:9).

It is also instructive to ask the question of how the tithes in the Old Testament were used. There were at least three different ways Old Testament tithes functioned:

To support the full-time religious workers. This tithe was given to the Levites, who had no inheritance in the land (Num. 18:8 – 32). In turn, the Levites were commanded to give a tenth of this tithe to the priests, who had no other means of income (Num. 18:26 – 28).

To provide a community meal for fellowship and celebration of God's goodness. This tithe of crops and livestock was to be shared in joy with family and community, including the poor and especially the Levites (Deut. 12:5 – 19; 14:22 – 29).

To help the poor. This "triennial" tithe, given every third year, went to the local storehouses to be distributed not just to the Levites but also to the poor and marginalized: the aliens, fatherless, and widows (Deut. 14:28 – 29; 26:12 – 13).

These giving priorities teach us that it is impossible to love God wholeheartedly unless we consider the needs of others to be as important as our own. In sum, while various principles of tithing, such as proportional and planned giving (cf. 1 Cor. 16:1 – 4), provide helpful guidelines as we strive to develop a lifestyle of greater generosity, it was and still is possible to "tithe" faithfully, yet fail to give generously. As Jesus himself said, "Woe to you, scribes and Pharisees, hypocrites! For you tithe mint and dill and cumin, and have neglected the weightier matters of the law: justice and mercy and faithfulness. These you ought to have done, without neglecting the others" (Matt. 23:23).

The subtle temptation when we think that only 10 percent of our income must be *given* to God is to begin to act as if only 10 percent of our lives *belong* to him. He can have Sunday morning, an occasional offering of my time when someone is in need, but not much more than that. Yet the truth is that when it comes to our time, talents, and treasures, it is not 10 percent that belongs to God, but 100 percent. And because of the cross of Christ, we again belong fully to him; thus, as we image Jesus, we offer him everything (Rom. 12:1 – 2). In other words, such giving cannot be easily calculated on one's tax returns.

Jesus' example of living and giving fully expresses the heart and identity of God. Jesus reveals what God is like and what we are to be like. His call is not for 10 percent but for us to take up our cross and follow him. When we look to this *person* and not just to a *percentage*, we are reminded of the fundamental character of Christian discipleship: all things hold together in Christ. We do not partition stewardship and generosity off from our discipleship as a whole, dividing our obedience into "a variety of segments, each with its own norms and modes of behavior."[21] We fix our eyes on

Jesus, the author and perfecter of the faith (Heb. 12:1–2), and looking to him our lives are reshaped.[22]

Imitating Jesus

There has been considerable confusion (and even some controversy) throughout church history with regard to what it actually means to imitate Jesus. Debates have swirled around a variety of different questions, including the question of what it is about Jesus that we are called to imitate. We know, for example, that in his early life Jesus lived as a carpenter. Later, after he began his public ministry, we know that he traveled about the countryside as an itinerant preacher without acquiring any personal property of his own. We also know Jesus never married. But Christians are never directly commanded to imitate any of these aspects of Jesus' example.[23] So, what are we to imitate?

The Cross, Not the Career

The short answer is that Christians are called to imitate Jesus' self-giving love on the *cross*, not his crown as a king or his career as a carpenter. As Dietrich Bonhoeffer famously put it, "When Christ calls a man, he bids him come and die."[24] A handful of passages illustrate this point of emphasis:

> If anyone would come after me, he must deny himself and take up his cross and follow me. (Mark 8:34 NIV)[25]

> This is my commandment, that you love one another as I have loved you. Greater love has no one than this, that someone lay down his life for his friends. (John 15:12–13)

> Be imitators of God, therefore, as dearly loved children and live a life of love, just as Christ loved us and gave himself up for us as a fragrant offering and sacrifice to God. (Eph. 5:1–2 NIV)

> To this you were called, because Christ suffered for you, leaving you an example, that you should follow in his steps." (1 Peter 2:21 NIV)

> This is how we know what love is: Jesus laid down his life for us. And we ought to lay down our lives for our brothers. (1 John 3:16 NIV)

We could go on multiplying examples, but the point is clear: Jesus' *cross* provides the primary pattern for our faithfulness to God in the present.[26] It is not primarily his career but the sacrificial gift of his cross that we are called to imitate.[27] In other words, imitation is not so much about slavishly mimicking all of the different things Jesus did while he was on earth, but of creatively reenacting the *virtue* of his unselfish love in countless and different situations.[28]

When we remember just how radical the cross is, keeping in mind how it was considered "folly" to worship a crucified Lord, we see how radical this metaphor becomes for shaping the Christian life.[29] Much confusion arises from a lack of attention to this emphasis on the exemplary significance of the cross in contrast to Jesus' life more generally.[30] Many are distracted, for example, by debates about Jesus' specific social and economic identity. "How poor was Jesus?" they ask. "Might he have actually been middle class?"[31] In fact, this preoccupation with the normativity of Jesus' socioeconomic identity is commonplace, both in some traditional approaches to the imitation of Christ and in more recent trends.

For example, the imitation of Jesus' life of poverty became especially popular in the thirteenth century under the influence of St. Francis of Assisi (1181–1226) and the monastic order he founded.[32] According to the example of St. Francis—who famously renounced his large family inheritance, exchanged clothes with beggars, and kissed lepers—the imitation of Christ involved an attempt to mimic, as nearly as possible, all of the sufferings of Christ, especially his life of poverty.

By way of contrast, in response the tradition of *imitatio Christi* and to Ronald Sider's more recent emphasis on Jesus' life of poverty in *Rich Christians in an Age of Hunger*, John Schneider argues that while there is, indeed, an "awesome lowliness about the entire Incarnation," the narrative of Jesus' early life was relatively comfortable, perhaps even affluent by the standards of his day.[33] Instead of focusing on the exemplary significance of Christ's cross, Schneider emphasizes Jesus' early career as a carpenter:

> Until he was about thirty, it is assumed, Jesus worked in Nazareth—perhaps he even inherited the family business, since there is no mention of Joseph in any narratives of his adult life. At any rate, that is how people identified him; he was known in his hometown as Jesus "the carpenter" (Mark 6:3). For the greater part of his life, then, it seems that Jesus worked this trade.... We know nothing about Jesus' income or personal habits of investment, savings, or charity. All we can say, perhaps, is that a builder's son in Nazareth may not have been rich, but he would have had much to be thankful for compared to the majority of his countrymen.[34]

Schneider goes on to mention that because of a huge stimulus from Roman construction activity that took place in Galilee during our Lord's lifetime, Jesus might actually have done quite nicely for himself.[35] He employs this point to defend the "good of affluence" more generally, as God's ideal for Christian economic life, saying that the specific form of Jesus' social and economic experience "implies a very strong identification on God's part with the sort of human personhood that it was"[36]— that is, a socioeconomic identity and experience that were "of some little affluence."[37]

But this preoccupation with Jesus' social and economic identity— whether asserting his relative poverty or affluence—misses the point. We are never explicitly called to imitate Jesus' early life or career. These aspects of Jesus' example are never directly identified as the framework for the economic life of Christians, though they obviously influence us (e.g., his associations with tax collectors and sinners). But we are specifically commanded, over and over again, to imitate Jesus' unselfish giving on the cross.

To be sure, we are not all necessarily obligated to enter into a life of voluntary poverty. But we cannot claim Christ's cross as the *source* of our lives without allowing the same cross to shape the whole *course* of our lives. Our faithfulness is not to be judged by where we fit into the socioeconomic ladder, but by the degree to which our daily decisions and life story as a whole correspond to Christ's self-giving example on the cross.

Imitating Paul and Others

It is also important to recognize that imitating Jesus' self-sacrificial obedience is something we are to do, not as isolated individuals but in the context of community. *The call to sacrificial generosity in the New Testament is addressed to the community as a whole.*[38] As Richard Hays has observed, this communal dimension of giving is particularly striking in passages like Romans 12:1–2, where Christians are called to lay down their individual "bodies" (plural) as "a living sacrifice" (singular).[39] In other words, the idea of this one "living sacrifice" that is made of many Christian lives describes the vocation of the community as a whole.

Unlike our Lord, who suffered alone, we follow after Jesus in fellowship with a "so great a cloud of witnesses" like Moses, who chose to be "mistreated with the people of God" and "considered the reproach of Christ greater wealth than the treasures of Egypt" (Heb. 11:25–26; 12:1). Consequently, following the pattern of Jesus' obedience always involves learning from the example of others who have gone before us. The Christian life is designed by God so that much of our growth comes through imitating godly examples, imperfect though they may be.[40]

The apostle Paul, as the primary case in point, repeatedly summoned his readers to progress in their faith by imitating his example.[41] His life, which was meant to imitate the cross of Christ, provided a concrete example for his fellow believers to follow after.[42] Believers follow not simply his words but also his concrete sacrificial actions. As he says, "Be imitators of me, as I am of Christ" (1 Cor. 11:1).[43]

The Abundance of the Cross

The most profound moment in the movement of divine generosity is the moment that takes us from death to life, from the cross to the resurrection. For as we will see in the next two chapters, it is ultimately in the bright light of Easter morning that we finally get a clear look at what God's generosity is all about—the new creation for which our bodies are now yearning. Yet, it is important for us to realize that even in this ultimate movement, Christ's cross is not left behind.

Had the cross been merely a means to an end, a simple "tool" in the larger scheme of God's purposes, early Christianity might have chosen a different image as the great sign and symbol of the faith. But as history has shown us, this was not the case. The cross remains at the center of everything, even after the resurrection; and not only for understanding the salvation God has accomplished in the past, or only as the pattern for our own obedience, but also for our experience of God himself and his abundance in the present.

We see this unique perspective on the abiding centrality and significance of the cross in passages like Philippians 3:10–11, where Paul says,

> ... that I may know him and the power of his resurrection, and
> may share in his sufferings, becoming like him in his death, that
> by any means possible I may attain the resurrection from the dead.

What is so striking here is that Paul begins by expressing his desire to know the power of Christ's resurrection, but then he returns to cross![44] That is, "to share in his sufferings." Shouldn't this go the other way around? Of course, the obvious answer is yes, at least logically speaking. But here is a taste of some divine "foolishness." For we only truly experience the present abundance of Christ's resurrection in powerful tension with the "sharing in his sufferings." Christ's resurrection stands behind us. Our resurrection is held out before us. But in between the power of the resurrection stands our present fellowship with Jesus through the cross.

How Should We Then Live and Give?

But how are we supposed to do what we have examined in this chapter? On a practical level, what does it actually mean to imitate Jesus in our giving? After all, it is one thing to say that our lives ought to be shaped by the cross. But it is another thing to hazard an explanation of how this is actually done. Nitty-gritty questions of this kind make all of us uncomfortable.

We must also be careful before trying to specify certain behavioral norms since even the most devout and thoughtful Christians can differ *widely* over such details, and our individual callings and particular situations will inevitably impact the way Christ's cross takes shape in our lives. As Michael J. Gorman has astutely observed, the way of the cross cannot be neatly defined or legislated:

> It can only be remembered and recited, hymned and prayed, and then lived by the power of the Spirit and the work of inspired individual and corporate imagination.[45]

This important word of caution does not mean, however, that the call to imitate Jesus lacks any clear implications for our lives. There is *freedom* within Jesus' example, but there is also a basic *form*. Thus, the challenge we face is always the challenge of *knowing Jesus more* so that we can discerningly apply his example more and more *freely within form*—like a jazz soloist who is able to improvise long rifts because he is so intimately familiar with the basic beat of the song. Let us conclude this chapter by describing two aspects of that "basic beat," which can be summarized in terms of giving up rights and giving up resources.

Giving Up Rights

Nothing is more basic to the self-giving pattern of Jesus' example than his willingness to *give up his rights*. As Paul explains in Philippians 2:5–8, Jesus' death on the cross was not some sudden or spontaneous act of generosity. It was the climactic conclusion of his long-standing decision to forego the use of his rights as God. Our attitude, Paul says, should be the same as that of Christ Jesus:

Who, being in very nature God,
> did not consider equality with God something to be grasped,
but made himself nothing,
> taking the very nature of a servant,
> being made in human likeness.
And being found in appearance as a man,
> he humbled himself
> and became obedient to death —
>> even death on a cross! (NIV)

Here we see that the Son of God takes the path of humility, of lowliness. Jesus obediently submitted to one progressively degrading situation after another until he was finally in a position — stretched out and exposed — to give what we most desperately needed. In Jesus' humble renunciation of his divine rights, we discover the genius of God's generosity and the crucifixion of our common sense.

One of the reasons giving up our resources is so difficult for us, and often spectacularly ineffective, is because we try to give away our resources while clinging to our rights. But Jesus set aside his rights *before* he gave up his resources. In God's grace and provision, the use of our rights and resources are always connected.

By way of contrast, sometimes we hear philanthropists and celebrities speak about the thousands of people who die every day from easily preventable diseases. With good intentions, they will often call for more foreign aid and private donations. But the truth is that such expenditures are all but meaningless if they are not drenched in *humility*.

As development economist William Easterly has observed, the West has spent over 2.3 trillion dollars on foreign aid over the last five decades. But with that mountain of money it has accomplished precious little.[46] Why? Easterly does not use biblical language or categories to explain his diagnosis. But in the final analysis, this respected secular economist ultimately concludes that the problem has been rooted in pride. The West, according to Easterly, has made its "Big Plans" to help the poor and given away lots of money. But it has failed to listen to the voices of the poor in the process. A lack of feedback mechanisms from the beneficiaries of aid to those giving the aid has made many programs dangerously ineffective. Donor countries, institutions, and individuals are tempted to dole out money, but they are reluctant to sacrifice their privileged positions of power and authority.[47]

This is a struggle for all of us, but the poor need to be heard and valued as image bearers, not projects. But we can only hear their voices when we humble ourselves and genuinely listen and engage their lives. Thus, biblical generosity always involves not just giving, but also walking with the poor and "associating with the lowly" (Rom. 12:16). This applies, of course, not merely to donor countries and institutions, but to each of us as individuals in meaningful communities.

Of course when it comes to giving up our rights, we are all much like the man in Fyodor Dostoevsky's novel *The Brothers Karamazov*, who declares his heroic intentions but scratches his head at his inability to follow through.

> "I love mankind, but I am amazed at myself: the more I love mankind in general, the less I love people in particular.... In my dreams," he said, "I often went so far as to think passionately of serving mankind, and, it may be, would really have gone to the cross for people if it were somehow suddenly necessary, and yet I am incapable of living in the same room with anyone even for two days.... As soon as someone is there, close to me, his personality oppresses my self-esteem and restricts my freedom. In twenty-four hours I can begin to hate the best of men.... I become the enemy of people the moment they touch me," he said. "On the other hand, it has always happened that the more I hate people individually, the more ardent becomes my love for humanity."[48]

Like Dostoevsky's character, we may daydream of sudden sacrifice, perhaps even imagining ourselves going to the cross in an instant of heroic necessity. But our good intentions remain an illusion. So long as we cling to our personal rights instead of the fellowship of Christ's sufferings, we will never find ourselves in situations where cross-shaped generosity is possible.

The point here is not that there is anything *wrong* with our *rights*. After all, there was certainly nothing wrong with the privileges Jesus enjoyed from all eternity as the only Son of God. Instead, the point is that there is something which is *better* than our rights, something that Jesus revealed by giving his away (Acts 20:35).[49]

The truth is that we are often faced with *relative choices* — choices that are not necessarily black and white, but are between two or more *relative goods*. Jesus had to choose between the enjoyment of his divine rights and the salvation of sinners. And he chose the cross, which has now become the great sign and symbol of God's wisdom in choosing what is *best*. "Into the immeasurable calm of the divine blessedness," Benjamin Warfield once said:

He permitted this thought to enter, "I will die for men!" And so mighty was His love, so colossal the divine purpose to save, that He thought nothing of His divine majesty, nothing of His unsullied blessedness, nothing of His equality with God, but, absorbed in us, — our needs, our misery, our helplessness — He made no account of Himself. If this is to be our example, what limit can we set to our self-sacrifice?[50]

Thus, we also have decisions to make — some big and others small. Where should we live? Where should we send our children to school? What kind of car should we buy? What should we do for vacation? With whom should we spend our time and energy? How are we to make such decisions? How will we know what is *best* if not by looking to the cross? Here is where we need the genius of Jesus' generosity, which is also the folly of the cross (1 Cor. 1:18 – 25). Regarding this foolishness, this wisdom increasingly moves us to give up our positions of power and privilege rather than grasp after our personal rights and prerogatives.

Giving Up Resources

While clinging to our rights can render the gift of our resources ineffective, several key passages make it clear that there is, nevertheless, an iron-clad connection between *material generosity* and the way of the cross:

> Whoever does not bear his own cross and come after me cannot be my disciple ... any one of you who does not renounce all that he has cannot be my disciple. (Luke 14:27, 33)

> For you know the grace of our Lord Jesus Christ, that though he was rich, for your sakes he became poor, so that you through his poverty might become rich.... You will be made rich in every way so that you can be generous on every occasion, and through us your generosity will result in thanksgiving to God. (2 Cor. 8:9; 9:11 NIV; cf. 2 Cor. 6:10; Heb. 10:34)

> This is how we know what love is: Jesus Christ laid down his life for us. And we ought to lay down our lives for our brothers. If anyone has material possessions and sees his brother in need but has no pity on him, how can the love of God be in him? (1 John 3:16 – 17 NIV)

But how are we to understand this connection between financial generosity and the way of the cross? In conclusion, let us just briefly take a closer look at the last of these three texts.

It is, after all, with striking simplicity that John provides the ultimate summary of how we know love: "Jesus Christ laid down his life for us." That is how we know love. Our sure knowledge of God's love hinges on this singular event of Christ's self-giving death on the cross.

Astonishingly, however, 1 John 3:16–17 then moves all the way from the loftiest of subjects to the practical use of our financial resources! Without missing a beat, John rapidly goes from God's love, to Jesus' death, to our laying down of our own lives after his example, which is then immediately spelled out in terms of what we do (or don't do) with our *material possessions*. The movement here is surprising and convicting, and it can also be liberating. Yet this movement really should not catch any serious student of Jesus by surprise. For it was our Lord himself who taught his disciples that "where your treasure is, there your heart will be also" (Matt. 6:21). Luke Timothy Johnson artfully explains this connection by pointing out:

> Possessions are symbolic expressions of ourselves because we both are and have bodies. Every claim of ownership, therefore, involves an ambiguity; we say, this is *mine*, but we imply as well, this is *me*. Our possessions extend not only our bodies as possessions into the world but also our bodies as our *selves*.... When I open wide my *arms* to greet you, I am stating a welcome; when I open wide the *doors* of my house as you walk by, I am making precisely the same statement. The disposition of our possessions symbolizes our self-disposition in the same way that our bodies symbolize our selves.[51]

For the apostle John, there is a connection between how we understand the nails in Christ's hands and what we do with the cash in ours. Jesus chose what was best by going to the cross. We have a similar opportunity to choose what is best by giving up our rights and our resources. In such sacrifice we inevitably experience genuine pain and loss, but there is also joy. For in pouring out our lives after Christ's example, we know that we have a "better possession" that is still before us — "and an abiding one" (Heb. 10:34).[52]

The Christian life in its entirety is to be subsumed under the category of resurrection.

Richard Gaffin[1]

The problem of the bodily resurrection [of Jesus] is not just an example of Christian curiosity; it is related to a major theme in theology: God's ultimate purpose in creating.

Raymond Brown[2]

The claim [of Jesus' resurrection] advanced in Christianity is of that magnitude: Jesus of Nazareth ushers in not simply a new religious possibility, not simply a new ethic or a new way of salvation, but a new creation.

N. T. Wright[3]

What is sown is perishable; what is raised is imperishable. It is sown in dishonor; it is raised in glory. It is sown in weakness; it is raised in power.

1 Corinthians 15:42 – 43

chapter eleven

Resurrection Faith and Work

Death and Life

Christians have a strange relationship to death. It is not easily categorized and thus is often misunderstood — and mis-*lived*. Christians are told not to fear death because Jesus — the risen Messiah — has conquered it.[4] As the apostle Paul once said: "To live is Christ, and to die is gain" (Phil. 1:21). This should remind us of the gambler again, who goes all in. I've said we risk everything and nothing at all. For the Christian a fearlessness in the face of death comes when we understand our life is in the risen Christ, who cannot truly be taken from us. We can risk everything because we are risking *nothing*. Whatever we pour out is still ours in Christ.

However, we know that some people who have lost their fear of death have also become dehumanized in the process. We have all heard of people, both past and present, who in a fit of zealotry have rushed into death for the sake of a cause, a belief, a hope. But their fearlessness also involved an utter disregard for life or even hatred of this world. Such people have blown up innocent people with car bombs or pillaged villages while on crusade, often doing so in the "name of God." The hatred at the root of this fearlessness therefore excludes it as an option for Christians (cf. Matt. 5:38–48; John 13: 34–35; 1 John 4:20; 3:16; 4:7–21).

But then how are we to face the reality of death? How are we to approach all of the painful smells, sights, and sounds of all that accompanies death and dying? Death is serious, and trivializing the reality of this horror is to belittle the victory won for us by the Lord of life. It is perhaps most painful as we see loved ones facing the realities of death. There is nothing easy about this. But thanks be to God in Christ, who has taken the sting of death into himself (1 Cor. 15:54–57); as a honeybee dies after stinging someone, so Christ absorbs and exhausts the sting of death that we might live. Death is swallowed up in victory.

Messiah Jesus, the crucified and risen Lord, has transformed both life and death. *His* death and resurrection are the keys to *our* own living, dying, and rising. In the following two chapters we will focus on the power and gift of Christ's resurrection: those who encounter and trust in the risen Lord find their lives changed—not yet perfectly, but truly. A new world unfolds before us, and this vision fills us with a love and compassion for the world rather than a bitter hatred or indifference to it.

Christ's resurrection points us back to creation, but also forward to heavenly life. Though it may seem strange, this connection is related to the classic question of the relationship between faith and good works. Jesus' resurrection is a key to understanding the dynamic connection between our faith and actions. It profoundly illumines not just our hope for the future, but also the way we can *live into* that future today. The gift of Christ's resurrection shows us how to interpret not only death but also life.

Good Works: The Call and the Crisis

At the heart of the sixteenth-century Protestant Reformation was the theological debate about the relationship between faith and works—specifically, the question of what one needs to do to be saved. How does a sinner become acceptable to a holy God? While we certainly cannot attend to all the historic details here, I do want us to think afresh about the place of what are sometimes called "works." What is the role of human activity in relationship to God and life in his world?

I am a Protestant.[5] Sometimes Protestants like me are prone to say negative things about the value of human works. In some ways this is understandable, since we long to highlight God's free and radical grace. There is nothing you need to "do" to be saved, since Christ has completed that work (Heb. 9:12, 26). On the cross Christ took our sin and put it to death, casting our transgressions as far from us as the east is from the west; by his grace he makes us whiter than snow and draws us into his holy love.

Salvation is an unearned gift from God. As the Reformation slogan goes, "We are saved by grace alone, through faith alone, in Christ alone." That is a liberating truth, and one I believe the Scriptures clearly teach—in fact, this is central to the idea of the "gift" that runs through the entire book you hold in your hands. Yet in our zeal to celebrate God's grace, we can make deeply faulty, even untrue, claims about the significance of "work" in our lives. Therefore I want to revisit the call to good works. Interestingly, this will eventually take us to resurrection.

Created to Do Good Works

Let's begin with a couple of questions:

What were we made to do?
How were we created to live?

When God created this world, he delighted to make human beings as the crown of his creation. We were designed to respond to God, to love him, to enjoy his presence, and to serve him joyfully. Creation was not static but dynamic, and God's relationship to his human creatures was not static but relational and dynamic.

God made us for communion with himself, with each other, and with the rest of the created world. That means that even before the fall—that is, before there was sin or the need for anything like redemption or justification—God's people (Adam and Eve) actively cared for one another, cultivated the land, and did whatever good work God put before them. We sometimes forget that the call to do good work came before sin entered the world.

We were created to do good works. In fact, by doing the good work that God had given, our first parents glorified him and were destined to experience his blessings in joy. Good works, properly understood, are nothing other than outward and concrete expressions of love. We express God's gifts in our acts; we were not made to be passive but to play an active part in God's care for his world. This brings us to the crucial point: God did not love Adam and Eve because they did good work, but *they were given good work to do because God loved them.*

God did not create his people to be passive in relation to himself or to the rest of his creation. Instead, as one of the old Protestant catechisms declares, God made humankind "after his own image, in knowledge, righteousness, and holiness, with dominion over the creatures."[6] Adam and Eve were created good and whole and able to relate affectionately to God and the rest of the creation. They were to echo God's care and love in their own acts, knowing God to be good and treating each other and the rest of creation with dignity and wisdom. Good works were their appropriate response to God's gifts, the outworking of love and delight.

We All Sense the Call to Good Works

Let's approach this topic from a slightly different perspective. Do you know non-Christians who care deeply about the environment? Do you have friends who work hard to support the local homeless shelter? Have you met nonreligious folks who try to care for their neighbors because they just sense a connection to them and so they do what they can to help? These are people who sense the call to do "good works."

Are their instincts wrong? To be sure, our ability to rightly respond to this call is impossible apart from the presence of faith and love (Rom. 14:23; cf. 1 Cor. 13:1–3). Something deep inside of us calls us to work. But are not such people onto something true? We should not get distracted here with a theological debate about what makes a work "good."[7] I think we can all agree that when someone lifts the spoon for an elderly person so that they can enjoy their soup, that is a "good" thing. It is a "good" work when a person heroically jumps in front of a bus in order to save a distracted child.

People instinctively do such actions because they sense, in a primal kind of way, that they were created for good, not evil. These works are "good," not because they are sufficient to earn God's favor or save us from our sins, but because they are useful in promoting life and because they ultimately point back to God's purpose in creating. Thus, we celebrate such moments, those tastes of purity, even when they are far from perfect.[8] We may not be able to explain it, but something in all of us longs to do good work, to create flourishing relationships, and to find meaning in life. And we can all relate to this, Christian and non-Christian alike, because we were created for such work.

But try as we might, at some point the weight of the work and the heaviness of the need comes crashing against our own struggles, our own inadequacies, our own needs. We try to do good work, but it never seems enough. The homeless shelters never empty, every environmental victory is matched by a new and more disturbing challenge, and our motives never remain pure. What once seemed hopeful and promising starts to feel exhausting and endless; the struggles of life simply do not disappear.

Worse than that, we all sense something inside us that aches. We sense the futility, vanity, and weariness of life that has been handed down to us through the generations (cf. the book of Ecclesiastes; also 1 Peter 1:18). The pain is not just outside of us, but within us as well. That ache points back to the good of creation, just as it reminds us that something went wrong along the way. Things are still not the way they are supposed to be. Something is off in our relationship to one another, in our relationship to the earth, and ultimately in our relationship to God. And our work does not fix it. But let us not belittle those who attempt to do "good." Doing good works is not really their problem or ours. In fact, their desire for good, meaningful work may be the very thing we can use to point them to Jesus, the risen King.

So what is the problem?

Paul's Attempts at Good Work

The apostle Paul valued good work. Saul, as he was known before he started following Jesus, was a deeply religious man (Gal. 1:13 – 14). He valued not just good work in general, but religious work — effort expended in order to please God. But he also discovered that his zeal for work did not satisfy. He clearly remained unsettled. Something was wrong; something was missing.

In Philippians 3, Paul argues against a group known as Judaizers — folk who believed that Gentile Christians still needed to be circumcised like Jews in order to be right with God (see also Acts 15:1 – 35; Gal. 2:11 – 3:29). "They made obedience to the law *a necessary pre-condition* of salvation, at least in the fullest sense of that term."[9] Their insistence on circumcision implied that the Gentiles had to perform some act to become and stay acceptable to God and thus to earn his favor. The "good work" of becoming a Jew was the thing that the Judaizers thought secured one's good standing before God.

Paul was not persuaded by their arguments, and he reacted vehemently against them. In his response, he listed his own credentials and accomplishments, making it clear he was no slouch:

> If anyone else thinks he has reason for confidence in the flesh, I have more: circumcised on the eight day, of the people of Israel, of the tribe of Benjamin, a Hebrew of Hebrews; as to the law, a Pharisee; as to zeal, a persecutor of the church; as to righteousness, under the law blameless. (Phil. 3:4b – 6)

So what in Paul's list is bad? Wasn't it God who commanded circumcision of the Jews on the eighth day (Gen. 17:9 – 14; Lev. 12:3)?[10] Moreover, it was God who made his covenant with Israel, Benjamin being one of the blessed tribes. Paul's credentials were impeccable: he was a real Hebrew through his birth, by the covenant, and in God's promise.

Furthermore, even his persecution resulted from a desire to protect divine truth. As a man zealous for God, he was willing to persecute those he viewed as a threat to his religion. Now, was it a bad instinct for him to protect Yahweh's people from what he thought were blasphemous sectarians? And who would deny that this man was rigorous in keeping the law? Elsewhere Paul clearly states that God's laws and commandments are "holy and righteous and good" (Rom. 7:12). The law was not the problem. God had graciously entrusted the Jews with the oracles of God, and this was meant as a blessing (Rom. 3:1–2). Paul knew he was called to good work, and so he poured himself into it. He kept the law carefully and as closely as possible. The problem was not the things Paul did (e.g., circumcision, keeping the law, etc.). So what was the problem?

Good Works Can Become Our God

Looking back at his performance-driven life, Paul says that all the things he had done and all the credentials he had accumulated did not draw him to God. The Old Testament consistently treated God's law as a gift, a joy, and a blessing (e.g., Ps. 19:8–9; 119). Yet Paul says that this law, meant to be a blessing, had become a curse for him. How did this happen?

The entrance of sin into the world has plunged us into profound conflict, both within ourselves and between us and all else. The call to love God and neighbor did not evaporate with the fall, just our ability and willingness to faithfully respond to it (cf. Rom. 1:1–3:20). God's law points us back to God, to his good creation, and to right relationships that flourish under him. But God's law can never empower good work; it just outlines it.[11] Good works, including obedience to God's law, must derive their power and motivation from a preexistent and loving relationship with God.

Everyone feels the pull to do good, but our relationships with God, each other, and the rest of the earth are ruptured. We know our profound inability to care for others and to commune with God. As Luther commented, "Neither silver, gold, precious stones, nor any rare thing has such manifold alloys and flaws as have good works."[12] We are called to the good, especially as expressed in God's law, but we can't keep even part of it, much less the whole of what God commands (cf. James 2:8–11).

In our flight from God, we try to substitute our work, even our religious law keeping, for God. Sin takes even the blessing of the law and of our work and bends it back in upon us. *Our work now becomes our god rather than a gift from God*, and thus we end up missing God himself.

Fearing God and the blinding light of his perfect righteousness, which exposes our weakness and sin, we try various schemes of "self-improvement." Rejecting our call to be God's beloved, we attempt to create an alternative meaning and purpose through our efforts apart from him. We try to close the perceived distance between God and us, sometimes reasoning, "If I do ... God will love me." But we never escape our brokenness because we continue to reinforce the contradiction that caused it. Seeking to do good, we only do so to become gods ourselves, and we are pathetic gods that neither satisfy ourselves or others.

When we worship our work, we worship an idol. But the answer to this problem is not to become indifferent to it or to oppose the value of work. We can easily overvalue our work, thinking that we are "made" by what we do. But we can just as easily undervalue the astonishing gift of being both made and remade for good work — *a gift that is simultaneously our act.*

Paul Meets the Risen Christ

What changed Paul's evaluation of his works? To answer that we must go to the Damascus Road event (Acts 9:1 – 22), where Paul encountered the risen Jesus and was changed forever. Jesus the Messiah, against whom Paul was fighting, showed himself to be the very Yahweh whom Paul had thought he was serving. The crucified Jesus was not dead but alive. The God of creation has come to earth in Jesus, and he makes all things new. He has come to heal, to forgive, and to free us.

Jesus alone was able to love God and neighbor without compromise. He alone was able to fulfill the law (Matt. 5:17 – 20). But more than that, Jesus was willing to unite himself irrevocably to those who would believe in him (Rom. 3:21 – 26). By faith in Christ believers share in his love, and they are declared righteous — not based on their own actions but based on the faithfulness of Christ (cf. Rom. 5:19; Gal. 3:11). This is what Paul is getting at in Philippians 3 when he declares that he was willing to give up everything he had, all his work and credentials, for the sake of Christ:

> I count everything as loss because of the surpassing worth of knowing Christ Jesus my Lord. For his sake I have suffered the loss of all things and count them as *rubbish*, in order that I may gain Christ and be found in him, not having a righteousness of my own that

comes from the law, but that which comes through faith in Christ, the righteousness from God that depends on faith. (Phil. 3:8 – 9, italics added)

Our current Bible translations like to clean things up a bit, but let's just say that the old King James translation of *skybala* as "dung" ("rubbish" in ESV, NIV) captures Paul's point more fully. He now considers his works—his efforts at keeping the law and doing good—to be excrement, refuse, or a rotting corpse.[13] Whether or not Paul has in mind the imagery of dung or garbage, I think the same idea holds true. So what is his point? Dung is that which has come out of the body after the body has extracted all the useful components of food. It is missing all nutrients. Dung is not what one eats, but what is meant to come out *after* one has eaten.

Paul is not saying that everything he had done was bad. God commanded his people to keep his law. Calvin comments that Paul "divested himself—not of works, but of that mistaken confidence in works, with which he had been puffed up."[14] Attempting to survive on his credentials proved to be Paul's terrible error, for he thought he could be justified by his works. He was trying to eat dung; he found himself scrounging in the waste bin for nutrients, and it was killing him. Good works were always meant to flow out of one's relationship with Yahweh, but they were never intended to be the cause of that relationship. Getting this wrong didn't make a small difference; rather, it made all the difference.

When Paul meets the risen Christ, he turns from the dung to a feast. He is confronted with a stark contrast: he looks at Jesus, and then he looks at his own efforts to love God and neighbor. He realizes that before him are two meals: one is a feast, the other is a pile of you know what. One nourishes his soul, the other's nourishment has already been used up. Paul's credentials and his law keeping were never meant to give him life. Properly experienced they come out of life, but they do not give it and were never intended to.

The Reformers Did Not Oppose Good Works

The great German Reformer Martin Luther talked about "works" negatively in order to argue that we are saved by grace and not by works. But what was it about works that Luther found so objectionable? Was it that Luther thought it was better for people to do "bad" works rather than "good" works? Did Luther discover that "works" are antithetical to genuine human flourishing?

While Luther did say many negative things about "good works," it is a profound misunderstanding to conclude that he believed our actions are irrelevant to God or others. It was Luther, after all, who pronounced: "We do not, therefore, reject good works; on the contrary, we cherish and teach them as much as possible."[15] How does that come from the mouth of the man who also wrote, just pages earlier: "This is the height of folly and utter ignorance of Christian life and faith, that a man should seek to be justified and saved by works and without faith"?[16] It wasn't that doing "good" was evil; *it was the attempt to gain God's approval through one's works that was hopeless.*

Luther rejected the idea that one can gain God's love and acceptance by working for it. Yet this monk also understood that we are all called to good work, not just the spiritual elite or full-time ministers.[17] But those of us who are soaked in religion sometimes try to do good apart from Christ and devoid of faith; when we do this, the results are deadly. We have lost sight of the gift of Christ's resurrection.

Feasting on Christ

So now Paul feasts on Christ. He gains Christ and is found in him (Phil. 3:9). He gives up all the rest "that I may know him and the power of his resurrection" (3:10). In the risen Christ, Paul gains perfect and full righteousness, which he could never have achieved by keeping the law. He finds real life in Jesus, and he realizes that he has been starving.

How does Paul feast? He believes. He recognizes that only by being connected to Jesus can he be reunited to his Creator. And union with Christ also reunites him to his neighbor. Jesus transforms Paul, and his writings describe that transformation. Paul no longer seeks to put others to death in a zealous effort to achieve purity for God's people, but his new life in Christ liberates him to suffer for the sake of others, which thereby points them to the crucified and risen Messiah.

When the risen Christ confronts and converts Paul, he puts Paul into a new relationship with God. This is a gift, not a result of Paul's own effort. And that new connection is the very thing that finally frees Paul to engage properly in the works he was created and recreated to do. As with Paul, outside of Christ our attempts to gain meaning become rubbish, for we cannot "have" anything that is not under the lordship of the risen King. The resurrected Christ takes us to a new creation, where we are shaken from our foolish forgetfulness.

Unquestionably, we lose nothing when we come to Christ naked and stript of everything, for those things which we previously imagined, on false grounds, that we possessed, we then begin really to acquire ... how great the riches of Christ, because we obtain and find all things in him.[18]

All things belong to the Creator God, who comes as Redeemer and reclaims what was lost. Meeting the Redeemer plunged Paul into life with God, no longer to be drowned by the doom of sin and death.

To claim anything outside of God's lordship is to lose everything; it is to follow the path of death rather than life. Paul, accordingly, expounds what belonging to God means and how this renews his work for God:

> Not that I have already obtained this or am already perfect, but I press on to make it my own, *because Christ Jesus has made me his own.* Brothers, I do not consider that I have made it my own. But one thing I do: forgetting what lies behind and straining forward to what lies ahead, I press on toward the goal for the prize of the upward call of God in Christ Jesus. (Phil. 3:12–14, italics added)

We belong to Christ because he died for our sins and rose for our justification (Rom. 4:25). He claims us as "his own." This brings us back to the pivotal importance of the resurrection, the victory over the grave. What we discover is that our Redeemer, by reclaiming us, has not only overcome the power of death, but he has given us the ability to experience the newness of life and work even now in this fallen world. This is a gift that calls for action. To this idea we now turn.

Jesus said to her, "I am the resurrection and the life. Whoever believes in me, though he die, yet shall he live, and everyone who lives and believes in me shall never die. Do you believe this?"

John 11:25–26

The stone is rolled back, not paper-mache,
not a stone in a story,
but the vast rock of materiality that in the slow
grinding of time will eclipse for each of us
the wide light of day.

John Updike[1]

The first day belongs to the head of the church, Our day, the Lord Christ, you see, does not end in a sunset.

Augustine[2]

chapter twelve

Resurrection Life in Action

The Greed of the Grave

If Jesus is dead, he has *nothing* to give us. But if he is alive, he has *everything*. Thus, with the bodily resurrection and ascension of Jesus the movement of divine generosity comes full circle. In dying and rising Jesus has reclaimed all by giving all away. He has overcome the greed of the grave.

Scripture often personifies the grave as exceedingly greedy; here is an all-devouring foe with a ravenous appetite. Sheol, as the grave is sometimes called in the Old Testament, comes with its entangling cords of death (2 Sam. 22:6; Ps. 18:5; 116:3), its mouth wide open as it greedily licks up life and swallows all it encounters (Ps. 141:7; Prov. 1:12; Isa. 5:14; cf. Num. 16:30).[3] No one can escape its pull. Proverbs 30:15–16 declares that just as the "leech has two daughters" who constantly cry "Give," so Sheol is never content; it never cries, "Enough."[4]

But Jesus defeats this all-consuming foe by way of *gift*, that is, by pouring out his soul into death (Isa. 53:12). By sending his Son to die, God fills up to overflowing even the depths of death itself with the uncontainable fullness of his own infinite life. Only God could do this. The gift of God alone satisfies that which is "never satisfied." Within the miracle of Jesus' deep descent, the grave is forced to cry out "Enough!" It cannot hold God.

Here we notice the extreme irony of this picture: the grave itself becomes a *giver*, yielding before Jesus' infinite life. After the three days, the grave spews forth the life-giving One, the Son, just as the great fish "vomited Jonah out upon the dry land" (Jonah 2:10; cf. Matt. 12:38–42; Luke 11:29–32). Thus, everything changes. Jesus' resurrection brings new creation and new life.[5]

Resurrection Life

None of the New Testament's teaching on good works, and especially Jesus' radical demand for sacrificial giving, would make any sense if Jesus had not risen from the dead. Apart from this joy set before us, the call to carry our crosses would be a cruel joke. Indeed, if we fail to read the New Testament's teaching on good works and generosity in light of this future hope of resurrection, as Richard Hays has astutely observed, "either we will fall into a foolish utopianism that expects the world to receive our nice gestures with friendly smiles, or we will despair of the possibility of living under the 'unrealistic' standards exemplified by Jesus."[6]

But because Jesus is risen, our good works are no joke. Indeed, because Jesus is risen, Paul concludes his most extensive statement on the resurrection with this final exhortation to engage in good work:

> Therefore, my beloved brothers, be steadfast, immovable, always abounding in the work of the Lord, knowing that in the Lord your labor is not in vain. (1 Cor. 15:58)

We have a new King, and we are called to *live into* his new kingdom. Those who encounter the risen Christ are, like Paul, changed, and this in turn changes not only our inner life but also how we address the world around us. Christians, justified and liberated by our risen Lord, are called to do unexpected deeds that challenge people and transform communities. And because of Christ's resurrection, none of this work is in vain.

Resurrection Life: Reversal and Reward

Someone may naturally ask, "What does this resurrection life actually look like? On a practical level, what does it mean?" Here, as observed in a previous chapter, we must exercise caution. We must be careful before trying to specify behavioral norms. Yet our freedom does not leave us without a path to follow, shaped by the radical reversal of a dead man rising.

When Jesus refashions the world by his resurrection, he does so in a way that surprises, offends, and delights us. Jesus envisions a world flipped upside down, or better, right side up. The dead are made alive, the foolish are wise, the humble are exalted, the hungry are filled, and the poor are made rich. Jesus invites us to affirm the goodness of creation without denying the harsher realities of our sin-soaked world.

For example, Jesus affirms the joy of a festival, the laughter of a party, and the warmth of gathering together. These are good things, not bad. And yet, the feast of faith in the resurrection of Jesus also refashions the feasts we give ourselves. For Jesus says that these celebrations are at their best when they resemble not the pattern of this fallen world but the blueprint of his kingdom. Listen, for example, to Jesus' remarks to a man who invited him over for dinner, and imagine how we might respond to such words spoken at one of our own parties:

> When you give a dinner or a banquet, do not invite your friends or your brothers or your relatives or rich neighbors, lest they also invite you in return and you be repaid. But when you give a feast, invite the poor, the crippled, the lame, the blind, and you will be blessed, because they cannot repay you. For you will be repaid at the resurrection of the just. (Luke 14:12 – 14).

How strange Jesus' advice must have seemed! Don't invite your friends and family. Jesus' logic is startling. Don't invite those who might be able to pay back anything at all. Isn't this odd? But are Jesus' words strange because he is absurd or because we live in a world that is terribly twisted?

The challenge in Jesus' advice about dinner parties is the challenge of faith in the resurrection itself. "To put it at its most basic," N.T. Wright has said, "the resurrection of Jesus offers itself . . . not as an odd event within the world as it is but as the utterly characteristic, prototypical, and foundational event within the world as it has begun to be."[7] Jesus' resurrection is not "an absurd event within the old world but the symbol and starting point of the new world."[8] And his advice about how to throw a dinner party follows suit. It is not strange advice but is now the "new normal," grounded in re-creation itself, that is, the resurrection from the dead.

King Jesus does not invite those who can pay him back to his feast, to his lordly supper. He invites us in our sin, in our nakedness. What could we possibly give him as repayment? Christ invites us when we have nothing to offer but our sin. And we respond in faith, giving him our sin, our failure, our weakness, our pain.

In this gospel reversal he takes our poverty and gives us his riches. We therefore feast with Christ and invite others to join the celebration. We eat and drink the body and blood of Christ, not to mourn his death but to celebrate his resurrection life in which we share. We celebrate that our death-deserving sins, pride, and failures have been replaced by his life-giving resurrection. Our debt is paid and our accounts have been filled. In Christ we now have an inheritance that is secure, eternal, and liberating (Eph. 1:11, 14, 18; Col. 3:24; 1 Peter 1:4). Although our earthly riches will disintegrate and disappear (James 5:2), we cannot lose God's riches manifested in forgiveness and grace (Rom. 2:4; Eph. 1:7; 2:7; Col. 1:27; 2:2).

Jesus' resurrection must change the look of our tables because we have eaten at his table. We now feast with the King, and therefore we should go to the highways and byways, inviting not only those who have resources, but especially the marginalized of this world. Unlike earthly kings who surround themselves with the elite, the wealthy, and the power brokers, this King delights to have his supper with the dejected, the voiceless, the wounded, the sick, and the dying (cf. Luke 14:15 – 24). Our tables, our fellowships, our communities should now aim to reflect this new kingdom.

Responding to the Power of Christ's Resurrection

The beginning of the book of Acts tells about those who encountered or believed in the resurrected Jesus. This is the history of early Christianity, and the rising of Jesus is central to the church's self-understanding and mission from the beginning.

Acts 4 in particular begins with Peter and John, among others, publicly "teaching the people and proclaiming in Jesus the resurrection from the dead" (Acts 4:2). This upset the authorities, especially the religious ones, so they arrested the apostles; but those who believed their message multiplied to almost five thousand (4:3 – 4).[9]

Though these apostles appeared "uneducated" and "common," they also had a power that unnerved the political leaders. They had, in the name of the risen Christ, publicly healed a forty-year-old beggar, disabled since birth, and no one could deny it (Acts 3:1 – 10; 4:9, 14, 22). As with the coming of Messiah Jesus, so the message of the risen Christ was accompanied with the healing of the disabled beggar and proclamation of the kingdom to the poor. Even when the authorities demanded they stop proclaiming Christ, Peter and John knew silence was not an option.

As soon as they were released from prison they started again: "With great power the apostles were giving their testimony *to the resurrection of the Lord Jesus*, and great grace was upon them all" (Acts 4:33, italics added). What did they preach? What witness did they give? They proclaimed not merely a crucified Messiah, but a risen and reigning Lord (Matt. 28:18; John 20:28; Acts 2:36; Rom. 1:4; 10:9; 1 Cor. 12:3; Phil. 2:11).

But we should not stop there. As their message about the risen Messiah was received and believed, the result was transformative—the believers started doing good works! They became united in heart, and "no one said that any of the things that belonged to him was his own, but they had everything in common" (Acts 4:32). Belonging to Christ, they also belonged to one another. What was the result?

> There was not a needy person among them, for as many as were owners of lands or houses sold them and brought the proceeds of what was sold and laid it at the apostles' feet, and it was distributed to each as any had need. (Acts 4:34–35).

Now let's go ahead and admit what we often think after reading these words: this is just wrong. Don't their actions go against our Western sense of ownership and private property?[10] What were they thinking? Yes, it is good they believed in Jesus and his resurrection. They should do that; we all should do that. But why did they give up their rights to their possessions? What did that accomplish? Were they trying to earn God's love by these works? No, no, no.

Think again about Acts 4:32: no one claimed ownership of anything, they shared everything, and no one was in need. Doesn't that sound like a return to the garden, to original communion with God and neighbor? Each was taken back to the realization that all things ultimately belong to God, and thus they lived freely and responsibly with God and each other, secure in God's love and grace.[11] Having believed in Christ and the power of his resurrection, they were liberated from endlessly seeking their own welfare, from trying to "work" for themselves.

Like the transformation of Paul after he met the risen Christ, so in Acts 4 the people were transformed in their minds, their hearts, and their actions. Because Jesus was their Lord, they were not only reconnected to God, but also to their neighbors. They now did good work toward others in response to God, not in order to earn God's favor, but as the natural overflow of resurrection life. Love of God and neighbor was reestablished. That is the power and gift of Christ's resurrection.

Raised That We Might Die

Just as we turn this corner, we run into a paradox. The gospel, the good news of the crucified and risen Messiah, frees us from sin's condemning power and from the exhausting efforts to save ourselves. We receive the new life God gives in Christ, so that we now are able to give our lives to others. Again, few have said it more wonderfully than Martin Luther:

> A Christian lives not in himself, but in Christ and in his neighbor. Otherwise he is not a Christian. He lives in Christ through faith, in his neighbor through love. By faith he is caught up beyond himself into God. By love he descended beneath himself into his neighbor. Yet he always remains in God and in his love.[12]

Acts 4 and other passages of Scripture show us that preaching the resurrection of Christ produces a deepened concern for this present life and for the needs of this world.

You have probably heard the comment, "You are so heavenly minded you are of no earthly good." But we should be able to say of Christians, "You are so heavenly minded you are of utmost earthly good." Our overly spiritualized expectations about eternal life can give us the dangerous impression that God only came to redeem our "souls." But the Father sent his Son to die and rise for our bodies as well as our spirits. As Randy Alcorn observes, "He came to redeem not just 'the breath of life' (spirit) but also 'the dust of the ground' (body)."[13] The resurrection forbids us from ever forgetting the fullness of our connection to the rest of God's creation.

When people experience the power of Jesus' resurrection, they do not detach themselves from this world; rather, they invest in it! Believers find themselves more linked to the real physical pains of those around them, concerned for their welfare and seeking to meet their needs. The power of the resurrection does not take us away from the sorrows, pains, and poverty of this world. Rather, it liberates us to enter into those sorrows, into those pains, into that poverty (cf. Matt. 25:31–46). For we need no longer fear that they will consume us. We cannot handle them, but we can take that poverty, that pain, that despair, and we can bring it to the King who alone can make things right. We do not worship a dead prophet but a risen Messiah. We worship the God of creation, who is also the God of re-creation.

The Good Work of Re-Creation

Though the call to engage in good works has not disappeared, it has been transformed. Again Luther says: "We do not become righteous by doing righteous deeds but, having been made righteous, we do righteous deeds.

This in opposition to the philosophers."[14] We do good works not to earn God's love or favor, nor to clean ourselves up in some misguided attempt to become presentable to God or others. Rather, united to the risen Christ, we experience God's favor and we freely extend ourselves to others. As Paul said, knowing the power of Christ's resurrection we may now share in his sufferings, becoming like him in his death.

But here we face a sobering question: How faithfully do we follow Christ in reaching out to others? How does the world view Christians, especially in America? To be honest, I think they view us as angry, arrogant, and disconnected. And I don't think they often accuse us of doing too many good works.

If we went to random street corners across America, asking people for their first reaction to a word, what do you think we would hear after saying "Christian" or "evangelicals"? Most of us know it wouldn't be pretty. What would it be like, however, if their reactions were something like this:

- "Christians are incredibly generous."
- "No one cares for the poor like those evangelicals."
- "When I am with evangelicals, I just sense so much grace."
- "They seem more concerned with the welfare of others than concerned about themselves."
- "I can't think of any group that is quicker to enter into people's pain, suffering, and struggles than Christians."

Now I know the "world" is not going to be quick to praise Christians, and I don't want us to change our lives *in an effort to gain* their praise.[15] That would be foolish and misguided. Yet people all over this world who know almost nothing about Christianity generally know that Jesus died and that his death was for the sake of other people. How are we known?

Paul connects Christ's death and resurrection with our concern for others. He reminds us that those who have experienced the gift of the resurrection power of Jesus are also united with Christ's suffering, "becoming like him in his death" (Phil. 3:10). Elsewhere he writes, "For as we share abundantly in Christ's sufferings, so through Christ we share abundantly in comfort too" (2 Cor. 1:5). Similarly, Peter encourages his readers: "But rejoice insofar as you share Christ's sufferings, that you may also rejoice and be glad when his glory is revealed" (1 Peter 4:13). Sharing in Christ's sufferings means pouring oneself out for the sake of others, willingly taking the path of humility that others might be raised up to see God (cf. Rom. 8:17; 15:1–7; Phil. 2:1–11; Col. 1:24).

Four Important Clarifications

It is important to make four quick observations that may help avoid misunderstandings.

First, *"good work" is not easily categorized.* It covers everything from wiping a baby's bottom to wiping other people's tears away. It includes visiting prisoners and clothing the naked. We also engage in God's good work through praying alone in the dark and when we offer simple words of encouragement. All our work points to God's work of redemption. If our definition of "good work" excludes Christians who are young, aged, sick, and mentally or physically disabled, then we have become overly rigid in our definitions.[16]

Second, *busyness is not the same thing as good work.* Especially in America, where we often gain our identity from our flurry of activities, we need to beware of this danger. Simply being busy is not the same thing as doing good work. Part of this confusion comes from our love of instant gratification. But God's good creation is often slow to develop, and we need patience. It takes time and seasons for the seed to grow into a flower. Yes, seeds need to be watered and attended, but too much water creates a flood that destroys everything around. And the gardener often needs to cut away some of the weeds that grow too quickly around the plant; the weeds of busyness can suffocate real growth.

How much is too much? When (and to what) should a person say yes and when (and to what) should a person say no? These are not easy questions, and they are certainly ones I struggle with all the time. So while I could give some principles for helping determine how to best use one's time, I would prefer instead to offer a simple encouragement.

Listen to God. Quiet yourself; humbly and attentively listen and respond to God's nudges. Our Creator knows us better than we know ourselves. He has given us all the time we need. He knows how he has gifted us. He knows our stamina—or lack thereof. He knows our mixed motives, and he knows our temptations. He knows how to liberate his people so that we will enjoy the good work laid before us. Yes, sometimes it is exhausting, but it is also life-giving. God does not desire busybodies; he calls for faithfulness. And faithfulness is not measured by one's busyness, but by one's love toward God and neighbor.

Third, *all of God's people get to participate in and enjoy good works.* Good works are not just for those employed in full-time Christian ministry or for select believers who love the smell of incense and dark monasteries. Part of what Martin Luther opposed so strongly was the idea of "self-elected" good works that became exclusively associated with religious institutions, but excluded the laity, and especially the poor.[17] Good works are for all of God's people, not just those who receive their paychecks from the church.

Rich or poor, slave or free, educated or uneducated—all of God's people, having received God's gifts, are called to participate in the ongoing movement of divine generosity. And we are to do what we can to free others to serve Christ as he has called them.[18] We are one body in Christ, working together in response to God's good work of re-creation.

Fourth, *when our opportunities or abilities for good work diminish, we should honestly admit that it hurts all of us.* Once, after preaching on the relationship between the resurrection and good works, I received a wonderful email from a loving husband about his wife, who was caring for her elderly Christian mother. Part of the note read (names have been changed):

> Sue's mother has been in a nursing home for a couple of years now, and due to her age-related infirmities she is unable to do anything "useful."[19] She was always such a dynamic person, full of energy and service. Now she laments her inability to do anything but wait. Sue has worried that her mother tied her relationship to God to her good works. But as you reminded us Sunday, we were created to do good works, and she is simply reflecting that.

Yes, it is deadly to make our works our god. But we can also appreciate the pain that comes when opportunities to work begin to diminish. Sue's mother is certainly still "useful," and her son-in-law knows that. But he expresses candid pain about what he calls "a deep pool of troubling duties and experiences" that come with elder care, and we need to hear that pain for not just the aged mother but for all involved.

Let us not too quickly respond by overspiritualizing this situation. We should mourn with this elder saint. We can join with her because when God's people lose their abilities to serve, we all sense a loss. But ultimately this grandmother and the whole church rest not in the ability or inability to work, but in God's good work finished in Christ. So Sue's mother still "works," but there is no doubt it now looks and feels different, and so we look longingly for the final resurrection.

Re-Creation Work Occurs in a Fallen World

Finally, we always need to remember that unlike creation before the appearance of sin, we now live in a world ruptured, violated, and scarred by sin. All of us share in that brokenness. But the gift and power of the resurrection has set us free to do good amid this fallenness. Believers are encouraged to be "zealous for good works," responding to God's mercy by bringing the peace of Christ to this tumultuous world (Titus 2:11 – 14; cf. 1:16; 2:7; 3:1, 4 – 8, 14).

The goal of our good works is not to win the "culture wars" or to elect certain people to political office. Our good works are political, but political because they are understood as service to the King and his kingdom. Therefore, in a fallen world our good works will look a lot more like a cross than a state capital. They will sound a lot more like suffering than like political bantering. And when we do these works, they will feel a lot more like dying than like living. But paradoxically, to be raised with Jesus means we die with him, and by dying with him we rise.

We were created for that good work, and now we have been redeemed for that good work. Listen to Paul connect all of these themes — death, resurrection, faith, grace, and good works — holding them together as a harmonious whole. Read his words slowly and carefully.

> But God, being rich in mercy, because of the great love with which he loved us, even when we were dead in our trespasses, made us alive together with Christ — by grace you have been saved — and raised us up with him and seated us with him in the heavenly places in Christ Jesus.... For by grace you have been saved through faith. And this is not your own doing; it is a gift from God, not a result of works, so that no one may boast. For we are his workmanship, created in Christ Jesus for good works, which God prepared beforehand, that we should walk in them. (Eph. 2:4 – 10)

Let us take up the cross and follow our Savior, for even while he leads us through death for the sake of others, he has overcome the power of sin and death. He has risen, risen indeed. And we who are found in him, who enjoy his righteousness and grace, are set free to join in the movement of divine generosity, no longer fearing death. We open our hands, our hearts, our lives to others, and in this we reflect the heart of Christ. We reflect the heart of God.

I will make my dwelling among you. . . . And I will walk among you and will be your God, and you shall be my people.

Leviticus 26:11 – 12

So powerful is participation in the church that it keeps us in the society of God.

John Calvin[1]

Question 55: What do you understand by "the communion of saints"?

Answer: First, that believers one and all, as partakers of the Lord Christ, and all his treasures and gifts, shall share in one fellowship.

   Second, that each one ought to know that he is obliged to use his gifts freely and with joy for the benefit and welfare of other members.

The Heidelberg Catechism[2]

So a thriving place is full of intention, a sufficiency awaiting expectation, teasing hope beyond itself.

Marilynne Robinson[3]

chapter thirteen

Receiving Life Together

Believing in the Church

Hands up, who believes in the church? I doubt many hands are raised at such a question. What does it mean to "believe" in the church anyway? Formulated in the early centuries of Christian history, the last part of the Apostles' Creed reads: "I believe in the Holy Ghost; the holy catholic church; the communion of saints...." The most basic Christian confession — our *credo* — includes belief in the church as part of our confession of the Holy Spirit. So in what sense are we to have "faith" in the church?

Across the centuries we see countless divergent expressions of Christian commitment. Our world today is full of diverse confessions and denominations, covering everything from the large Eastern Orthodox and Roman Catholic communities to the thousands of independent Protestant congregations all around the globe. There are Baptist, Anglican, Assemblies of God, Presbyterian, Nazarene, and Methodist churches. Which "church" are we supposed to believe in? How can you believe in "the church" when our churches are so often divided and seemingly impotent? It suddenly makes sense. Believing in the church is truly an act of faith.[4]

Pontificating about "the church" in abstract terms can produce an idealism that never touches reality. If you move from the romanticized visions of the church to an actual localized gathering of people, such idealism quickly fades. Anyone who has been a part of a worshiping community for any extended period of time will have experienced moments of frustration, deep disappointment, hurt, and struggle. As Swedish theologian Gustaf Aulén once wrote, "Only faith can see the holiness of the church."[5] Why? Because its holiness is not always readily apparent. Not just outsiders, but insiders who have felt the sting of pain from their involvement in a church will have difficulty believing in it. Quickly, the wounded saint will say: "I don't believe in the church; I believe in God."

And yet, as we will see, to believe in God is to believe in his church, to enter Yahweh's community of peace and sacrificial love and to reach out from it. This is a crucial part of living in the movement of divine generosity. In fact, Paul goes so far as to describe the church as "the fullness of him who fills all in all" (Eph. 1:23). But living in the church is always an act of faith, demanding not only our intellectual assent, but also our time, our savings accounts, and most of all our love for people and places different from us. It demands what would be impossible if it were not first given.

God Creates the Church

Lest we despair, we need to acknowledge that God himself, by his Word and Spirit, creates and sustains the church. "I will take you to be my people," Yahweh declares, "and I will be your God" (Ex. 6:7; cf., Jer. 7:23; 11:4; 30:22; Ezek. 36:28). We are God's people because he first loved us, gave himself to us, drew us in, and embraced us (1 John 4:10, 19; cf. Deut. 7:6–8; 10:15; 14:2, etc). Receiving this life *together* liberates us to then give our life *together* away.

Jesus asserted his primacy in relationship to the church, programmatically announcing to Peter, "On this rock *I will build my church*, and the gates of hell shall not prevail against it" (Matt. 16:18, italics added).[6] This is *Christ's* church, *his* work; we are his people, who have received God's mercy in Christ by the Spirit. To scattered and diverse congregations Peter declares, "Once you were not a people, but now you are God's people; once you had not received mercy, but now you have received mercy" (1 Peter 2:10).

Take a deep breath and relax for a moment. Hear this, really hear it. The church is not something that we are ultimately responsible for; rather, this is Christ's church, his body, and his bride. We need to hear this because, especially in Western evangelical churches, we easily believe the church's survival rests on us. How often, for example, do we identify a church by the pastor's name, such as "Jim's church"? So what happens if Jim stumbles, if he is unfaithful, if his charismatic personality no longer draws the crowds? Yes, Jim is the pastor, but whose church is it? How often do crises of faith come to God's people because they believe that the church's survival rests on a particular person or movement rather than on God himself?

Similarly, the church's continued existence does not depend on who is in the White House or which political party is in power. Nor does the church's health depend on how well we keep up with cultural and technological trends. When we forget these things, we often mistake ourselves for God; we begin to act as if we, rather than King Jesus, are messiah. We must never forget this is Christ's church.

Although God delights to work through us as he grows and sustains his church, fundamentally this is God's work, his people, his church. The "gates of hell will not prevail" because King Jesus leads the charge. Surely hell would prevail if it were up to our inconsistent attitudes, doctrinal fidelity, cultural relevance, and advocacy for justice in the world. We, the people of God, are often faithless, but "he remains faithful — for he cannot deny himself" (2 Tim. 2:13). Hell will not prevail.

God himself calls into existence our life together as the church. He is the Lord of the church. French Reformer John Calvin expressed this in a remarkable way:

> So powerful is participation in the church that it keeps us in the society of God ... all those who, by the kindness of God the Father, through the working of the Holy Spirit, have entered into fellowship with Christ, are set apart as God's property and personal possession.[7]

Thus, the church is not merely a group of people who "have a shared taste for religion or the creation of some kind of human community spirit. It is not," explains Lutheran theologian Christoph Schwöbel, "a community devoted to a common cause or to the realization of a common aim, and in this the church differs from other organizations." This is because "the Church is created by the divine Word insofar as it evokes the human response of faith."[8] God creates and sustains the church through his Son and his Spirit.

The church, as the "blessed community," is made up of those who have found themselves bound together in the love of the Father, the grace of the Son, and the fellowship of the Spirit (2 Cor. 13:14). This divine embrace cuts across racial barriers, educational distinctions, geographical limitations, and political parties. As we will see later, this unity is our basis for extending ourselves out to others, even our enemies, as we participate in the movement of divine generosity. But this is not something we have originated ourselves. It is something we must first receive together as God's covenant community.

We have received grace and the healing of God's presence together as God's people, and out of that collective experience we extend our hearts and hands to others. We participate in God's work as he grows his church and loves his world. Dietrich Bonhoeffer declared, "Christian brotherhood is not an ideal which we must realize; it is rather a reality created by God in Christ in which we may participate."[9]

Christ declares "my church," and yet, as those who belong to Christ, we echo that this is also "our church." It is ours, not because we are so effective at community organization or so persuasive with our use of arguments; instead, it is ours because in Christ we belong to God. "So let no one boast in men. For all things are yours, whether Paul or Apollos or Cephas or the world or life or death or the present or the future — all are yours, and you are Christ's, and Christ is God's" (1 Cor. 3:21 – 23). We are in the divine embrace, and Christ extends his presence to the world through this imperfect community (Eph. 1:22 – 23). Receiving this life together takes faith! And that faith results in action.

Entering and Extending Divine Hospitality

We need to be drawn more deeply into the community of God's people if we are to reach out beyond it, releasing what we have received in the world. The gift of coming together as God's peculiar people must be savored if it is to be spread.[10] It is only in entering more and more deeply into this particular community — gathered around God's gifts — that we can be collectively filled up and poured out for the world.

As we discussed in a previous chapter, to understand Messiah Jesus one needs to pay attention not simply to his words but also to his actions. Not only is this true about Jesus; it must be true about his church. We bring the good news both by the words that come out of our mouths and by the actions that flow from our hands.[11] Hospitality, the most common form of generosity found in the New Testament, holds these different dynamics together, capturing the connections between entering and extending, discourse and deed.

John's Vision of the "Truth" of Hospitality

John's letters provide a fascinating example of how divine hospitality both draws us to God and at the same time it draws us to the church. He opens his first letter by inviting others to join in their fellowship [*koinōnia*], which he sees as an extension of divine hospitality, the fellowship of the triune God.

> That which we have seen and heard we proclaim also to you, so that you too may have *fellowship with us*; and indeed *our fellowship is with the Father and with his Son Jesus Christ*. (1 John 1:3, italics added)

Fellowship with the people of God is connected to fellowship with the triune God. As those who have then experienced God's welcoming hospitality and grace, God's people will be a community that extends hospitality and love to others in their need. This community, this place, this people is where God most clearly makes himself known in word and action.

John contrasts a love for God with a love for the world. But, as we noted in chapter 4, "world" in John often represents all that is set against God in his holy love; it represents our rebellion. "Do not love the world," John says, because the world loves the wrong things: "the desires of the flesh and the desires of the eyes and pride in possessions" (1 John 2:15 – 16). No, the people of God belong to Jesus, who has become our desire just as we are *his* possession. Thus, all we are and have is a gift from him, a gift that looks for opportunities to be used for others.

Consequently, the sign and symbol of fellowship with God are love and care for those in need (1 John 3:16 – 17). John encourages the flock, "Let us not love in word or talk but *in deed and in truth*" (1 John 3:18, italics added). Notice, while he says not in "talk," he still calls us to "truth" [*alētheia*]. His point is not that we should be silent about Jesus, since his whole letter aims to make Jesus known. But *we make Jesus known "in deed and truth."* The "truth" of Jesus is not simply something a person rationally accepts; it is something that is felt, experienced, and known.

When truth is present, it manifests itself in hospitality. Thus, when John writes his second letter to the "elect lady and her children," he refers to them as those "whom I love *in truth*, and not only I, but also *all who know the truth*, because of *the truth that abides in us and will be with us forever*" (2 John 1 – 2, italics added; cf. v. 4). The gospel is not a philosophy; instead, it is the truth of Jesus (John 14:6; 18:37; cf. Col. 2:6 – 8). He lives in his people, and where he dwells his light shines through acts of love and mercy. Faith and life are connected, according to John:

If anyone says, "I love God," and hates his brother, he is a liar; for he who does not love his brother whom he has seen cannot love God whom he has not seen. And this commandment we have from him: whoever loves God must also love his brother. (1 John 4:20–21)

John connects the hospitality of God with the fellowship of the saints, and he claims that this loving fellowship is best expressed as hospitality toward the one in need. Mirroring the gospel, such hospitality is the natural extension of the gospel as it is always "bearing fruit and growing" (Col. 1:6) — "whoever loves God must also love his brother."

Such a pattern does not belittle the spoken word; rather, it expects that Christians will be agents who extend that word in concrete acts of love. One of the main ways we experience God's love is through the love of others as we give and receive: we need each other. But this is not merely a program of social improvement. Those who go "out into the world" without a connection to the incarnate Christ are outside of the truth (2 John 7, 9–11). Word and deed always go together. The apostle Paul used "the same language for proclaiming his message (e.g., *diakonia* in 2 Cor. 3:3, 7–9; 4:1; 5:18; 6:3; 11:8) and for social ministry (*diakonia* in 2 Cor. 8:19–20; 9:1, 12–13)."[12] Sadly, we tend to choose between these, but a biblical understanding of divine hospitality holds them together.

John's third letter again associates divine truth with Christian fellowship. He loves Gaius "in truth" and is thankful that all reports describe this small church "walking in the truth" (3 John 1–3). These believers were being faithful in the truth as they welcomed traveling Christians, most likely missionaries. Their hospitality provided relief for the travelers, and in that way they helped their fellow saints in their mission to the Gentiles (3 John 5–8). In contrast with our individualistic tendencies, this united community had a collective *purpose*. In similar ways the apostle Paul saw himself as a preacher to "the Gentiles in faith and truth" (1 Tim. 2:7), sent and encouraged by the various churches who shared his concern and enabled his efforts. "We might call hospitality," writes John Koenig, "the catalyst for creating and sustaining partnerships in the gospel."[13]

One of the great signs of being outside of the truth is a spirit of inhospitality (3 John 10). By way of contrast, the Jews of Jesus' day saw Abraham, whom Christians know as the "father of the faithful," as a kind of "patron saint for hosts."[14] Accordingly, the apostle John challenges his readers by saying, "Beloved, do not imitate evil but imitate good" (v. 11). In his letter John links "evil" with inhospitality (cf. the behavior of Diotrephes, vv. 9 – 10) and the "good" with generosity (cf. the positive examples used throughout). Thus, the truth of God's hospitality toward us in the gospel constitutes the basis and motivation for the church's life together and in its outreach to the needy world.

Welcoming the Stranger, Helping the Hurting

Hospitality is itself a kind of gift that is not so much received and possessed as it is entered into and shared. It is an ever-expanding gift of new stories and surroundings. God calls his people to live out the gospel pattern of welcome and generosity. "Therefore," Paul says, "welcome one another as Christ has welcomed you, for the glory of God" (Rom. 15:7; cf. vv. 1 – 7; Ps. 69:9b).[15]

Sadly, Christian history is littered with countless examples of churches that proclaimed an orthodox theology while demonstrating more hate than love. One could give examples of churchmen through the ages saying belittling things about women, or Luther in his old age decrying the Jews in ways that are repulsive, or nineteenth-century conservative, white Presbyterian ministers espousing horrific racist views that linger with us to this day. What do we make of theologically "orthodox" congregations that would bring slaves into the sanctuary, chain them up in the balcony, and then preach to them about Jesus' love? How is that, in any sense, living in the truth?

While it may be easy for us to condemn the sins of others in the past, how well do we do? Are we genuinely hospitable in the truth? We all struggle to live our theology. Too often we behave like the unforgiving servant, who obtained forgiveness of his great debt to the king and then denied his own debtor that same grace. This two-faced behavior denies the graciousness of our King (Matt. 18:23 – 35), and it puts us in danger of severe discipline. We too easily view the needy as lazy, morally compromised, or somehow unworthy. Such contempt for others is often a sign we have forgotten who we are, or more importantly, *whose* we are. We have started to think we are the King, but sadly we don't act anything like him in his patience or mercy.

Sometimes I read Jesus' words and I ask myself, "Are we taking him seriously?" In his most famous sermon he rejects the common wisdom of the day that concluded you should love those who love you and hate your enemy (see Matt 5:43). Instead, Jesus goes against our self-serving impulses by saying, "Love your enemies and pray for those who persecute you. . . . For if you love those who love you, what reward do you have?" And then he makes the connection with hospitality: "And if you greet only your brothers, what more are you doing than others?" (5:44, 46–47). This is what everyone does, Jesus says, but you should be different by extending yourself to the vulnerable and loving those who might not be easily lovable. He concludes, "You therefore must be perfect, as your heavenly Father is perfect" (5:48).

Notice that Jesus defines his Father's perfection in terms of his hospitality toward the undeserving! Jesus calls us to live out his love to those in need, and to do it quietly, not making a fuss or public display of our generous actions (Matt. 6:1–4). We do not announce our hospitality and care to the world, because that so easily creates a self-righteous focus on ourselves. The goal of hospitality is worshipful communion in the "truth." It fosters the fellowship we have with God and neighbor.

Now since we—including me—tend to gravitate to Jesus' statements of love and forgiveness, at the same time downplaying his demanding statements of discipleship and judgment, we need to listen to Jesus' own words here as he speaks of true hospitality, of the gathering of all the nations, and of final judgment and blessing. It is a long quotation, but we need to exert the love it takes to really listen. Jesus says:

> When the Son of Man comes in his glory, and all the angels with him, then he will sit on his glorious throne. Before him will be gathered all the nations, and he will separate people one from another as a shepherd separates the sheep from the goats. And he will place the sheep on his right, but the goats on the left. Then the King will say to those on his right, "Come, you who are blessed by my Father, inherit the kingdom prepared for you from the foundation of the world. For I was hungry and you gave me food, I was thirsty and you gave me drink, I was a stranger and you welcomed me, I was naked and you clothed me, I was sick and you visited me, I was in prison and you came to me." Then the righteous will answer him, saying, "Lord, when did we see you hungry and feed you, or thirsty and give you drink? And when did we see you a stranger and welcome you, or naked and clothe you? And when did we see you sick or in prison and visit you?" And the King will answer them, "Truly, I say to you, as you did it to one of the least of these my brothers, you did it to me."

> Then he will say to those on his left, "Depart from me, you
> cursed, into the eternal fire prepared for the devil and his angels.
> For I was hungry and you gave me no food, I was thirsty and you
> gave me no drink, I was a stranger and you did not welcome me,
> naked and you did not clothe me, sick and in prison and you did
> not visit me." Then they also will answer, saying, "Lord, when did
> we see you hungry or thirsty or a stranger or naked or sick or in
> prison, and did not minister to you?" Then he will answer them,
> saying, "Truly, I say to you, as you did not do it to one of the least of
> these, you did not do it to me." And these will go away into eternal
> punishment, but the righteous into eternal life. (Matt. 25:31–46)

Is this not one of the most frightening passages you have ever read in your life? The goats are condemned, not for anything they have done, but for what they have failed to do. It is as if, as C. S. Lewis once observed, the heaviest charge against each one of us turns on things that we may never have even dreamed of doing.[16] So what are we to make of this passage? What are we to make of Jesus?

When we read this, we quickly sense how unfaithful we are. When was the last time we thought of visiting a prisoner? How often have we failed to welcome the stranger, clothe the naked, or care for the sick when it was in our power? Yet Jesus reveals a startling insight, saying we honor or neglect him precisely insofar as we honor or neglect those who are poor and vulnerable! "Whoever is generous to the poor lends to the LORD, and he will repay him for his deed" (Prov. 19:17; cf. Matt. 10:42; 18:10; Mark 9:41; Heb. 6:10). To visit a prisoner is to visit Jesus; to provide shelter to a child is to welcome the Lord.

And "do not neglect to show hospitality to strangers," writes the author of Hebrews, "for thereby some have entertained angels unawares" (Heb. 13:2; cf. Gen. 18:1–15; Judg. 6:11–24; 13:3–24). To neglect a brother in need is not only to reject our neighbor, it is to reject Jesus. "So then," Calvin comments on Matthew 25, "whenever we are reluctant to assist the poor, let us place before our eyes the Son of God."[17]

The Sacraments and God's Hospitality

My goal here is not to overwhelm us with guilt. But I am not opposed to provoking us—you and me—to repentance. To be honest, writing this book is one of the hardest things I have ever done, because one cannot study, meditate, and then write on these things without examining oneself. And so often I am found wanting. So often I live far more concerned about myself than about others, especially those in the greatest need. How about you?

Jesus is not joking around when he talks about the sheep and the goats. He is serious, and we need to make sure we have not cut passages like this out of our Bibles because they make us feel bad or uncomfortable. We need to hear his words, we need to examine our hearts and our lives, and we need to repent. But genuine repentance is not about entering a pit of despair and self-abuse; it is about rediscovering the extravagance of God's grace and the liberating power of his Spirit. Repentance means confessing things about ourselves, confessing things about God, and then trusting the Giver that we can be changed (see ch. 5). Repentance leads to life, not death (Acts 11:18).

Acknowledging how often we fall short should lead us to reconsider what it means to receive life together in the church. Here we are taken back to the sacraments of baptism and the Lord's Supper. These are visible signs of invisible grace that remind us who we are and what kind of God we are dealing with, and they give us renewed impetus for extending divine hospitality to others. The sacraments of the church are another way we are taught faith and receive life in this peculiar community. They are another way to believe and experience God's gifts.

Baptism. There is no way into God's church except through the humbling recognition that we are unclean. The public mark that one is part of the people of God, his church, is baptism. Whether a person comes as a child or a college student, a middle-aged worker or a senior citizen, the imagery reaffirms that we all need to be washed, cleansed of the grime and filth that has crept into our every crevice. Sin is not a small spot of dirt easily brushed aside; it requires a flood. Thus, I am sympathetic with Christians who ask new converts to be immersed in baptism, not simply sprinkled.

After hearing what sounded like a pious statement that just one drop of the blood of Christ could bring redemption, John Owen countered, if one drop was all that was needed, why in the world did he die?[18] No, our sin is deadly, fatally serious. We enter the community of the forgiven, not by just ironing our clothes or washing our faces, but by affirming that we are naked and dirty, and the only thing we bring is the muck of our sin. But God specializes in baths: he makes brilliantly clean what seems irreversibly dirty. He does this as we are united to the crucified and risen Lord.

Not only when we ourselves are baptized, but when anyone enters the community of faith, we are reminded of our baptismal vows. Witnessing these baptisms, we are not meant to steel ourselves to try harder, but to return to our need and to God's gifts. We are brought back to the embrace of the Father through the Son and Spirit. We are brought into a kingdom from which we fled, but God has given us eyes to see it and feet to enter in. Renewed by God's gracious promise, we go afresh into his world with the purpose of extending his hospitality to others.

Lord's Supper. Like baptism, the celebration of Communion is central to the rhythm of the Christian life. While this sacrament has many spiritual and physical aspects, it is never less than *Eucharist*, a meal of thanksgiving. In it we celebrate the death of Jesus. Bread and wine represent the body and blood of Jesus. Yes, flesh and blood.

You don't have to believe that the elements of the Lord's Supper turn into Christ's material body and blood to realize how offensive this imagery is. But if it is grotesque to us, it would have been all the more outrageous to the Jews of Jesus' day. If you are a Jew, you do *not* drink blood. You do not even eat meat with traces of blood in it. The Old Testament said that blood belongs to God because life is in the blood (Lev. 17:14). That truth begins to dawns on us. And this potentially grotesque and offensive meal becomes the most beautiful and inviting banquet in history, and God's people, God's church, repeat it forever.

In celebrating the Lord's Supper we look back to Christ's sacrificial death and life-giving resurrection, and we look forward to that great banquet feast in heaven, when all things will be made right in Christ. There will be a party in heaven filled not only with abundant food and drink, but with a feast of fellowship, laughter, contentment, and peace. But the Lord's Supper, in which we partake now, also reminds us what it cost God to prepare this meal. This meal is the gift of Jesus, God's Son.

The Lord's Supper reminds us that *we* are the hungry, the impoverished; we are those who will starve without this bread and wine of heaven. Our thirst cannot be quenched and our hunger cannot be satisfied apart from this meal. Only Jesus can provide the food and drink that nourishes the soul and satisfies the longing heart. As the meal of Communion brings us back to God's hospitality, the Spirit renews us, and we then reach out to the world in a spirit, not of damnation but of compassion.

The cultural markers of hospitality in Jesus' day included greeting (removal of isolation), washing feet (removal of dirt), and feeding (removal of hunger). As the church extends God's hospitality to believers through the spoken Word, baptism, and Lord's Supper, believers are then to turn and offer hands of encouragement, food, and physical comfort to the world. In this way we are able to give, to give together, for we have entered into the community of faith that is carried along and sustained in the movement of divine generosity.

But who am I, and who are my people, that we should be able to give as generously as this? Everything comes from you, and we have given you only what comes from your hand.

1 Chronicles 29:14 NIV

Let us ... contribute whatever we have — wealth, diligence or care giving — for our neighbor's advantage.... For nothing is so pleasing to God as to live for the common advantage.

Chrysostom[1]

You will be made rich in every way so that you can be generous on every occasion, and through us your generosity will result in thanksgiving to God.

2 Corinthians 9:11 NIV

Thanks be to God for his inexpressible gift!

2 Corinthians 9:15

chapter fourteen

Giving Life Together

God Gives His People as a Gift

As Yahweh's "called-out ones," his people become God's gift to the world. We are not simply a country club, an environmental advocacy organization, or a place for group counseling. Having experienced the forgiveness of sins, the fellowship of Christ's suffering, and the power of his resurrection, we now gather as agents of God's work and continued concern for his world. Paradoxically, this means that as we gather, we should look outward. We are called to be a community focused on "the other" rather than on "self."

This has always been the pattern of God's redemptive work in history. God calls a particular people to himself and blesses them, with the purpose that they will then be a blessing to the nations (Gen. 12:2–3).[2]

> God chooses not only to make Abraham and his offspring the *object* of his blessing but also to make them the *instrument* of his blessing to the world. This person, family and nation who are to be blessed by God will be the means of others coming into the same blessing.[3]

In other words, God blesses the particular in order to be a universal blessing; he works not generically, but through real people gathered in real communities. From the Abrahamic covenant to Christ's gathering the Twelve, and then the growing of the disciples and the formation of his church, God has always gathered his people to serve as a light to the world, bringing the gift of salvation (cf. Isa. 42:6; 49:6; Luke 2:25–32; Acts 13:46–48).

There is a difference of relative emphasis, however, in the pattern of how God's people care for the nations. According to Charles Scobie, "In the OT the ingathering of the Gentiles involves the nations coming to Israel, not Israel going to the nations. Here [in the NT] the reversal is even more striking: the basically *centripetal* movement of the OT is replaced by the *centrifugal* movement of the NT." Scobie further explains, "The OT 'come' [Isa. 60:3; 66:23; cf. 45:14; 60:5, 14; Mic. 7:12; Tobit 13:11] is replaced by the NT 'go' [Matt. 28:19; Mark 16:15; Acts 1:8]."[4]

The people of God became the normal avenue for the world to encounter God's presence and redemptive activity in the world. At first the pattern primarily moved "from the periphery to the center" in order to draw the nations in, but now the focus is primarily from the center out. Certainly we would not want to be overly rigid in distinguishing the different patterns between the Old and New Testaments, since one can find examples in each Testament that breaks this general rule. For our purposes, however, the point is that both of these movements (centripetal and centrifugal) are forms of divine hospitality and the extension of grace.

The mission of Jesus — the mission of God — is a movement of inclusion, not exclusion; a movement of grace, mercy, and love, not of rejection, hatred, and fear. It is good news, after all. Yes, it calls for repentance, as we discussed earlier in the book. It requires us to come before the holy God, in an encounter that reveals our great sin and need. This is why there were sacrifices to be offered. This is why the great sacrifice of Christ was offered (Heb. 9:11 – 28). But this is also why this mission centers on *good* news. It captures us, frees us, and then moves us toward God and toward each other. Thus the repeated biblical refrain, "how beautiful are the feet of those who preach the good news" (Rom. 10:15; cf. Isa. 52:7; Nah. 1:15; Eph. 6:15).

Belonging to God does not mean we escape this world but that we bring God's life, light, and hope further into it. We hear this movement echoed in Jesus' prayer to his Father just before he was arrested: "As you sent me into the world, so I have sent them into the world" (John 17:18; cf. vv. 15 – 18). As disciples of Jesus we belong to God, not to justify a hatred or frustration with this world, but so that divine love may move through us to others. We go out to the world not representing perfection or superior etiquette, but as shattered sinners who have been reconciled with the holy God.

> So if anyone is in Christ, there is a new creation.... All this is from God, who reconciled us to himself through Christ, and has given us the ministry of reconciliation; that is, in Christ God was reconciling the world to himself ... entrusting the message of rec-

onciliation to us. So we are ambassadors for Christ, since God is making his appeal through us; we entreat you on behalf of Christ, be reconciled to God. (2 Cor. 5:17–20 NRSV)[5]

As those who have tasted God's grace and forgiveness, we are now his ambassadors, willingly carrying this message of hope even if it means our suffering (Eph. 6:20). This is not retreat: this is movement forward, outward. This is the movement of divine generosity, a movement that is meant to pulsate through God's church to the world.

A People Known for Hospitality

So what does hospitality look like? I think Christine D. Pohl is right: "Part of the mystery [of Christian hospitality] is that while such concrete acts of love are costly, they nourish and heal both giver and recipient."[6] We are healed as we move with God in his motions of generosity. God's gifts are wonderfully ironic; we often experience his love for us most when we love others. As conduits of his love we find ourselves strangely reinvigorated through hard work and humble service. It is only when we see how much we have been forgiven that we can participate in God's grace to others. At their (and our) most faithful moments, this is how Christians have been known: not because they wielded great political power, but because they wielded great sacrificial service.

In a fascinating book called *The Rise of Christianity*, sociologist Rodney Stark reconsiders the early developments of the fledgling church after Christ's death, trying to understand how it was that this small group of believers in an obscure Jewish Messiah rose to become such a dominate presence in the world in just a few centuries. He found that the empirical evidence points to a few massive and deadly epidemics as a crucial time of numerical growth for the early Christians. Why? Because during this deadly period of plagues, their faith provided not just a doctrine that carried explanatory force, but one that also "provided a prescription for action."[7] The Christian faith combined word and deed.

While we may take the idea for granted, Stark argues that the thought of loving your neighbor, especially the vulnerable stranger, was a revolutionary Christian concept, foreign to paganism.[8] As an epidemic spread, people abandoned the cities and homes, commonly even leaving loved ones who had been infected. Based on their pagan beliefs and worldview, it was the only rational thing to do. These people had no eternal horizon.

But many Christians stayed behind, first caring for their own and then for others who were abandoned in their illness. The Christian bishop Dionysius wrote of his fellow believers, "They were infected by others with the disease, drawing on themselves the sickness of their neighbors and cheerfully accepting their pains.... The best of our brothers lost their lives in this manner." Even Emperor Julian, clearly no friend of Christians, found himself frustrated by how well the "Galileans ... devoted themselves to benevolence" and thus far outshone the pagans.[9] Elsewhere Julian wrote:

These impious Galileans [i.e. Christians] not only feed their own poor, but ours also; welcoming them into their *agape* [love], they attract them, as children are attracted, with cakes.... Whilst the pagan priests neglect the poor, the hated Galileans devote themselves to works of charity, and by a display of false compassion have established and given effect to their pernicious errors. See their love-feasts, and their tables spread for the indigent. Such practice is common among them, and causes a contempt for our gods.[10]

Clearly not all Christians engaged in this heroic work, but the evidence shows that a great many did. This defined the church's character for the pagans around them. Christians in their small networks and local connections extended the love of the crucified and risen Savior by entering into the poverty, pain, illness, and isolation of others. In this way they became the avenue by which others were received and welcomed into the hospitality of God.[11]

The Collection: Participating in Divine Generosity

The earliest Christian communities never limited their expressions of sacrificial generosity to their local fellowships. From the outset they looked beyond their own immediate communities. To be sure, the early church delighted in the breaking of bread and table fellowship that radically reduced the poverty among them (Acts 2:42–47; 4:32–37). But this joy also overflowed. Their giving spread and expanded. Nowhere do we see the expansive and unifying force of the early church's generosity more clearly than in the enterprise that came to be called "The Collection."

It is indeed striking that the first thing we are told that believers did after being called "Christians" for the first time was to take up a collection for the poor (Acts 11:19–30, esp. vv. 26–29). When believers in Antioch heard of a famine that was about to hit Judea and Jerusalem, they immediately *decided to give*. These gifts went to fellow believers whom they had never met because they lived far away. This collection and the collections that would follow also played a formative role in the life and mission of the apostle Paul.

Early in his ministry, the elders of the church at Antioch asked Paul with Barnabas to deliver this relief fund. In Galatians 2:1–10 Paul recounts the common concern for the poor that he also shared, not only with the leadership at Antioch, but also with the "pillars" of the church in Jerusalem. Such shared concern was as a natural outworking of their unity in the gospel:

> … and when James and Cephas and John, who seemed to be pillars, perceived the grace that was given me, they gave the right hand of fellowship to Barnabas and me, that we should go to the Gentiles and they to the circumcised. Only, they asked us to remember the poor, the very thing I was eager to do. (Gal. 2:9–10)

Commenting on this passage in Galatians, New Testament scholar Scot McKnight says, "Little did the Jerusalem leaders know that their suggestion would become Paul's *obsession* for nearly two decades."[12] This may come as a surprise for many of us who know Paul primarily for his letters — his words. But if we think we know Paul's theology and remain ignorant of his work on behalf the poor, we should reread those letters (esp. Romans, Galatians, and 1 and 2 Corinthians). Although we cannot fully unpack this here, studying Paul's theology apart from the Collection is very much like studying the presidencies of George Washington or Abraham Lincoln apart from the Revolutionary and Civil Wars, or the speeches of Martin Luther King Jr. apart from the Civil Rights Movement. To be sure, Paul did many different things, but this campaign consumed such a great deal of the apostle's energy and imagination that we cannot rightly understand the one apart from the other.[13]

The Purpose of the Collection

James Dunn has said that the Collection held a "peculiar significance" for Paul: it "sums up to a unique degree the way in which Paul's theology, missionary work, and pastoral concern were held together as a single whole."[14] N. T. Wright similarly insists, "This project cannot have been a mere whim, a nice idea dreamed up as a token gesture. Paul must have wanted very, very badly to do it."[15] But why? Paul appears to have been willing to give up his very life to complete this project (Rom. 15:31; cf. Acts 20:3, 24).[16] But why was it such a priority?[17]

The short answer is that the Collection appears to have been a campaign that combined a rich variety of implicit and explicit purposes. These different motivations and aims seem to have included the following.

To relieve poverty. Whatever we say about the meaning and purpose of the Collection must include the obvious fact that it displayed a deep concern for the poor (Acts 11:27–30; Rom. 15:25; Gal. 2:10; 2 Cor. 8:4, 13–15; 9:12). Paul and the early church repeatedly exhibited their desire to help fellow Christians in need.[18] At a basic level, then, Paul viewed the Collection as "a matter of fairness" (2 Cor. 8:13). The parallels with the priorities of Jesus' own life, preaching, and ministry are obvious (Matt. 5:42; 6:2; 25:34; Mark 10:21; Luke 4:18–19; 7:22; John 13:29).

Jesus meant the church, his body, to be identified by her sacrificial concern for those in need. In this way, whatever the church owns was, ideally, made liberally available to the poor. In fact, John Calvin even observed, "You will frequently find in both the decrees of synods and in ancient writers, that all the church possesses, either in lands or in money, is the patrimony [i.e., inheritance] of the poor."[19] Luther similarly concluded, "After the preaching of the Gospel, the office and charge of a true and faithful pastor is, to be mindful of the poor."[20] This has always been an abiding concern of "Christians" since they are called by that name (Acts 11:19–30).

To unify the church. Yet, we cannot reduce the significance of the Collection to poverty relief alone. For Paul himself saw fit to accept contributions from the Macedonians who themselves were *poor* and whose "abundance of joy and their extreme poverty," Paul says, "overflowed in a wealth of generosity on their part" (2 Cor. 8:1–2). Thus, there must have been some significance that transcended even the practical purpose of the project, important though that was. Part of the greater purpose of this gift, in Paul's mind, seems to have been that it was not only for the recipients but also for the *givers.* This collection came primarily from Gentile converts and was directed primarily to Jewish believers in their season of poverty. Paul therefore clearly hoped that this Collection would help establish *unity* within the church as a whole, bringing Jew and Gentile together. N. T. Wright has expressed this point beautifully, describing the Collection as

a massive symbol, a great prophetic sign, blazoned across half a continent, trumpeting the fact that the people of God [were being] redefined around Jesus the Messiah [as] a single family.[21]

In other words, Paul saw the Collection as a project that would defy on a practical level the divisions that threatened the unity of the church. To overcome the conflict between Jewish and Gentile believers, Paul sought *spiritual solidarity* through *generous giving*, allowing Gentile Christians the opportunity to "express tangibly their spiritual debt to Jewish believers" (Rom. 15:27).[22] In this light, Paul's decision to delay his trip to Rome makes sense (Rom. 15:22–29). The unity of the church was the foundation for her growth.[23]

To participate in God's grace. From a pastoral perspective, Paul not only envisioned the Collection as a means of relieving poverty and promoting the unity of the community. He also saw the Collection as an opportunity for each contributor to actively participate and share in God's grace.

When we discover that two whole chapters of Scripture are devoted to a single topic, it tends to capture our attention. In 2 Corinthians 8–9, at the heart of one of Paul's major letters, this is precisely what we find: two chapters entirely devoted to the Collection. In these chapters the word grace (*charis*) appears no fewer than ten times. This is one of the most concentrated uses of one of the most important words in Paul's vocabulary that we find in the New Testament. As Keith F. Nickle has said, "If any one phrase could summarize Paul's theology, it would be 'the grace of God in Christ.' "[24]

God's grace, supremely manifested in Jesus Christ, is Paul's greatest theme and he applies it to the Collection in an astonishing variety of ways:[25]

- as the inexpressible gift that made participation in the Collection possible (2 Cor. 8:1; 9:8, 14–15)
- as the act of participation in the Collection itself (2 Cor. 8:6)
- as the result of participation in the Collection (1 Cor. 16:3)
- as a direct expression of Christian fellowship (2 Cor. 8:4, 7)
- as an activity stimulated by the grace of Christ's example (2 Cor. 8:9)

After holding up the example of the grace God gave to the Macedonians, Paul appeals to the ultimate example of generosity: "For you know the grace of our Lord Jesus Christ, that though he was rich, yet for your sakes he became poor, so that you through his poverty might become rich" (2 Cor. 8:9 NIV). It's worth taking a moment here to stop and consider the incredibly *practical* situation that gave rise to this much loved verse on the mystery of Christ's incarnation. We often quote it out of context as an opportunity to talk philosophy. But Paul is not giving a lecture on systematic theology at this point. He is fund-raising. Thus, for Paul, practical participation in the church's collective work of generosity brings into fruition our knowledge of God's grace. Raising money for the needy provides the perfect setting and environment for doing true theology and engaging in true worship. For Paul, the Collection demonstrates what the knowledge and truth of God's grace really look like in the life of a community.

Thus, it would be a mistake to think of the Collection as if it were somehow marginal to Paul's message or mission; rather, it takes us to the very heart of the gospel. Only because people know God's grace are they able to give with true and voluntary abandon after the example of their Lord. Thus, flowing out of our confession of the gospel, the church's collective generosity is to be experienced as a participation in God's grace that results in his glory and our good. "Thanks be to God," Paul concludes, "for his inexpressible gift" (2 Cor. 9:15).

To prefigure the future. While it is nowhere stated as one of Paul's explicit purposes for organizing the Collection, this project bears some striking similarities to various Old Testament prophecies. A time in the future was anticipated in the Old Testament when Gentiles would come bringing gifts to God's people in Jerusalem.[26] When Paul, as the apostle to the Gentiles, comes together with his foreign companions to bring their gifts from Macedonia, Achaia, Galatia, and Asia, they certainly appear to be, at least partially, fulfilling some of these ancient expectations so long foretold:

> Then you will see and be radiant;
>> your heart shall thrill and exult,
> because the abundance of the sea shall be turned to you,
>> the wealth of the nations shall come to you.
> (Isa. 60:5; cf. vv. 3–4, 6–7, 11, 13, 17; 2:2–4; Mic. 4:13; Hag.
>> 2:7–8; Zech. 14:16–21)

Regardless of whether the Collection should be read directly in light of such texts from Isaiah and the other prophets, it is clear that one final day is coming when all the wealth of this world will come rushing back in worship to God. When Paul remarks that all things are not only from God, but also through him and to him (Rom. 11:36), he reminds us that God's ownership points not just to the past but to the future as well.[27] In the Collection we see a picture of God's people manifesting the truth of this good future.

The beginning of the Bible's grand story shouts to us of God's ownership of all things. The end of the narrative also highlights all things rushing back to him (Rev. 21:24–26). Here we discover again just how far God's redemptive rule will reach: to every tribe, tongue, people, and nation. Near and far, they will all come bearing gifts. And the Collection appears as a concrete symbol of this great expectation. We belong to each other. We belong to the Lord!

Stewards of the Gospel

In light of this emphasis on the "collection for the saints" (1 Cor. 16:1), we observe that fundamental to the church's life together is also the idea of *stewardship*. Despite our tendency to reduce this language to purely monetary matters, most often the New Testament uses this vocabulary in reference to the gospel itself. Beginning with Paul and his missionary team, the apostolic call was to be "stewards [*oikonomoi*] of the mysteries of God" (1 Cor. 4:1–6).[28]

The apostolic proclamation is entrusted to ministers and preserved in local congregations (2 Tim. 1:13–14; 2:2; 3:14). This trust calls God's people, and particularly shepherds of God's flock, to be stewards of the good news (Col. 1:24–27). Consequently, ministers who steward this message are told to be "above reproach" (1 Tim. 3:2). Such an "overseer" must not be "arrogant or quick-tempered or a drunkard or violent or greedy for gain, but hospitable, a lover of good, self-controlled, upright, holy, and disciplined" (Titus 1:7–8). Not only must leaders quench their greedy impulses, but also the first positive trait they must cultivate is hospitality. They represent, in proclamation and action, God's immense generosity and grace.

This message of salvation has been entrusted to the leaders of the church as "the stewardship of God's grace that was given to me [Paul] *for you*" (Eph. 3:1–3, italics added). Paul expresses the movement of grace given from one to another rather than withholding from each other. These mysteries are now revealed; they have been shared with us that we may spread them around. The mysteries are not abstract speculations but rather what God has made known in Christ and what we have received by faith (e.g., 1 Tim. 1:3–7; cf. Rom. 16:25; Eph. 1:6; 3:3; 6:19; Col. 1:26–27). Having received this gift from God, thus entrusted with the care of his gospel, our reaction should not be pride; rather, we should delight in offering this word of hope freely and whenever possible (1 Cor. 9:16–18).

Ultimately all Christians are to act as stewards of the gospel, spreading this truth by word and deed. Peter connects the imagery of gift and stewardship, challenging us to live together in a way that promotes the praise of the Triune God through sacrificial service:

> As each has received a gift, use it to serve one another, as good stewards of God's varied grace: whoever speaks, as one who speaks oracles of God; whoever serves, as one who serves by the strength that God supplies—in order that in everything God may be glorified through Jesus Christ. To him belong glory and dominion forever and ever. Amen. (1 Peter 4:10–11)

This is how God's people should be known, as servants of Christ and stewards of the varied grace that God has given us.

Conclusion

As we said earlier, divine hospitality is a gift that is not so much possessed as entered into. It is the gift of new surroundings and stories. Hospitality says, "Come with us into the joy of our Lord; join the feast at the table of God." Gathered around the bread and wine, we are reminded that God manifests his love and lordship supremely as gift. He reveals his sovereignty in self-giving. As those who belong to God, we extend his love and lordship to others, inviting them into the feast of communion with their Creator, who redeems and sustains his world.

God calls his people to live out together the gospel pattern of gift. Even as God has given himself to us in our lowliness, caring for us in our great need, so now God calls the church to care for the poor, the oppressed, and the downtrodden. In this way God includes us in his ongoing movement of grace and love, promising that such giving wastes nothing but leads to "life that is truly life" (1 Tim. 6:19 NIV).

God So Loved, He Gave

Then the Pharisees went and plotted how to entangle him in his words. And they sent their disciples to him, along with the Herodians, saying, "Teacher, we know that you are true and teach the way of God truthfully, and you do not care about anyone's opinion, for you are not swayed by appearances. Tell us, then, what you think. Is it lawful to pay taxes to Caesar, or not?" But Jesus, aware of their malice, said, "Why put me to the test, you hypocrites? Show me the coin for the tax." And they brought him a denarius. And Jesus said to them, "Whose likeness and inscription is this?" They said, "Caesar's." Then he said to them, "Therefore render to Caesar the things that are Caesar's, and to God the things that are God's." (Matt. 22:15–21)

The Creator of all things, including humanity, comes: he comes himself, entering the chaos, the brokenness, the poverty, and the shame. He comes quietly, humbly, truly. And when he comes, he does the scandalous, for God becomes a human being. And in the end this man, Jesus the Messiah, suffers, dies, rises, and ascends. In this we learn what is called the "gospel," the good news of God. God has reestablished our belonging to him not by taking, but by *giving*!

This good news is about God's liberation of sinful humanity, bringing forgiveness, freedom, hope, and restored communion with the Creator. Here is the work of renewing creation—all things have been made new in Christ.

In Christ we discover again the joy of belonging to God. Those captured by this gospel enjoy the inexhaustible grace of God. The people who understand and live in this forgiveness and freedom find themselves also giving themselves, their resources, all they have for the sake of making known again the great King and his advancing kingdom.

The people of God and the good news of his coming both reflect God's own pattern of working, not primarily through power or fame but through weakness and love. The paradoxes of God also mark his people. They discover that it really is better to give than to receive. We see the humble exalted and the exalted brought low. Those who serve come to power and those who give come to wealth. We discover the freedom of being a slave to Christ. We discover the blessing of weeping with those who weep and rejoicing with those who rejoice. We experience the unquenchable delight of participating in God's generosity as we enter into the movement of divine grace: all things are from him, through him, and to him. Here is freedom. Here is redemption. Here is life.

Those who belong to God participate in his kingdom work. Therefore, the church embodies and gives away the good news. And just as this good news of Jesus' coming shows us God's concern for us as the weak, the poor, and the oppressed, so also the life of God in us will inevitably cause our hearts to burn with compassion for all vestiges of weakness and poverty around us. God's impartiality makes him partial to the poor. In fairness he favors the fatherless and receives the rejected. They have a special place in his affections because God is not blind to the harsh inequalities of this world. The material world matters to God. When we forget this, we become blind to the fullness of redemption and the joy of our kingdom work.

The kingdom of God comes to earth, not to deny our physicality but to show us how to live by the Spirit in this physical world that God created and is redeeming. Those who belong to Christ thus reflect his heart, his mission, his work. We seek to set the captives free from sin through the finished work of Jesus on the cross; this we proclaim by the spiritual preaching of the Word, through the material administration of the sacraments, and through the physical application of aid to the circumstances of those in need. In this way, those in the kingdom find themselves following the way of the cross by service, sacrifice, and even suffering. Life and proclamation should always be tied together in the generosity of God's people who know that they belong to their Master. He has set us free to live as agents of grace, hope, and love. Thus we enter the story and participate in God's good news: For God so loved, he gave.

Acknowledgments

THIS BOOK SHOULD NOT EXIST. The story of how it came to be is too long to tell here, but the short version is that what began as a small idea soon came to dominate my life. I want to thank (and blame) Daryl Heald, Justin Borger, and David Arthur in particular, since each of you early on, normally over a meal when I was weak and vulnerable, convinced me that this was an idea worth exploring. The result was that it took over my life! I became convinced—through those conversations and my study—that when the Christian story is approached through the lens of "Gift," this story and our lives open up before God's glorious and empowering grace.

My late mentor, Colin Gunton, taught me (as much by example as through word) that the best theology is theology done in community. This truth has shaped me in many ways, and there are few greater joys than for a teacher to see students grow in grace and truth. Working with Justin, my former student, has been a wonderful example of this delight as he has proven to be not only an able researcher and thinker, but a trusted friend—your prayers in the dark times mean more to me than you will ever know.

Justin has thought long and hard about the topic of generosity, and he proved invaluable to this project in countless ways. But while Justin has been my trusted assistant on this book, he represents countless other students who were not only willing to challenge my thinking but who also provided needed encouragement and prayers. To my students who kept asking me to write on something "besides Owen" and to take some of the ideas from class and present them in a written form, I can finally say, "Take up and read." Thank you for being willing to take your teacher seriously, but not too seriously.

I would also like to thank others in my "community." Besides our loving family, it has been our neighborhood, our church, and Covenant College that have been incredible instruments of grace during the writing of this book. Each group loved our family in concrete ways as we faced some awfully challenging days. To our families, thank you for being flexible and supportive of the Kapic madness—we love you. New City Fellowship in Chattanooga has modeled the reality of divine generosity, and certainly your influence should be felt throughout the pages in this book.

Some others warmly deserve mention: Danny Kapic, David and Kelly Paschall, Jim and Dayle Seneff, Roger and Rebecca Sandberg, Jeff and Lynn Hall, Randy Nabors, Duane and Jerilyn Sanders, Jay Green, Jeff Morton, Paul Morton, Matt and Joan Vos, and John Holberg. How thankful I am for my colleagues at Covenant College, who provide such a rich interdisciplinary environment to think and live out of. I am also deeply thankful to Covenant College for the sabbatical during the fall of 2009, without which I would certainly have not been able to finish this book.

I would like to especially thank the members of my department (Scott, Jeff, Dan, Ray, Herb, Ken, and Roger), as each lent their expertise, ear, and friendship at different times in the writing of this book. John Yates painstakingly read most of the manuscript and provided invaluable feedback at all levels. John Muether lent his expertise with the indexes. Katya Covrett of Zondervan has not only been an incredible editor, but also a valuable friend—thank you for not only believing in this project from early on, but for caring about my family throughout the process.

As I sit here, my mind rushes through the last two years, thinking of how God turned our world upside down, and yet, in many ways, he made it right side up. Cancer is terrible. Yet God has been absolutely present and merciful. And Tabitha, you are beautiful and full of strength. You embodied the truth that God's grace is often found in weakness and sacrifice. Thank you for your love, faith, courage, and most of all, the way you call me, Jonathan, and Margot to a kingdom perspective. The three of us sometimes just look at you, shake our heads, and smile as we say, "Mama." This book is dedicated to you, Tabitha, because you have helped me and many others live in the glory of God's great gifts.

Kelly

• • •

We would like to express particular thanks to God for the strong support and partnership we have received from Generous Giving and the Maclellan Foundation throughout the course of this project. These are two of a growing number of Christian organizations responsible for pioneering a renewed emphasis on the biblical message of generosity, and it is no exaggeration to say that this book would never have been written apart from the support of Daryl Heald, Bill Williams, and other members of their leadership teams.

Kelly and Justin

•   •   •

It is appropriate that I begin by thanking God for my parents and grandparents, who have not only taught me what it means to belong to God but have lived lives poured out in generosity. Nothing has impacted my life more profoundly than watching the gift of their faith being worked out in love.

Because this project has developed over a number of years, I find it impossible not to mention a special group of family, friends, and former colleagues who have so deeply influenced my understanding of the depth and diversity of God's gifts. These are people whom God has used in profound and providential ways throughout the course of this project, not only offering helpful feedback, but also by prayer and consistent encouragement: Jason Hood, Jasper Reynolds, David Author, Julie Wilson, Ben Borger, Joni Owen, David Cross, Ryan Casselberry, Lowen Howard, Cathy Matherly, Diane Talley, Melinda Eller, Fritz Schalmo, Donny Friederichsen, Tim Trouten, and Charles MacKenzie.

The congregations of Evangelical Presbyterian Church of Annapolis, Maryland, and St. Paul's Presbyterian Church of Orlando, Florida, also deserve special thanks for their fruitful participation in several months of classes taught from early drafts of this manuscript.

Finally, it is appropriate that I end by thanking God for Kelly, who has not only been a profound mentor but has become a beloved friend. The depth of humility and relentless availability Kelly has shown to me throughout the course of our work together has truly been one of the sweetest gifts I have ever received.

Justin

Discussion Questions for Each Chapter

The following questions can be used for small group discussion or personal reflection.

Chapter 1: All Things Belong to God

1. To whom do you belong, God or competing posers? Have you personally experienced the burden of self-ownership? What possessions are keeping you from fully experiencing the joy of belonging to God? What will you do about it? In what ways are you currently clinging to your own life and self as your ultimate possession?

2. What does it mean to embrace God's ownership—or the reality of belonging to God—as good news? How is this different from other ways that the good news has been explained to you?

3. Did God have to create? How does the Trinity show us that God does not need creation in order to love or be loved? What does it say about God's character that although he did not need to create, he did?

4. How does the reality of God's absolute ownership confront and comfort you?

5. How does the dynamic nature of God's ownership (flowing from him, through him, and to him) activate your imagination? What are the implications of this dynamic for a life of stewardship and generosity?

6. Why does the Bible ground God's ownership in the work of creation? What are the implications of this for our stewardship over creation? What does it mean to enjoy the Giver through his gifts, the Creator through his creation?

7. Why is it important for us to remember that everything God created is *good*—especially when we are talking about issues of stewardship and generosity?

8. "We own nothing, but we manage everything." What are the most important things God has entrusted you to manage? Why do you believe they are the most important? Are you managing them in a way that glorifies you, or God? What changes might this prompt you to make in managing them?

9. What do we mean when we say that "God owns by giving"?

10. How does the good news of belonging release us to give ourselves away (to God and to others) in ways that are impossible for those who treasure their lives as their own?

11. In what way is God's ownership not only a thing of the past but of the future as well?

Chapter 2: Everything Appears Lost

1. In what kind of environment did humanity first begin to doubt God's generosity? Can you describe the shape or character of the first temptation and sin?

2. How has your own vision been twisted by an emphasis on God's *prohibition* instead of his *provision*? Do you ever feel as if God is holding out on you in spite of all that he has given?

3. There's a certain irony in the story of humanity's fall: Adam and Eve *lose everything* when they reach out to *take something*. By contrast, Jesus saves all by giving all away. Have you experienced similar ironies in your own life? Have you ever lost something by taking or gained by giving? Explain.

4. We fall from belonging into bondage. Can you list and describe some of the different forms of bondage spoken of in this chapter? Which form of bondage is most troubling or obvious to you? Which form of bondage do you tend to forget or ignore?

5. What makes bondage to sin so deeply personal, social, relational, creational, and even demonic?

6. How can personal evil be simultaneously strengthened and disguised by social structures and relationships? Can you think of examples? What social/structural sins have you participated in, perhaps without even realizing it?

7. Jesus says that money has a peculiar power that can profoundly capture us, taking on a quasi-divine status and creating a sort of bondage (Matt. 6:24). Have you ever experienced this power that money has? Have you been possessed by your possessions or consumed by your consumerism?

8. We easily trivialize and downplay the significance of sin and the powerful ways in which sin, Satan, and death hold us under bondage. How has this chapter helped you to reconsider sin's catastrophic consequences?

Chapter 3: The Coming of the King

1. What message did Jesus begin to proclaim from the outset of his public ministry? Why is this important?

2. What did Samuel say when Israel asked for a king "like the other nations"? Was it wrong for Israel to want a king?

3. What did Samuel warn that a king "like the other nations" would be like? What kind of activity did Samuel say would define such a king's rule? How does this activity compare with the way God rules as King?

4. Have you set up a king over Yahweh in your life (person, privilege, or possession)? What has been "taken" from you as a result?

5. How did Jesus respond to John the Baptist when he asked the great question, "Are you the one who is to come, or shall we look for another?" (Matt. 11:3). How might Jesus' answer have surprised John and, perhaps, transformed his expectations about the Messiah? How does the answer he gave to John's question surprise and challenge your assumptions about the nature of God's Messiah and his kingdom?

6. Why is Jesus' emphasis on proclaiming good news to the poor such an important indication of his true identity? How does this affect your outlook and approach to the poor?

7. Can you list some of the different signs of the King and the kingdom spoken of in this chapter? What do these signs show us about Jesus' identity and his relationship to the kingdom?

8. How do these different signs of the kingdom show us that Jesus was reclaiming that which belonged to God?

Chapter 4: The Gift of the Son

1. How does Jesus' answer in response to the Pharisees' question about paying taxes move us beyond politics? How does Jesus take us back to creation with his answer? What does it mean to "Render to Caesar the things that are Caesar's, and to God the things that are God's" (Matt. 22:21)?

2. Here is a theme or a question running throughout the Bible as a whole: Insofar as God's possessions have been plundered and ransacked as a result of humanity's fall into sin, how is God going to get everything back? How does the most famous verse in the Bible help us to answer this question?

3. Who is the "world" in John 3:16 and why does it matter?

4. Is God's love for the world in John 3:16 the same kind of love that we are warned against having for the world in 1 John 2:15? If not, how do they differ?

5. How does the story of Abraham and Isaac in Genesis 22 help us to understand that there can be no substitute for the gift of the Son?

6. We normally give gifts to celebrate an achievement or to mark a joyous occasion, such as a birthday, anniversary, or graduation. But God gives a gift in John 3:16 for a different reason. Explain what that reason is.

7. In what ways is the gift of the Son like a multifaceted jewel? Describe some of these facets and explain their importance.

8. Why was the cross necessary? Why couldn't God just forgive us without Jesus' death on the cross?

9. How does Jesus' parable of the lost son illustrate that God's grace does not primarily consist in what we hold in our hands but in whose hands we are held?

Chapter 5: Believing the Gift

1. What does faith involve? How does the story of Nicodemus help us to answer this question? Is mere belief in God's existence or

an intellectual assent to the God of the Bible sufficient? Why or
why not?

2. What does the story of the men who lowered the paralytic through
the roof teach us about the costly, risk-taking nature of faith?
What risks does faith involve for you and for the church today?

3. What truths does faith in the gift of Jesus call us to confess
about ourselves? In what fundamental problem do we find ourselves before having received this gift? What continuing needs
does this gift meet on a daily basis even if we have been believers
for many years?

4. What truths does faith in the gift of Jesus call us to confess
about God? What does the nature of this gift, and specifically
the way it was offered on the cross, tell us about the kind of God
we are dealing with here?

5. What are the three dynamics that help us to understand faith as
a gift?

6. Compare and contrast John's characterization of Nicodemus's
first encounter with Jesus in John 3 and his last appearance in
John 19.

7. How does trusting in God's gift change us? How might recon-
sidering Nicodemus's last appearance in the gospel of John help
us to answer this question?

Chapter 6: The Gift of the Spirit

1. Why is it significant that the Holy Spirit is called "the gift of
God" in the New Testament? What does it mean to say that the
Holy Spirit is a triune gift?

2. Can God really be given? How does Augustine anticipate John
Biddle's objection? What can we learn from Biddle's astonishment at the idea that God could be given?

3. Why are the two ways of referring to the Spirit — as both *holy*
and *given* — strikingly paradoxical?

4. What does it mean that the Holy Spirit is "a gift from the
future"? How do the metaphors of the Spirit as guarantee, firstfruits, seal, and water help to answer this question?

5. What was the significance of the firstfruits in the Old Testament? To whom were the firstfruits given? How does Paul build
on the idea of firstfruits in Romans 8:23?

6. What does it mean that Christian joy and security is not about the absence of grief or suffering, but the presence of the Spirit?

7. Can you list some of the many different ways in which the Bible speaks of believers as belonging to God?

8. What happens when the life-giving waters of the Spirit are poured out on people in Isaiah 44:3–5? How do the people respond? How should this insight impact our lives as recipients of God's Holy Spirit?

Chapter 7: Experiencing the Gift

1. How does the Holy Spirit enable believers to enter the movement of divine generosity? How does this empowerment help us to see that God's giving is more than a past basis for Christian obedience but the continuous source of our giving as well?

2. What does it mean and why is it important to distinguish between the gift of the Spirit and the gifts that he gives? What does it mean to experience both his person and his work, both his presence and his different blessings?

3. Why is the Holy Spirit called the Spirit of adoption? What are the rights and responsibilities of adoption which we experience now, and what will we experience in the future?

4. What two activities especially characterize those who have been filled by God's Spirit? Give examples from both the Old and New Testaments. By way of contrast, what kinds of behavior characterize those who have been filled by Satan (cf. Acts 5:1–11; 13:9–10)?

5. Do you share Annie Dillard's desire to bear fruit? What do such longings, found even among non-Christians, tell us about ourselves and the purpose for which we were created? Why is the imagery of spiritual fruit important? What can we learn from this metaphor about life in the Spirit?

6. What underlying goal must guide our understanding of the gifts of God's Spirit? Why is this goal or purpose of the gifts so easily abused?

7. What three main actions for celebrating the year of Jubilee were outlined in the Old Testament? What characterized the "Roman triumph"? How do these two historical themes relate and inform our understanding of Christ's ascension and the outpouring of the Spirit at Pentecost?

Chapter 8: The Gift of the Kingdom

1. Jesus, John the Baptist, and Peter all begin their preaching about the kingdom with a call for repentance. Why is repentance of such central importance to their message about the kingdom?

2. The apostle Peter himself had to repent. He had to change his view of God, of himself, and of the world—and this necessarily entailed a kind of disorientation and reorientation that simultaneously shook up and revitalized every area of his life. How have you experienced this kind of shake-up and revitalization in your own life? What areas of your life are still most in need of the disorientation and the reorientation of repentance?

3. The call to repentance and faith often appear side-by-side in Scripture. Why is it important to hold them together?

4. We do not tend to think of the kingdom as gift. We might affirm that the kingdom of God is real, that it is the reign and rule of God, but what does it mean to think of it as something that is given? What does Jesus mean when he comforts his disciples with the words: "Fear not, little flock, for it is your Father's good pleasure to *give* you the kingdom" (Luke 12:32, italics added)?

5. Why is the rich man in Jesus' parable called a fool? Would Jesus call you wise or foolish by these standards? How should this parable change the way we think about our financial future and retirement plans?

6. Why does Jesus say that people who are worried about their material welfare should sell their possessions and give to the poor in Luke 12:32–34? What grounds for giving does he provide in this passage?

7. What is the relationship between the gift of the kingdom of God and the gift of eternal life?

8. What does it mean that "God's sovereignty is revealed in self-giving"? How ought such an understanding of God's reign transform the way we think about the essential character and awesome power of biblical generosity?

Chapter 9: Living in the Gift

1. What does it mean that the kingdom of God is inaugurated, but not fully realized? How did Oscar Cullmann use the historical example of D-Day and VE-Day to illustrate the tension existing between the already and the not yet of God's kingdom?

2. What are the governing dynamics of the kingdom? How does God reign over the universe that belongs to him? Why are justice and righteousness fundamental to answering this question?

3. What passages indicate that generosity is the positive characteristic of justice and righteousness?

4. What are some passages that indicate the negative sides of God's justice and righteousness? Why is it important that we do not downplay or neglect these negative, judgmental aspects of God's justice and righteousness?

5. Does biblical justice involve more than fair punishment and procedures? If so, give some examples.

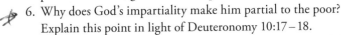 6. Why does God's impartiality make him partial to the poor? Explain this point in light of Deuteronomy 10:17–18.

7. How does Bruce Waltke distinguish between the essential characteristics of the righteous and wicked in the book of Proverbs? Cite the proverb he coins in order to contrast the righteous from the wicked.

8. How does John Calvin summarize the nature of God's rule as King?

Chapter 10: Following a Crucified Lord

1. Why is it belittling and humiliating only to receive and never to give? How does the story of Justin's relationship with Tammy illustrate this painful reality? How does the movement of divine generosity, both to us and through us, ultimately overcome this kind of experience?

2. What does Bruce Waltke mean when he says that Scripture does not present God as "anthropomorphic" but humanity as "theomorphic"?

3. Why is it so important for us to continually reexamine our lives in light of (1) the amazing gift and (2) the costly demand of the cross? What does it mean to embrace the cross as both the *source* of your life and the *course* of your life?

4. The biblical standard for Christian generosity is ultimately a *person*, not a *percentage* of our income. But there are still important lessons to be learned from the Old Testament laws concerning the tithe (cf. 2 Tim. 3:16–17). What are some of the most instructive aspects of the Old Testament laws concerning the tithe for Christians today?

5. What is it, exactly, about Jesus that we are called to imitate?

6. How is imitating Jesus similar to being a jazz musician? What does it mean to imitate Jesus freely within form? How is knowing Jesus similar to knowing the "basic beat of the song"?

7. Nothing is more basic to the imitation of Christ than giving up our rights. What rights are you holding that keep you from giving up your resources effectively? How does Jesus' example of giving up his divine and heavenly rights show us, not simply what is good or bad, but what is "best"?

8. What does Luke Timothy Johnson mean when he says that our possessions are "symbolic expressions of ourselves"? How does 1 John 3:16–17 support this conclusion? What does your own use of possessions say about who you are and what you love?

Chapter 11: Resurrection Faith and Work

1. How does Christ's resurrection simultaneously point back to creation and forward to heavenly life?

2. For what purpose does God first create and then recreate humanity? Why is it important for us to keep this purpose in mind whenever we discuss the relationship between faith and good works? How might we be in danger of belittling or trivializing the importance of good works?

3. Everyone feels the pull to do good, but our relationships with God, with each other, and with the rest of the earth are so ruptured that we are unable to do good. How does the resurrection, through its fundamental connection to creation, deal with this problem?

4. What are some ways in which good work may be functioning as your god rather than as a gift from God?

5. Did the Reformers, like Martin Luther, reject the importance of good works? Explain your answer.

6. To claim anything outside of Christ's lordship is to lose everything. But to be claimed by Christ's lordship is to gain everything. Explain.

Chapter 12: Resurrection Life in Action

1. How did Jesus overcome the greed of the grave? What does this say about the power of Christ's resurrection for overcoming the grip of greed in our own lives?

2. What are some of the dangers of trying to imitate Jesus' self-giving love on the cross without also looking ahead toward the resurrection? How might focusing on Christ's cross apart from his resurrection lead to a sense of foolish utopianism or a sense of pragmatic despair?

3. How does Jesus apply the reality of the resurrection to our table fellowship? What does the resurrection have to do with the idea of reversal and reward? Why is Jesus' challenging advice about whom to invite to our dinner parties really the challenge of faith in the reality of the resurrection itself?

4. What's wrong with the old adage, "You're so heavenly minded that you're no earthly good"?

5. What are the four clarifications listed at the end of the chapter? Why are these important?

6. Why is it important to recognize that re-creation work occurs in a fallen world? What difference does this recognition make?

Chapter 13: Receiving Life Together

1. Do you believe in the church? Why is belief in the church included in our most basic Christian confession—the Apostles' Creed?

2. We often refer to various churches as "Jim's church" or "John's church." But why is it important for us to remember that the church ultimately belongs to Christ? What are some of the practical dangers of neglecting to recognize this basic reality?

3. How is belonging to the church different from belonging to other communities like Christian ministries or nonprofit organizations? What did Dietrich Bonhoeffer mean when he said, "Christian brotherhood is not an ideal which we must realize; it is rather a reality created by God in Christ in which we may participate." Why is this truth so encouraging?

4. Explain the dynamic between entering and extending divine hospitality. Why might we need to be drawn more deeply into the community of God's people if we are to extend ourselves out of it to others?

5. Why is it important to understand biblical "truth" as a category that applies equally to our words and our actions? Do you share John's vision of the "truth" of hospitality? What are some ways in which hospitality may be practiced outside of the truth? What

does this look like? How can we be genuinely hospitable in the truth? What does this look like?

6. Whom does Calvin say we ought to place before our eyes whenever we feel reluctant to assist our poorer brothers and sisters? Do you believe Jesus' words in Matthew 25 when he says that whatever we do or fail to do for the poor, we do or fail to do for Jesus and, therefore, God himself?

7. Why are the sacraments of baptism and the Lord's Supper essential to our understanding and practice of hospitality? What are the dangers of trying to practice hospitality apart from availing ourselves of these means of grace? What are some of the ways in which being washed in Christ's blood and filled at Christ's table should transform our own table fellowship?

Chapter 14: Giving Life Together

1. What does it mean that "God blesses the particular in order to be a universal blessing"? Why is it important to understand that God works, not generically, but through real people gathered in real communities?

2. Why is Genesis 12:1–3 an essential text for understanding the missional movement of divine generosity?

3. What role did generosity play, according to Rodney Stark, in the rise of Christianity? How might Stark's historical observations challenge our assumptions about the role that sacrificial giving should play in contemporary Christianity and the future of the church?

4. What was the first thing that Christians did after being called Christians for the first time in history? Compare and contrast that with what Christians are known for today.

5. What were the four implicit and explicit goals of Paul's Collection for the poor among the saints in Jerusalem? What do these different purposes say about the importance of the Collection for Paul and the early church?

6. What is the significance of the fact that the words for stewardship in the New Testament are used primarily in reference to the gospel? Why is it important for us to embrace the gospel as the greatest resource the church has received as God's steward? What are the implications of this observation as the church seeks to share the best of what it has received with the world?

Notes

Chapter 1: All Things Belong to God

1. John Locke, *The Second Treatise of Government*, 5.27.

2. Luke Timothy Johnson, *Sharing Possessions: Mandate and Symbol of Faith* (London: SCM, 1986), 57–58.

3. John Webster, "God's Perfect Life," in *God's Life in Trinity*, ed. Miroslav Volf and Michael Welker (Minneapolis: Fortress, 2006), 145.

4. M. Douglas Meeks, *God the Economist: The Doctrine of God and Political Economy* (Minneapolis: Fortress, 1989), 115.

5. Heidelberg Catechism Q. & A. 1, in Mark A. Noll, *Confessions and Catechisms of the Reformation* (Grand Rapids: Baker, 1991), 137.

6. John Locke, *The Second Treatise of Government*, 5.27.

7. Victor Paul Furnish notes the importance of the "Pauline 'genitive of belonging,'" which he calls "frequent and characteristic." See, e.g., Rom. 1:6; 1 Cor. 3:23; 15:23; 2 Cor. 10:7; Gal. 3:29; 5:24. Victor Paul Furnish, *Theology and Ethics in Paul* (Nashville: Abingdon, 1968), 179.

8. Blaise Pascal, *Pensées*, rev. ed. (London; New York: Penguin, 1995), 141.

9. From Kuyper's *Souvereiniteit in Eigen Kring* (Amsterdam, 1880), 35, quoted and translated by James D. Bratt in *Dutch Calvinism in Modern America: A History* (Grand Rapids: Eerdmans, 1984), 231.

10. Cf. Gen. 14:19, 22 [KJV]; Lev. 25:23; Deut. 10:14; 1 Chron. 29:11–12; Job 41:11; Ps. 24:1–2; 50:10–12; 89:11; 100:3; Ezek. 18:4; Hag. 2:8; 1 Cor. 3:21–23; 6:19–20; 8:6; Col. 1:16. For an extensive commentary on the entire Bible's concerns related to God's ownership and our stewardship, see the *NIV*

Stewardship Study Bible (Grand Rapids: Zondervan, 2009) and Generous Giving's "Stewardship Bible Study Notes" found at www.generousgiving.org.

11. "God hath all life, glory, goodness, blessedness, in and of himself," Westminster Confession of Faith 2.2.

12. Aiden Wilson Tozer, *The Knowledge of the Holy: The Attributes of God* (New York: Harper, 1961), 38. Italics added.

13. "Message of the Holy Father Benedict XVI to the Youth of the World on the Occasion of the 22nd World Youth Day, 2007," Libreria Editrice Vaticana. Can be accessed online at: www.vatican.va/holy_father/benedict_xvi /messages/ youth/documents/hf_benxvi_mes_20070127_youth_en.html.

14. Saint Augustine considered how the nature of love might point back, in some way, to God himself. "Now love means someone loving and something loved with love. There you are with three, the lover, what is being loved, and love" (see Augustine, *The Trinity*, trans. Edmund Hill, *The Works of Saint Augustine: A Translation for the 21st Century* [Brooklyn, NY: New City Press, 1991], 6.14; p. 255).

15. Mark 1:11; 9:7; John 3:35; 5:20; 14:26; 17:23–26; Rom. 5:5, 15:30; Eph. 1:3–14; Titus 3:4–7; 1 John 4:9, 16.

16. C. S. Lewis, *The Four Loves* (New York: Harcourt Brace Jovanovich, 1991), 127.

17. The language of the final end or goal of creation was *finis creationis*. See Heinrich Heppe, *Reformed Dogmatics: Set out and Illustrated from the Sources*, ed. Ernst Bizer, trans. G. T. Thomson (Grand Rapids: Baker, 1978), 195.

18. Walter Brueggemann, *Theology of the Old Testament*, 9th ed. (Minneapolis: Fortress, 2007), 529.

19. Sabbath rest (Ex. 16:23; 20:8–11; 31:15; 35:2; Lev. 23:3), the celebration of the firstfruits (e.g., Ex. 23:19; Deut. 26:2; Neh. 10:35–36), Feast of Harvest (Ex. 23:16; 34:22), New Moon feast (Num. 10:10; 29:6; 1 Sam. 20:5; Ps. 81:1–3), etc. It is worth noting that at the end of an extended discussion of the festivals and feasts in the Old Testament, C. E. Armerding concludes that they represent "joyful solidarity with Yahweh and his people, in tune with the rhythms of creation, combined with concern for the poor and needy and ultimately all the nations of the world," in C. E. Armerding, "Festivals and Feasts," in *Dictionary of the Old Testament: Pentateuch*, ed. T. Desmond Alexander and David W. Baker (Downers Grove, IL: InterVarsity Press, 2003), 300–313, quote from p. 313. Later in the book we will explore in more depth these connections between creation, redemption, the poor, and the call of God's people.

20. As we will discuss later, the most important regular celebratory event is the Lord's Supper, which brings the thanksgiving for what God has done in Christ.

21. Walter Brueggemann, *The Message of the Psalms: A Theological Commentary* (Minneapolis: Augsburg, 1984), 26, 28.

22. James Luther Mays, *Psalms* (Louisville: John Knox, 1994), 120.

23. While it is cost prohibitive to quote her lyrics here, I encourage you to listen to her "Laughing With," from her album *Far* (Warner Bros. 2009). This song shows how she wrestles through these questions.

24. Ex. 6:6–7; 19:4–5; Deut. 4:20; 29:13; 2 Kings 11:17; 2 Chron. 23:16; Jer. 24:7; 31:33; 32:38; Ezek. 37:27; Zech. 2:11–12; 8:8; 2 Cor. 6:16; Heb. 8:10; Rev. 21:3. My italics.

25. Num. 6:24. My italics. As to how this blessing is picked up and has broader redemptive historical and theological significance, see Kelly M. Kapic, "Receiving Christ's Priestly Benediction: A Biblical, Historical, and Theological Exploration of Luke 24:50–53," *Westminster Theological Journal* 67 (2005): 247–60.

26. Zacharias Ursinus, *Commentary of Dr. Zacharias Ursinus on the Heidelberg Catechism* (Phillipsburg, NJ: Presbyterian and Reformed, repr. of 2nd American ed., orig. 1852). 19.

27. Gerhard von Rad, *Old Testament Theology*, 2 vols. (Louisville: Westminster John Knox, 2001 [1957, 1960]), 1:146–47. See also J. Richard Middleton, *The Liberating Image: The Imago Dei in Genesis 1* (Grand Rapids: Brazos, 2005); D. J. A. Clines, "The Image of God in Man," *Tyndale Bulletin* (1968): 53–103.

28. Mark Allan Powell, *Giving to God: The Bible's Good News about Living a Generous Life* (Grand Rapids: Eerdmans, 2006), 29.

29. Cf., John Calvin, *Institutes of the Christian Religion*, The Library of Christian Classics (Philadelphia: Westminster, 1960), 1:255.

30. See Prov. 30:8–9; Dan. 4:28–36; Mark 10:25; cf. also Deut. 6:10–12; 32:13–15.

31. This idea is powerfully argued for by M. Douglas Meeks, *God the Economist*.

32. Although approaching this topic with different presuppositions and ending in some different places than our study does, see Stephen H. Webb, *The Gifting God: A Trinitarian Ethics of Excess* (New York: Oxford University Press, 1996), for another example of unpacking this type of argument.

33. Miroslav Volf, *Free of Charge: Giving and Forgiving in a Culture Stripped of Grace* (Grand Rapids: Zondervan, 2005), 50, my italics.

34. Reprinted in Hugh Kerr, *Readings in Christian Thought*, 2nd ed. (Nashville: Abingdon, 1990), 32.

35. "In seeking God's own glory," Volf says, "God merely insists on being toward human beings the God who gives." Miroslav Volf, *Free of Charge*, 39.

36. For this language and type of argument carried through every area of theology and the Christian life, see the writings of John Piper, beginning with John Piper, *Desiring God* (Leicester: Inter-Varsity Press, 1986).

37. Richard Preston, *The Wild Trees* (New York: Random House, 2008), 6–7.

38. Bette Midler, "From a Distance." Written by Julie Gold, on the album, *Some People's Lives*, Universal Publishing Group, Cherry Lane Music Pub. Co. for lyrics.

39. For a sustained attempt to present a "scientific theology," see Alister E.

McGrath, *A Scientific Theology*, 3 vols. (Grand Rapids: Eerdmans, 2003). The three volumes are individually titled *Reality, Nature,* and *Theory.*

40. From John Chrysostom, *Ad Populum Antiochenum Homilia* 2, 6–7 (PG 49:43), with translation by Charles Avila, *Ownership: Early Christian Teaching* (Maryknoll, NY: Orbis, 1983), 85–86.

41. For example, in Alton Park, Tennessee, there are pulp mills that spew out some of the most disgusting odors, making it difficult to stay outside. Of course, the only reason it is allowed to smell like this is because it is Alton Park, which is generally a poor community. Other more affluent communities would not tolerate that kind of thing and would have guaranteed that the factories were shut down or moved. Similarly, in the affluent West we ignore the devastating pollution in developing worlds caused by, for example, the hazardous electronic waste of the United States that is shipped overseas and then burned. See, e.g., "Electronic Waste: Harmful U.S. Exports Flow Virtually Unrestricted Because of Minimal EPA Enforcement and Narrow Regulation," United States Government Accountability Office, Report published Sept. 17, 2008. So in our day, there is often a difference between how the poor and rich enjoy the air, sun, water, etc.

42. Randy Alcorn, *Money, Possessions and Eternity* (Carol Stream, IL: Tyndale, 2003), 140.

Chapter 2: Everything Appears Lost

1. Emil Brunner, *Dogmatics: The Christian Doctrine of Creation and Redemption*, 3 vols. (Philadelphia: Westminster Press, 1950), 2:91.

2. Søren Kierkegaard, *The Sickness unto Death: A Christian Psychological Exposition for Upbuilding and Awakening*, trans. Howard Vincent Hong and Edna Hatlestad Hong (Princeton, NJ: Princeton University Press, 1980), 22.

3. Harrison's autobiography is titled *I, Me, Mine*, 1st Chronicle Books LLC ed. (San Francisco: Chronicle Books, 2002). "I Me Mine," by the Beatles, was a song written by George Harrison and was first released on the *Let it Be* album. When this song was recorded in 1970, it was the last official recording The Beatles did as a band, although by this point John Lennon's absence is noteworthy. For the full significance of this reference, listen to the chorus of that song.

4. Augustine, *Sermon* 158.7, cited by Peter Brown, *Augustine of Hippo: A Biography* (Los Angeles: University of Calfornia Press, 2000), 243.

5. Bruce Waltke with Cathi Fredricks, *Genesis: A Commentary* (Grand Rapids: Zondervan, 2001), 102.

6. Ibid., 101.

7. Ironically, there is another sense in which they also attempted to take what had *already* been given. After all, God had already created Adam and Eve to be "like" him (Gen. 1:26–27). But the snake succeeded in tricking them into

stealing something (i.e., God-likeness) they had already received (Gen. 3:5). As a result of taking what had already received, humanity lost everything!

8. By way of contrast, Jesus is exalted because of his willingness to empty himself of his personal rights and prerogatives (Isa. 53:12; Phil. 2:5–11).

9. Thankfully, in chapter 4 we discover the redemptive power of one person's actions (Rom. 5:15–21).

10. This translation is from *The Complete Jewish Bible* (1998), which is published by Jewish New Testament Publications, Inc.

11. John R. Schneider, *The Good of Affluence: Seeking God in a Culture of Wealth* (Grand Rapids: Eerdmans, 2002), 62.

12. G. K. Chesterton, *Orthodoxy* (New York: John Lane, 1911). See also ethicist Reinhold Niebuhr, in his monumental work, *The Nature and Destiny of Man: A Christian Interpretation* (New York: C. Scribner's Sons, 1949), 1:178–264. Niebuhr writes, "The truth is that, absurd as the classical Pauline doctrine of original sin may seem to be at first blush, its prestige as a part of the Christian truth is preserved, and perennially reestablished, against the attacks of rationalists and simple moralists by its ability to throw light upon complex factors in human behavior which constantly escape the moralists" (1:248–49). He then goes on to use the horrific persecution of the Jews in modern history as an example of the challenge we face when trying to understand human nature, complex motives, influences, etc. The doctrine of original sin, as classically expressed along the lines of Paul, Augustine, and others, can actually help explain both the brokenness of human nature as well as the continual responsibility of people for their actions. This discussion is well beyond anything we can explore in this book with its limited focus.

13. Reprinted in Richard Foster, *Devotional Classics: Selected Readings for Individuals and Groups*, rev. and exp. ed. (San Francisco: HarperSanFrancisco, 2005), 88.

14. For a detailed treatment of shalom and its Greek counterpart, *eirēnē*, see the combined articles of W. Foerster and G. Von Rad in Gerhard Kittel, ed., *Theological Dictionary of the New Testament* (Grand Rapids: Eerdmans, 1964), 2:400–420.

15. Cornelius Plantinga, *Not the Way It's Supposed to Be: A Breviary of Sin* (Grand Rapids: Eerdmans, 1995), 13–14.

16. Paul Krugman, "Poverty is Poison," *The New York Times* (February 18, 2008).

17. Benoit Denizet-Lewis, "An Anti-Addiction Pill?" *The New York Times* (June 25, 2006).

18. The "condition" even has a name—Compulsive Buying Disorder (CBD)—which is viewed as so real by some clinicians that there have been efforts to add it to the American Psychiatric Association's Diagnostic and Statistical Manual of Mental Disorders. See "Holiday Post-Mortem" at www.dailycamera.com.

19. "Obese" is here defined as having a body-mass index over 30. The Department

of Health and Human Services says obesity may account for 300,000 deaths a year, making it the second most common preventable cause of death after cigarette smoking. See Robin Marantz, "Fat Factors," *The New York Times* (August 13, 2006).

20. Data from Food For the Hungry, "Hunger Facts," www.fh.org/fact_sheets (accessed March 5, 2008). This and the above bullet point come from this fact sheet.

21. See, e.g., Adam Jones, *Genocide: A Comprehensive Introduction* (London; New York: Routledge, 2006); Benjamin A. Valentino, *Final Solutions: Mass Killing and Genocide in the Twentieth Century*, Cornell Studies in Security Affairs (Ithaca, NY: Cornell University Press, 2004).

22. Blaise Pascal, *Pensées*, rev. ed. (London; New York: Penguin, 1995), 142.

23. Albert M. Wolters, *Creation Regained: Biblical Basics for a Reformational Worldview* (Grand Rapids: Eerdmans, 1985), 55–56.

24. Interview with Pannenburg in *Books and Culture* (September/October 2001), 19–20. Quotes from 20. Emphasis added.

25. For brief discussion of the views of Augustine, Luther, and Melanchthon, with a particular eye toward Luther's understanding, see Margaret Daphne Hampson, *Christian Contradictions: The Structures of Lutheran and Catholic Thought* (New York: Cambridge University Press, 2001), 37. For a fair-minded discussion of some key expressions of *homo incurvatus in se* in the history of theology, see Matt Jenson, *Gravity of Sin: Augustine, Luther, and Barth on Homo Incurvatus in Se* (London; New York: T&T Clark, 2006).

26. Valpy Fitzgerald, "The Economics of Liberation Theology," in *The Cambridge Companion to Liberation Theology: Cambridge Companions to Religion*, ed. Christopher Rowland (Cambridge; New York: Cambridge University Press, 1999), 224–25. Fitzgerald adds, "As a personal sinner, an individual is seen as both responsible for and as a victim of these oppressive social structures."

27. Ronald J. Sider, *Rich Christians in an Age of Hunger: Moving from Affluence to Generosity*, 5th ed. (Nashville: Thomas Nelson, 2005), 108. The study that Sider draws upon is by Rodney Stark et al., "Sounds of Silence," *Psychology Today* (April 1970), 38–41, 60–67.

28. U.S. Department of State, "Trafficking in Persons Report 2007."

29. For information, see http://216.128.18.195/IJMpdfs/IJM_Rescue.pdf.

30. For more information on this type of problem in trafficking in persons, see, e.g., the 2004 report on "Victims of Trafficking and Violence," available at www.state.gov/g/tip/rls/tiprpt/2004/ or the website on Human Trafficking developed by the U.S. Embassy in Vienna, Austria: www.usembassy.at/en/policy/human_traff.htm.

31. Volf, *Free of Charge*, 38.

32. Sebastian Moore, quoted in Richard K. Fenn and Donald Capps, *On Losing*

the Soul: Essays in the Social Psychology of Religion (Albany, NY: SUNY Press, 1995), 226.

33. Makoto Fujimura, "Beauty without Regret," on Makoto Fujimura official website. www.makotofujimura.com/ (accessed November 5, 2008).

34. Here we should also note, however, that Hezekiah is generally regarded as a good king, who, like David (1 Chron. 29:2–5), Solomon (2 Chron. 2:1–5:1), Joash (2 Chron. 24:5), and Josiah (2 Chron. 34:9), spared no expense for the sake of God's worship in his temple (2 Chron. 31:3–21). Cf. Richard Pratt, *1 and 2 Chronicles: A Mentor Commentary* (Fearn: Mentor, 2006), 35–36.

35. Charles Avila, *Ownership: Early Christian Teaching* (Eugene, OR: Wipf & Stock Pub., 2004), 88.

36. This is a paraphrase of a quote of Arthur G. Gish, which Richard Foster draws upon in his book, *Celebration of Discipline* (San Francisco; Harper San Francisco, 1998), 80.

37. The Heidelberg Catechism (1563), Q. & A. 1, in Noll, *Confessions and Catechisms of the Reformation*, 137. Emphasis mine.

38. "It is impossible to use electric light and the wireless and to avail ourselves of modern medical and surgical discoveries, and at the same time to believe in the New Testament world of spirits and miracles"; Rudolf K. Bultmann, *Jesus Christ and Mythology* (Upper Saddle River, NJ: Prentice Hall, 1958), 5.

39. For an insightful way into better understanding this and other aspects of the global church's worldview, begin with Philip Jenkins, *The Next Christendom: The Coming of Global Christianity*, rev. and exp. (New York: Oxford University Press, 2007); idem, *The New Faces of Christianity: Believing the Bible in the Global South* (New York: Oxford University Press, 2006).

40. George Barna, *Online Research Archive: Beliefs: Trinity, Satan,* found at www .barna.org.

41. David Garland, *Colossians and Philemon*, NIV Application Commentary (Grand Rapids: Zondervan, 1998), 67.

42. Similarly, John writes that "whoever who says he is in the light and hates his brother is still in darkness" (1 John 2:9).

43. The only exception to this we can think of is found in the covenantal blessings and curses of Deuteronomy, where Moses explained to the children of Israel that the climactic curse for breaking the covenant would be that God's people would belong to no one but themselves: "The LORD will bring you back in ships to Egypt, a journey that I promised that you should never make again; and there you shall offer yourselves for sale to your enemies as male and female slaves, but there will be no buyer" (Deut. 28:68).

Chapter 3: The Coming of the King

1. George R. Beasley-Murray, *Jesus and the Kingdom of God* (Grand Rapids: Eerdmans, 1986), 24.

2. George Eldon Ladd, *A Theology of the New Testament*, rev. ed. (Grand Rapids: Eerdmans, 1996), 54.

3. Matt. 3:13 – 17//Mark 1:9 – 11//Luke 3:21 – 22//John 1:29 – 34.

4. James D. G. Dunn, *Jesus Remembered* (Grand Rapids: Eerdmans, 2003), 449 – 50.

5. Bruce Waltke has similarly observed, "The books of Genesis and Numbers unequivocally anticipate kingship as God's good gift" (Bruce K. Waltke and Charles Yu, *An Old Testament Theology: An Exegetical, Canonical, and Thematic Approach* [Grand Rapids: Zondervan, 2006], 687).

6. M. J. Selman, "The Kingdom of God in the Old Testament," *Tyndale Bulletin* 40 (1989):161 – 83, cited by Bruce Waltke with Cathi Fredricks, *Genesis*, 52.

7. Waltke with Fredericks, *Genesis*, 53 – 54.

8. Ladd, *A Theology of the New Testament*, 68.

9. While there are problems with his approach, E. P. Sanders is to be applauded for his profound contribution to the "Quest for the historical Jesus" when he reminded scholars that the debate cannot simply be about what Jesus said, and in critical scholarship, which words actually can be attributed to him. But Sanders argued that to understand who Jesus was, one needed to pay special attention to his actions, and then in that light his proclamations become more understandable. See, e.g., E. P. Sanders, *The Historical Figure of Jesus* (London: Allen Lane, 1993), idem, *Jesus and Judaism* (Philadelphia: Fortress Press, 1985).

10. Here I am sympathetic with N. T. Wright's concerns about the idea of competing language used by various scholars and laity, from "magic" to "miracle." I have no problems with Jesus performing "miracles" and believe he did such things, but given the history of this word over the last few centuries, I am concerned that using "miracle" language can actually mislead Christians and in subtle ways play into modernist notions that place God outside of a relationship to this world, and thus only on special circumstances does he get involved. But this complex discussion is far more than we can engage in here. For those interested, see N. T. Wright, *Jesus and the Victory of God* (Minneapolis: Fortress, 1996), 186 – 97.

11. For biblical references to water as a dangerous source of evil and chaos, see Dan. 7:3 and Rev. 13:1, where the beasts emerge from the sea; Job 38:8 – 11, where the sea is a chaotic force that only God can subdue; Ps. 89:9 – 10 talks about the raging sea and sea creatures that God subdues. Cf. William P. Brown's wonderful book, *Seeing the Psalms: A Theology of Metaphor* (Louisville: Westminster John Knox, 2002), esp. his chapter "The Voice of Many Waters: From Chaos to Community," pp. 105 – 132.

12. It is worth noting that the translation of being "demon-possessed" is disputed, since the Greek does not necessarily imply "possession." While I agree with that linguistic point, the fact is that the demonic functions in these episodes in a way that attempts to create the impression of possessing people, rather

than their living under God's rightful possession. So the battle between Jesus and the demonic is his battle to reclaim—or repossess—what has been taken from him. For more on this, begin with Graham H. Twelftree, *In the Name of Jesus: Exorcism among Early Christians* (Grand Rapids: Baker Academic, 2007); idem, *Jesus the Miracle Worker: A Historical and Theological Study* (Downers Grove, IL: InterVarsity Press, 1999).

13. Often found as a combination of nature and the demonic was the reality of sickness and death, and Jesus displays power and authority here as well. After Jesus has healed the man with the unclean spirit (Mark 1:21–28), he then goes on to immediately restore to health Simon Peter's mother-in-law (1:29–31). That evening "all who were sick or oppressed by demons" were brought to Jesus, and he brought freedom and healing to those in need (1:32–34). What does he do next? Everyone wants him to keep performing mighty deeds, but instead he says he needs to go out and preach (1:38–39). From that point on he weaves together his preaching (word) and miracles (deeds).

14. This is a particularly Johannine emphasis, since, for example, only John tells the story of Lazarus.

15. Note that throughout the Gospels Jesus wields power to heal and forgive, the power to rebuke death-causing evil and bring life-giving renewal. Jesus' physical healings were, as he indicates himself, demonstrations of his even greater authority to forgive sin (Matt. 9:5).

16. John Calvin, *Commentary on the Gospel according to John*, 2 vols. (Grand Rapids: Eerdmans, 1949), 1: 442.

17. D. A. Carson, "Matthew," in *The Expositor's Bible Commentary*, ed. Frank E. Gaebelein (Grand Rapids: Zondervan, 1976), 10:261.

Chapter 4: The Gift of the Son

1. From Emerson's 1844 "Gifts" essay reprinted in Alan D. Schrift, *The Logic of the Gift* (New York: Routledge, 1997), 26.

2. Quoted in Hans Boersma, *Violence, Hospitality, and the Cross: Reappropriating the Atonement Tradition* (Grand Rapids: Baker, 2004), 25.

3. Notice that in the Septuagint (LXX), the Greek translation of the Hebrew Bible, which was commonly used in the first century, used "icon" (*eikōn*) in the translation of the Hebrew throughout the opening chapters of Genesis where reference is made to man and woman made in God's image and likeness (Gen. 1:26, 27; 5:1, 3; 9: 6).

4. Cf. the use of *houtōs* that is translated by the word "so" in John 3:16 with the way it is used 3:14: "And as Moses lifted up the serpent in the wilderness, *houtōs* [so *or* in this way] must the Son of Man be lifted up." Commentators note that the idea of Christ's being "lifted up" is a key term in the gospel of John (cf. 8:12; 12:32, 34). It carries the beautiful double connotation of both Christ's death by way of [cf. *houtōs*] crucifixion and his resurrection.

5. For a thoughtful treatment of this text both within the context of Genesis, as well as within the larger context of the canon of Scripture, see R. W. L. Moberly, *The Bible, Theology, and Faith: A Study of Abraham and Jesus*, Cambridge Studies in Christian Doctrine (Cambridge: Cambridge University Press, 2000); idem, *Old Testament Theology: The Theology of the Book of Genesis* (Cambridge: Cambridge University Press, 2009), 179–99. Moberly concludes in this second book: "The gospel narratives of Jesus' death and resurrection are no less dangerous texts than Genesis 22, liable to misunderstanding and misuse in any number of ways.... Nevertheless, Christians believe that, rightly understood and appropriated, these texts point to an entry into anguished darkness that can also be a way into light and life" (p. 199).

6. Cf. John 3:16; Rom. 5:15–17; 6:23; 8:32; Gal. 1:3–4; 2:20; Eph. 2:8; 5:2, 25; 1 Tim. 2:6; 1 John 3:16.

7. Cf. other texts linking love and gift: Gen. 39:21; Deut. 7:13; 10:18; Ps. 119:88, 159; 136:21, 25; Song 7:12; Isa. 43:4; Gal. 2:20; Eph. 5:2, 25; 2 Thess 2:16; 1 John 3:16–17; 4:9–10.

8. This discussion of the multifaceted nature of the gift of the Son above is deeply influenced by Roger Nicole among others listed below, and the above image is adapted from Nicole's, "The Nature of Atonement," in *Standing Forth: Collected Writings of Roger Nicole* (Fearn, Ross-shire, UK: Mentor, 2002), 263, 245–82. When one's total view of Jesus' atoning work is limited to just one image, then other important New Testament images can end up neglected. Nevertheless, the theme of redemption is certainly a prominent biblical way to speak of the work of Christ. If this were a full study of Christ's atoning work, we would need to incorporate the full range of biblical metaphors, mentioned above, including battlefield, sacrifice, law court, marketplace, reconciliation, etc. Obviously there is often overlap between these different ideas, since they all ultimately point to the same truth. For some studies exploring this dynamic, see Colin E. Gunton, *The Actuality of Atonement: A Study of Metaphor, Rationality and the Christian Tradition* (Edinburgh: T&T Clark, 1988); Charles E. Hill and Frank A. James, eds., *The Glory of the Atonement: Biblical, Historical & Practical Perspectives: Essays in Honor of Roger Nicole* (Downers Grove, IL: InterVarsity Press, 2004).

9. Kevin Vanhoozer, "The Atonement in Postmodernity: Guilt, Goats, and Gifts," in *The Glory of the Atonement: Biblical, Historical and Practical Perspectives*, ed. Charles Hill and Frank James (Downers Grove, IL: InterVarsity Press Press, 2004), 380.

10. Originally in Tractate on Manlio Simonetti, *Matthew 1–13*, Ancient Christian Commentary on Scripture—New Testament; 1a (Downers Grove, IL: InterVarsity Press, 2001), 27.

11. Quoted in Richard A. Norris, *The Christological Controversy*, Sources of Early Christian Thought (Philadelphia: Fortress, 1980), 46.

12. For the best treatment of this theological challenge of how God can suffer, understood from a classic orthodox perspective, see Thomas G. Weinandy,

Does God Suffer? (Notre Dame, IN: University of Notre Dame Press, 2000). See also Paul L. Gavrilyuk, *The Suffering of the Impassible God: The Dialectics of Patristic Thought*, Oxford Early Christian Studies (Oxford; New York: Oxford University Press, 2004).

13. Horatius Bonar, *The Everlasting Righteousness; Or, How Shall Man Be Just with God?* (London: J. Nisbet, 1873), 3–4.

14. In fact, God makes it clear how offensive he finds it when a human judge declares wicked people innocent and innocent people guilty (see Prov. 17:15).

15. P. T. Forsyth, *The Cruciality of the Cross* (London: Independent Press, 1948), 29–30. "If we spoke less about God's love and more about His holiness, more about his judgment, we should say much more when we did speak of His love" (p. 39).

16. John Stott, *The Cross of Christ*, 20th ed. (Downers Grove, IL: InterVarsity Press, 2006), 64.

17. Leon Morris, *The Apostolic Preaching of the Cross*, 3rd ed. (Grand Rapids: Eerdmans, 1965), 12. Cf. Stott, *The Cross of Christ*, 174–75. Some humanitarian organizations have a "no-ransom" policy, in which they will not pay ransom money to people who kidnap their staff. Paying ransom actually puts their staff and others at risk as it can embolden kidnappers. But when thought of in terms of love, you willingly put up a ransom if that is what it takes. A father desperately concerned for his child is not an agency trying to protect itself and its people, but a man who willingly will give himself for the child. God is different; he tips his hand. It seems to lack wisdom—but not when you think of love.

18. Certainly such imagery is not the only biblical metaphor used to make sense of what Jesus accomplishes, as noted above in the discussion of the "The Gift, Like a Jewel," and especially the footnote connected with the chart in this chapter.

19. Stephen Webb describes this tendency in *The Gifting God: A Trinitarian Ethics of Excess* (Oxford: Oxford University Press, 1996), 46.

20. Calvin, *Institutes*, 3.1.1.

21. The early church father Origen, commenting on this verse, makes an interesting statement: "To the believer, Scripture teaches, belongs all the money in the world; to the unbeliever not even a penny. The unbeliever owns things as a thief does because he neither knows the right use of his wealth nor the God who created it. Because he fails to hear God when he says, 'The silver is mine, and the gold is mine [says the Lord]' (Hag. 2:8), he does not possess those things as from God. But we see that all things are ours. All the money in the world belongs to the believer, but not even a penny to the unbeliever." See Judith L. Kovacs, *1 Corinthians: Interpreted by Early Christian Commentators*, The Church's Bible (Grand Rapids: Eerdmans, 2005), 67.

22. Anthony C. Thiselton, *The First Epistle to the Corinthians: A Commentary on the Greek Text* (Grand Rapids: Eerdmans, 2000), 327.

23. Quoted in Robert W. Jenson, *Systematic Theology* (New York: Oxford University Press, 1997), 2:107.

24. Cf. Zacharias Ursinus, *The Commentary on the Heidelberg Catechism*, 19.

Chapter 5: Believing the Gift

1. Michael Gorman, *Cruciformity: Paul's Narrative Spirituality of the Cross* (Grand Rapids: Eerdmans, 2001), 163.

2. Sinclair Ferguson, *The Holy Spirit* (Downers Grove, IL: InterVarsity Press, 1996), 126.

3. Dietrich Bonhoeffer, *Life Together* (New York: Harper, 1954), 67.

4. Walter Marshall, *The Gospel Mystery of Santification* (London: Oliphants, 1954), 43.

5. This language is borrowed from C. S. Lewis, *That Hideous Strength* (New York: Scribner, orig. 1945, repr. 1996). E.g., Lewis writes: "The Hideous Strength holds all this Earth in its fist to squeeze as it wishes," 291.

6. Augustine, *Rudimentary Catechesis* 4.7, found in W. A. Jurgens, *The Faith of the Early Fathers* (Collegeville, MN: Liturgical Press, 1970), 3:55.

7. John Marsh, *Saint John*, Westminster Pelican Commentaries (Philadelphia: Westminster Press, 1978), 183, cited by Leon Morris, *The Gospel According to John*, rev. ed., New International Commentary on the New Testament (Grand Rapids: Eerdmans, 1995), 203.

8. It is possible that "their faith" included the faith of the paralytic, but that is unclear. I think the text more naturally reads (and assumes) that this mention is directed toward the four men carrying him. Whether this "faith" includes the paralytic has been debated by various exegetes throughout church history.

9. "Take heart" is the translation found in NIV, ESV, NRSV, etc. For more background see, e.g., *tharreō* for the use of *tharsei* in the *New International Dictionary of New Testament Theology*, ed. Colin Brown (Grand Rapids: Zondervan, 1978, 1986), 1:327–29 (abbr. *NIDNTT*).

10. I have changed the name in this story for obvious reasons.

11. Cf. Mary Douglas, *Purity and Danger* (New York: Routledge, 1966, rept. 2002), 64–65, but *passim*; idem, *Leviticus as Literature* (Oxford: Oxford University Press, 1999).

12. The language Jesus uses here is *teknon*, which can easily be translated as "child." But the point remains; it is a form of address that normally is reserved for one's family or highlights a connection through familial imagery, and this connection can highlight both privileges and responsibilities. But this is not normally just a generic way to address people. This is the case, at least, in the fourteen times the word is used in Matthew (see Matt. 2:18; 3:9; 7:11; 9:2; 10:21; 15:26; 18:25; 19:29; 21:28; 23:37; 27:25).

13. From sermon 97A on Luke 5:31–32, found in Augustine, *The Works of Saint Augustine: A Translation for the 21st Century*, ed. John E. Rotelle, trans. Edmund Hill (Brooklyn, NY: New City Press, 1990), 3.4.40.

14. Augustine, ibid., 3.4.41.

15. Cf., Acts 6:7, 13:8; Rom. 4:12, 16; 2 Cor. 13:5; Eph. 4:13; Phil. 1:27; Col. 1:23; Tit. 3:15, etc.

16. As Peter and John hear the cries of a crippled beggar outside of the temple, they turn to him and offer him more than silver and gold; they offer him healing in the name of Christ (Acts 3:6). As the crowds gather, Peter explains that this is the work of the God of Israel, who was glorified in Christ. Thus, while the "Author of life" had been crucified, he was raised from the dead (3:15). So it becomes the "name of Christ," by which Peter makes it clear he means "by faith in his name," that healing was taking place. This was the faith they offered, and this was the "repent" they encouraged. Peter declares to those watching: "Repent, therefore, and turn again, that your sins maybe blotted out, that times of refreshing may come from the presence of the Lord" (Acts 3:19–20).

17. Udo Schnelle, *Apostle Paul: His Life and Theology*, trans. M. Eugene Boring (Grand Rapids: Baker Academic, 2005), 521. What follows on this point is heavily indebted to Schnelle, who lays out this point more fully and cites many more Scriptures than I can here. I am here paraphrasing parts of his argument (see esp. 521–23) as well as adding to and expanding on his ideas.

18. For faith is a gift see Ezek. 36:26–27; Matt. 11:25–27; Luke 17:5; John 3:3–8; 6:44, 65; Acts 13:48; 16:14; Rom. 10:14–17; 1 Cor. 2:4–5, 14; 12:3; Eph. 1:17–19; 2:1–10; 1 Thess. 1:5, 6; 2:13; Heb. 12:2.

19. Schnelle, *Apostle Paul: His Life and Theology*, 522.

20. Cf. "Faith is not the act of God; it is not God who believes in Christ for salvation, it is the sinner. It is by God's grace that a person is able to believe, but faith is an activity on the part of the person and of him alone. In faith we receive and rest upon Christ alone for salvation," John Murray, *Redemption, Accomplished and Applied* (Grand Rapids: Eerdmans, 1955; repr., 1992), 106.

21. On this point, see his classic treatise on ethics: Søren Kierkegaard, *Works of Love*, ed. Howard Vincent Hong and Edna Hatlestad Hong (Princeton, NJ: Princeton University Press, 1995).

22. Steve Brown, *Approaching God* (New York: Howard, Simon & Schuster, 2008), 152. In Schnelle's terms, "The Spirit mediates the gift of faith and at the same time gives its content a characteristic stamp, thus giving unity to the Church. Spirit and faith are related in Paul's thought as cause and effect inasmuch as the Spirit opens the door to faith and the believer then leads his faith or her life in the power of the Spirit" (*Apostle Paul: His Life and Theology*, 522).

23. For a classic endorsement of this kind of argument, although anchored in a Roman Catholic understanding of some of these points, see Saint Thomas Aquinas, *Summa Theologiae*, 60 vols. (Blackfriars, 1963–1980), II-II.Q.6.Art.1. But Aquinas's argument is relevant for Protestants and Roman Catholics as he shows his opposition to the persistent threat of Pelagianism, which he rightly concludes misunderstands this point about faith as a gift.

24. For a thoughtful sermon unpacking this point, based on Eph. 6:23, see Sermon 168 in Augustine, *Works*, III/5, 216–21.

25. "One must not imagine that the Christian faith is a bare and mere knowledge of God or an understanding of the Scripture which flutters in the brain without touching the heart, as it is usually the case with the opinion about things which are confirmed by some probable reason," in John Calvin, *Instruction in Faith (1537)*, trans. Paul T. Fuhrmann (Philadelphia: Westminster, 1949), 39.

26. E.g., at the beginning of his gospel, John tells us that Jesus, the "light" himself, "shines in the darkness" (John 1:5). By way of contrast, John tells us that after Judas took a morsel of food from Jesus at the last supper, "he immediately went out [to betray him]. And it was night" (13:30).

27. Ben Witherington III, *John's Wisdom: A Commentary on the Fourth Gospel* (Louisville: Westminster John Knox, 1995), 312.

28. Tradition even has it that Nicodemus may have been a man who was later known for his generosity to pilgrims and strangers. As D. A. Carson points out, "the name Nicodemus was common in Greek, but transliterated and made into a Jewish name. This Nicodemus has sometimes been identified with Naqdimon ben Gorion, a wealthy citizen of Jerusalem who supplied water to pilgrims at the principal feasts, and who is known to have lived in Jerusalem at the time of its siege in the Jewish War (AD 70; *b. Ta'anith* 19b–20; *Giṭṭin* 56a; *Ketubbot* 66b). That would have made Naqdimon a very young man forty years earlier, during the ministry of Jesus, probably too young to have been *a member of the Jewish ruling council,* the Sanhedrin, unless he was a very exceptional person indeed." D. A. Carson, *The Gospel according to John* (Leicester: Inter-Varsity Press, 1991), 186.

Chapter 6: The Gift of the Spirit

1. Augustine, *On the Trinity*, in *Nicene and Post-Nicene Fathers*, 1st series, 15.26.46 [p. 224].

2. Thomas A. Smail, *The Giving Gift: The Holy Spirit in Person*, 2nd ed. (London: Darton, Longman and Todd, 1994), 15.

3. *Confessions*, 1.3.

4. Throughout the history of the church there is a long debate about what is called the *filioque* clause ("and the Son") that was added to the early creed. This debate was whether the Spirit came from the Father, or from the Father and the Son. We cannot get into this debate here, but for those interested, see the relevant sections in Gary D. Badcock, *Light of Truth and Fire of Love: A Theology of the Holy Spirit* (Grand Rapids: Eerdmans, 1997); Donald G. Bloesch, *The Holy Spirit: Works and Gifts* (Downers Grove, IL: InterVarsity Press, 2000); Yves Congar, *I Believe in the Holy Spirit*, Milestones in Catholic Theology (New York: Crossroad, 1997); Thomas C. Oden, *Life in the Spirit: Systematic Theology*, vol. 3 (San Francisco: HaperSanFrancisco, 1992); T. F.

Torrance, *The Trinitarian Faith: The Evangelical Theology of the Ancient Catholic Church* (Edinburgh: T&T Clark, 1988); Robert Letham, *The Holy Trinity: In Scripture, History, Theology, and Worship* (Phillipsburg, NJ: Presbyterian and Reformed, 2004).

5. Raymond Brown similarly notes the potential triadic pattern in the last supper, or certainly the "three types of divine indwelling" that are promised in John 14:15–24: the Spirit will dwell in the disciples (vv. 15–17), Jesus will dwell in them (vv. 18–21), and Father with Jesus makes his abode in the disciples (vv. 23–24). Brown concludes, "All these indwellings were thought to be accomplished through and in the Paraclete. The Paraclete is the presence of Jesus while Jesus is absent.... And since the Father and Jesus are one, the presence of the Father and Jesus (23) is not really different from the presence of Jesus in the Paraclete." See Raymond E. Brown, *The Gospel according to John*, Anchor Bible (Garden City, NY,: Doubleday, 1966), 642–43.

6. For the heart of this aspect of his argument, see John Biddle, *Twelve Arguments* (London: William Ley, 1647), 3–8.

7. Augustine, *The Trinity*, in *The Works of Saint Augustine: A Translation for the 21st Century*, trans. Edmund Hill (Brooklyn, NY: New City Press, 1991), 15.5.36 [p. 424].

8. Immanuel Kant, *The Conflict of the Faculties*, trans. Mary J. Gregor (Lincoln: University of Nebraska Press, 1992), 65.

9. "All salvation, every blessing, and blessedness have their threefold cause in God—the Father, the Son, and the Holy Spirit" (Herman Bavinck, *Reformed Dogmatics* [Grand Rapids: Baker, 2006], 2:256).

10. There are 92 verses to be exact: Matt. 1:18, 20; 3:11; 12:32; 28:19; Mark 1:8; 3:29; 12:36; 13:11; Luke 1:15, 35, 41, 67; 2:25, 26; 3:16, 22; 4:1; 10:21; 11:13; 12:10, 12; John 1:33; 14:26; 20:22; Acts 1:2, 5, 8, 16; 2:4, 33, 38; 4:8, 25, 31; 5:3, 32; 6:5; 7:51, 55; 8:15, 17, 19; 9:17, 31; 10:38, 44, 45, 47; 11:15, 16, 24; 13:2, 4, 9, 52; 15:8, 28; 16:6; 19:2, 6; 20:23, 28; 21:11; 28:25; Rom. 1:4; 5:5; 9:1; 14:17; 15:13, 16; 1 Cor. 6:19; 12:3; 2 Cor. 6:6; 7:1; 13:13–14; Eph. 1:13; 4:30; 1 Thess. 1:5, 6; 4:8; 2 Tim. 1:14; Titus 3:5; Heb. 2:4; 3:7; 6:4; 9:8; 10:15; 1 Peter 1:12; 2 Peter 1:21; Jude 20.

11. The Hebrew word is *qôdeš*. See especially R. Laird Harris, Gleason L. Archer, and Bruce Waltke, *Theological Wordbook of the Old Testament* (Chicago: Moody Press, 1980). 2:786–89. Norman Snaith points out that "even the profits of the renewed prosperity of the harlot Tyre, after her seventy years of trade depression, will be *qôdeš* to Jehovah, because, instead of Trye hoarding her own gains, they will come 'to those who dwell before the Lord,' i.e. to the Jehovah-priests or to the Jehovah-community in Jerusalem, Isaiah xxiii. 18. Or, again, the priest is *qôdeš*, not because, as the Oxford Lexicon suggests, he is a person connected with a holy place, but because he belongs to Jehovah"

(Norman Snaith, *The Distinctive Ideas of the Old Testament* [London: Epworth, 1944], 44).

12. Snaith, *The Distinctive Ideas*, 30.

13. Dietrich Bonhoeffer, *The Cost of Discipleship* (New York: Touchstone, 1995), 272.

14. Eusebius, *Ecclesiastical History* 6.2.11 (Nicene and Post-Nicene Fathers, 2nd series 1:250].

15. Congar, *I Believe in the Holy Spirit*, 2:83.

16. Quotes in this paragraph come from Augustine, *The Works of Saint Augustine: A Translation for the 21st Century*, 2nd series, 23.6–9 (pp. 59–60).

17. George Eldon Ladd, "The Holy Spirit in Galatians," in *Current Issues in Biblical and Patristic Interpretation*, ed. Gerald F. Hawthorne (Grand Rapids: Eerdmans, 1975), 214.

18. James D. G. Dunn, *The Theology of Paul the Apostle* (Grand Rapids: Eerdmans, 1998), 418.

19. Graham Cole, *He Who Gives Life: The Doctrine of the Holy Spirit* (Wheaton, IL: Crossway, 2007), 238.

20. E.g., Ex. 23:16, 19; 34:22, 26; Deut. 18:4; 26:2; Neh. 10:35–37; Prov. 3:9.

21. Sinclair Ferguson, *The Holy Spirit* (Downers Grove, IL: InterVarsity Press, 1996), 179.

22. Paul elsewhere connects the Spirit in us with our ability to see the present in light of God's completed and promised work: "If then you have been raised with Christ, seek the things that are above, where Christ is, seated at the right hand of God. Set your mind on things that are above, not on things that are on earth. For you have died, and your life is hidden with Christ in God. *When Christ who is your life appears, then you will also appear with him in glory*" (Col. 3:1–4, emphasis added). Consequently, even through our tears we can claim—not naively, but nevertheless with eschatological confidence—that "in all things God works for the good of those who love him" (Rom. 8:28 NIV).

23. St. Chrysostom, *Homilies on Ephesians*, Homily 2 (Nicene and Post-Nicene Fathers, 1st series, 13:56). Later Chrysostom anticipates the question—why didn't God just give everything immediately, why an earnest, a down payment? His answer, while partially problematic, is also stimulating: "Because neither have we, on our part, done the whole of our work. We have believed. This is a beginning; and He too on His part hath given an earnest. When we show our faith by our works, then He will add the rest" (13:56). Chrysostom's answer seems to make our final redemption depend on our works rather than on the very gifts—the Son and Spirit—that Paul emphasizes. And Paul does not base the effectiveness of the down payment, sealing, and promise of a coming inheritance on our diligence, but on the worth of the gifts.

24. Calvin, *Institutes*, 3.1.3.

Chapter 7: Experiencing the Gift

1. Eberhard Jüngel, *God as Mystery of the World* (Grand Rapids: Eerdmans, 1983), 320, 391.
2. Edmund P. Clowney, "The Biblical Theology of the Church," in *The Church in the Bible and the World: An International Study*, ed. D. A. Carson (Grand Rapids: Baker, 1987), 74.
3. Michael Downey, *Altogether Gift: A Trinitarian Spirituality* (Maryknoll, NY: Orbis, 2000), 34.
4. Quoted in Richard J. Foster, *Devotional Classics: Revised Edition: Selected Readings for Individuals and Groups* (San Francisco: HarperOne, 2005), 214.
5. Douglas Moo, *The Epistle to the Romans*, New International Commentary on the New Testament (Grand Rapids: Eerdmans, 1996), 745.
6. Cf. J. I. Packer, *Knowing God* (Downers Grove, IL: InterVarsity Press, 1973), 181; Sinclair Ferguson, *The Holy Spirit* (Downers Grove, IL: InterVarsity Press, 1996), 182; Joel Beeke, *Heirs with Christ: The Puritans on Adoption* (Grand Rapids: Reformation Heritage Books, 2008), 17.
7. Christopher R. Seitz, *Word without End: The Old Testament as Abiding Theological Witness* (Grand Rapids: Eerdmans, 1998), 257–59.
8. E.g., Ben Witherington and Laura Michaels Ice, *The Shadow of the Almighty: Father, Son, and Spirit in Biblical Perspective* (Grand Rapids: Eerdmans, 2002), 20–28. They trace Jeremias's famous argument, criticisms raised against it, and the general consensus that seems to have been reached. For the classic studies, see Joachim Jeremias, *The Prayers of Jesus*, Studies in Biblical Theology, 2nd series (London: SCM Press, 1967), 67; idem, *New Testament Theology* (New York: Scribner, 1971).
9. Witherington and Ice, *The Shadow of the Almighty*, 22.
10. Thomas A. Smail, *The Forgotten Father* (Grand Rapids: Eerdmans, 1981), 41. Smail, an Anglican churchman and theologian who has strongly emphasized the continuing work of the Spirit in today's church, reminds us elsewhere that "to bring us into relationship to the Jesus who is Kurios (Lord) and the God who is Abba (Father) is the primary charismatic work of the Spirit.... A Christian becomes charismatic — that is, enters the dynamic field of the Spirit's action — not when he speaks in tongues and prophesies but when he confesses Kurios and Abba" (*The Giving Gift: The Holy Spirit in Person*, 13). Only by the Spirit do we enter into God's family.
11. Johnson, *Sharing Possessions*, 87.
12. For more on adoption in the ancient world, see Brendan Byrne, *Sons of God, Seed of Abraham: A Study of the Idea of the Sonship of God of All Christians in Paul against the Jewish Background*, Analecta Biblica (Rome: Biblical Institute, 1979); Francis Lyall, *Slaves, Citizens, Sons: Legal Metaphors in the Epistles* (Grand Rapids: Zondervan, 1984); James M. Scott, *Adoption as Sons of God: An Exegetical Investigation into the Background of [Huiothesia] in the Pauline*

Corpus, Wissenschaftliche Untersuchungen zum Neuen Testament, 2nd Reihe (Tübingen: J. C. B. Mohr, 1992).

13. Frederick Dale Bruner, *A Theology of the Holy Spirit: The Pentecostal Experience and the New Testament Witness* (Grand Rapids: Eerdmans, 1970), 163.

14. Sinclair Ferguson, *The Holy Spirit* (Downers Grove, IL: InterVarsity Press, 1996), 89.

15. E.g., Mic. 3:8 LXX; Luke 1:41–42, 67; Acts 2:4; 4:8, 31; 13:8–10. Cf. *NIDNTT*, 1:733–741 (esp. 739), which notes being filled (*pimplēmi*) as connected with missionary boldness in speech, but leaves the repeated connection with the needy undeveloped.

16. Later, we also learn that Barnabas played a unique role in assisting Paul on his great collection for the poor of Jerusalem.

17. Robert Wuthnow, "Pious Materialism," see www.religion-online.org/show-article.asp?title=238

18. Christian Smith, Michael O. Emerson, and Patricia Snell, *Passing the Plate: Why American Christians Don't Give Away More Money* (Oxford: Oxford University Press, 2008), 87–91.

19. Ibid., 29, 34.

20. Ibid., 103–8.

21. Augustine, *The Confessions*, ed. Edmund Hill and John E. Rotelle, *The Works of Saint Augustine: A Translation for the 21st Century* (Brooklyn, NY: New City Press, 1997), 10.29.40 (p. 1:263).

22. Annie Dillard, *Pilgrim at Tinker Creek* (New York: HarperPerennial, 1998), 113, the second italics is mine.

23. The following paragraphs draw heavily from the suggestive explorations and language of Lancelot Andrewes, *Ninety-Six Sermons*, new ed., 5 vols. (Oxford: J. H. Parker, 1865–1871), 3:227; John Flavel, *The Fountain of Life: A Display of Christ in His Essential and Mediatorial Glory*, in *The Works of John Flavel*, 6 vols. (London: W. Baynes and Son, 1820 [orig. 1671]), 1:506; Thomas Goodwin, "Christ Set Fourth, on Rom. Viii. 34," in *The Works of Thomas Goodwin*, ed. John C. Miller, 12 vols. (Edinburgh: James Nichol, 1861–1866 [orig. 1651]), 4:46–48. For more variations of this motif and a larger exploration in terms of the ascension, see Kapic, "Receiving Christ's Priestly Benediction," 247–60.

24. For helpful background on Jubilee and its place within biblical, theological, and ethical discussions, see Christopher J. H. Wright, *Old Testament Ethics for the People of God* (Downers Grove, IL: InterVarsity Press, 2004).

25. For general background see Mary Beard, *The Roman Triumph* (Cambridge, MA: Belknap Press of Harvard University Press, 2007); Robert Payne, *The Roman Triumph* (London, New York: Abelard-Schuman, 1963); David Andrew Thomas, *Revelation 19 in Historical and Mythological Context* (New

York: Peter Lang, 2008); H. S. Versnel, *Triumphus: An Inquiry into the Origin, Development and Meaning of the Roman Triumph* (Leiden: Brill, 1970).

26. Cf., Johann Joachim Eschenburg and N. W. Fiske, *Manual of Classical Literature*, 4th ed. (Philadelphia: Biddle, 1843), 373.

27. Douglas J. Moo, *The Letters to the Colossians and to Philemon*, The Pillar New Testament Commentary (Grand Rapids: Eerdmans, 2008), 215.

28. As Lancelot Andrewes (1555–1626) said long ago, "Here is a captivity led in triumph. A triumph is not but after a victory, or a victory but upon a battle; and even a battle presupposeth hostility, and that some quarrel whereupon it grew. His ascension is His triumph, His resurrection His victory, His death His battle, His quarrel is about *hominibus*, about us 'men,' for another captivity of ours that had happened before this" (Andrewes, *Ninety-Six Sermons*, 3:227).

29. N. T. Wright, *The Resurrection of the Son of God*, Christian Origins and the Question of God 3 (London: SPCK, 2003), 656. While not making the exact points noted above, Wright observes that "the Christian ascension stories cannot be derived from the pagan ones; but they would certainly have been heard, in the second half of the first century, as counter-imperial" (656).

Chapter 8: The Gift of the Kingdom

1. Cited by Congar, *I Believe in the Holy Spirit*, 2:70.

2. Calvin, *Institutes*, 2.15.4.

3. Bavinck, *Reformed Dogmatics*, 3:247.

4. The word family of *metanoia*, which is often translated in various forms of "repent," basically means to change one's mind and will, to turn around, to be fully affected in the reorientation of one's life and view. Cf. *metanoia* in *NIDNTT*, 1:357–59.

5. Malachi prophesied that when the Messiah comes, he will work like a refiner's fire, bringing repentance that displays itself in changed lives. Prior to this the people "robbed" God not simply because of their limited giving, but more significantly because of their stiff hearts and improper view of God (Mal. 3:1–15). This change will come about as God claims them for his treasured possession and they respond by serving him (Mal. 3:16–18).

6. See *aphrōn* in *NIDNTT*, 3:1023–26.

7. In his Proverbs commentary, Tremper Longman argues that it is best to describe the book's teaching on wealth and poverty as "providing seven snapshots, none of which are complete in themselves." First, God blesses the righteous with wealth (e.g., 8:18–19). Second, foolish behavior leads to poverty (10:4–5). Third, the wealth of fools will not last (11:4, 18; 13:11). Fourth, poverty is the result of injustice and oppression (13:23). Fifth, those with money must be generous (28:27; 29:7, 14). Sixth, wisdom is better than wealth (16:16; 28:6). Seventh, wealth has limited value (11:4; 13:8; 23:4–5; 30:7–9). Tremper Longman, *Proverbs* (Grand Rapids: Baker, 2006), 573–76.

8. In his modern-day classic, Francis Schaeffer famously lampooned the West's worship of these two impoverished values of "personal peace and affluence." "Personal peace" Schaeffer said, "means just to be left alone, not to be troubled by the troubles of other people, whether across the world or across the city—to live one's life with minimal possibilities of being personally disturbed.... Affluence means an overwhelming and ever-increasing prosperity—a life made up of things, things, and more things—a success judged by an ever-higher level of material abundance." Francis Schaeffer, *How Should We Then Live?: The Rise and Decline of Western Thought and Culture* (Wheaton, IL: Crossway, 2005), 205.

9. "The kingdom is established by God's sovereign grace, and its blessings are to be received as gifts of that grace. Man's duty is not to bring the kingdom into existence, but to enter into it by faith, and to pray that he may be enabled more and more to submit himself to the beneficent rule of God in every area of his life." Anthony Hoekema, *The Bible and the Future*, (Grand Rapids: Eerdmans, 1979), 44.

10. George Eldon Ladd, *The Presence of the Future: The Eschatology of Biblical Realism* (Grand Rapids: Eerdmans, 1974), 205.

11. Andreas J. Köstenberger, *John*, Baker Exegetical Commentary on the New Testament (Grand Rapids: Baker, 2004), 122–23. Cf. Thomas R. Schreiner, *New Testament Theology: Magnifying God in Christ* (Grand Rapids: Baker, 2008), 80–95. For example, see the parallel in Matt. 19:16, 24.

12. Cited by Congar, *I Believe in the Holy Spirit*, 2:70.

13. C. C. Caragounis, "Kingdom of God/Heaven," in *Dictionary of Jesus and the Gospels*, ed. Joel B. Green, Scot McKnight, and I. Howard Marshall (Downers Grove, IL: InterVarsity Press, 1992), 417–30 (this quote from 425). See also Herman N. Ridderbos, *The Coming of the Kingdom* (Philadelphia: Presbyterian and Reformed, 1962), esp. 77: "the coming of the kingdom necessarily consists not only in its proclamation but carries the gift of salvation with it. Thus it may be said that in this gift we receive and possess the kingdom itself.... Such phrases [e.g., we enter the kingdom, we are in it, etc.] also make it clear that the kingdom of heaven can be shared in some way or other, that it changes the lives of those who receive it, that by virtue of God's act it becomes a gift, a possession, a vital domain off those to whom this privilege is granted."

14. Herman Bavinck, *Reformed Dogmatics: Sin and Salvation in Christ*, ed. John Bolt, trans. John Vriend (Grand Rapids: Baker, 2003), 3:250.

15. This kingdom should be zealously sought after (Matt. 5:20; 6:33; 12:44–46), and it is spoken of as a reward to be received in heaven (Matt. 5:12; 6:20; 19:21; 20:1–7; 24:45). Yet it is also viewed as a "gift that far exceeds all human work and merit (Matt. 19:29; 23:12; 24:47; 25:21, 24; Luke 6:32f.; 12:32, 37; 17:10; 22:29) and has as its content the forgiveness of sins (Matt. 9:2; 26:28;

Luke 1:77; 24:47), righteousness (Matt. 6:33), and eternal life (Matt. 19:16; 25:46; Mark 9:43) " (Bavinck, *Reformed Dogmatics*, 247).

16. Ridderbos, *The Coming of the Kingdom*, 186. The next sentence is also a paraphrase of Ridderbos as he continues his point on that same page.

17. Martin Luther, "The Freedom of a Christian," in *Martin Luther's Basic Theological Writings*, ed. Timothy F. Lull (Minneapolis: Fortress, 1989), 596.

18. Ridderbos, *The Coming of the Kingdom*, 169.

Chapter 9: Living in the Gift

1. Thomas Merton, *No Man Is an Island* (Boston: Shambhala, 2005), 3.

2. Quoted in Charles Avila, *Ownership: Early Christian Teaching* (Eugene, OR: Wipf & Stock, 2004), 77.

3. Dallas Willard, *Knowing Christ Today: Why We Can Trust Spiritual Knowledge* (New York: HarperOne, 2009), 83.

4. Cyprian, *Treatise* 4.13 (Ante-Nicene Fathers, 5:451).

5. Benedict, *Jesus of Nazareth* (New York: Doubleday, 2007), 60–61.

6. Here I am drawing heavily from George Eldon Ladd, *A Theology of the New Testament*, rev. ed. (Grand Rapids: Eerdmans, 1996), 45–46. See also, e.g., George R. Beasley-Murray, *Jesus and the Kingdom of God* (Grand Rapids: Eerdmans, 1986); George Eldon Ladd, *Jesus and the Kingdom: The Eschatology of Biblical Realism*, 2nd ed. (Waco, TX: Word, 1969).

7. For more on the biblical dynamic of God making things new by renewing his creation rather than starting over, see, e.g., Steven Bouma-Prediger, *For the Beauty of the Earth: A Christian Vision for Creation Care*, Engaging Culture (Grand Rapids: Baker, 2001).

8. Oscar Cullmann, *Christ and Time: The Primitive Christian Conception of Time and History* (Philadelphia: Westminster, 1950), 84. VE-Day stands for "Victory in Europe" day. For more on this see Kelly M. Kapic, "Are We There Yet? An Exploration of Romans 8," *Modern Reformation* 15/4 (2006): 22–27.

9. Carl E. Braaten, *The Flaming Center: A Theology of the Christian Mission* (Philadelphia: Fortress, 1977), 43, quoted by Donald K. McKim, *Introducing the Reformed Faith: Biblical Revelation, Christian Tradition, Contemporary Significance* (Louisville: Westminster John Knox, 2001), 177.

10. Ps. 89:14; 97:1–2; cf. 1 Kings 10:9; 2 Chron. 9:8; Heb. 1:8–9.

11. See also Ps. 9:4, 7–9; 45:6–7; 72; 89:14; 97:2; Prov. 16:12; 29:14.

12. "In the LXX the use of צְדָקָה [Heb. righteousness] for God's dispensing of salvation is carried to such a point that δικαιοσύνη [Gk. righteousness] can even be used for חֶסֶד [Heb. loving-kindness] (Gn. 19:19; 20:13; 21:23; 24:27; 32:10; Ex. 15:13; 34:7; Prv. 20:22; Mas. 20:28) when ἔλεος [Gk. mercy] is the more usual rendering"; G. Schrenk, in *Theological Dictionary of the New Testament*, 2:195.

13. This verse is the high point of the psalm. It shows us the power of righteousness

at work. The apostle Paul quoted this verse in 2 Cor. 9:9, at what may well be the climax of the New Testament's teaching on generosity (2 Cor. 8–9).

14. Ps. 72:1, 4; cf. 1 Sam. 2:2–8; Ezek. 16:49–50; Luke 1:46, 52–53; 6:20–25; James 5:1–6.

15. "God is δίκαιος [just] not merely as the righteous Judge who exercises justice, but also as the One who gives salvation.... The new factor [in the New Testament use of the word] is the absolute connection with the atoning death of Christ in which God shows Himself to be δίκαιος" (*TDNT*, 2:186, 188).

16. For a well-balanced discussion of holistic mission that integrates evangelism and social involvement, see Christopher Wright, *The Mission of God: Unlocking the Bible's Grand Narrative* (Downers Grove, IL: InterVarsity Press, 2006), 316–23.

17. For a highly readable discussion of the dynamic, restorative character of biblical justice, see also Ronald Sider, *Just Generosity: A New Vision for Overcoming Poverty in America* (Grand Rapids: Baker, 1999), 55–67.

18. Bruce K. Waltke, "Righteousness in Proverbs," *Westminster Theological Journal* 70, (2008): 236. Cf. Blaise Pascal comments: "There are two principles, which divide the wills of men, covetousness and charity. Not that covetousness cannot exist along with faith in God, nor charity with worldly riches; but covetousness uses God, and enjoys the world, and charity is the opposite" (quoted in Bruce K. Waltke and Charles Yu, *An Old Testament Theology: An Exegetical, Canonical, and Thematic Approach* (Grand Rapids: Zondervan, 2006), 654. For Waltke's magisterial treatment on Proverbs, see his *The Book of Proverbs*, 2 vols., New International Commentary on the Old Testament (Grand Rapids: Eerdmans, 2004).

19. Righteousness as human action [Heb. צְדָקָה] "suffers notable constriction in Rabbinic usage, being used for almsgiving as the most important fulfillment of the Law" (*TDNT*, 2:196. Similarly, Moses Maimonides (1135–1204), the leading figure of medieval Judaism, described eight stages or degrees of *sᵉdākâ* ("righteousness"), all of which were grounded in giving. "The highest degree," said Maimonides, "than which there is none higher, is the one who upholds the hand of an Israelite reduced to poverty by handing that person a gift or loan, or by entering into partnership with him or her, or by finding that Israelite work, in order to strengthen that person's hand, so that she or he will have no need to beg from others." See Os Guinness, *Doing Well and Doing Good: Money, Giving, and Caring in a Free Society* (Colorado Springs, CO: NavPress, 2001), 105–6.

20. Calvin, *Institutes*, 2.15.4.

Chapter 10: Following a Crucified Lord

1. William H. Willimon, "Repent," in *On a Wild and Windy Mountain and 25 Other Meditations for the Christian Year* (Nashville: Abingdon, 1984), 61.

2. Bonhoeffer, *The Cost of Discipleship*, 89.

3. Martin Luther, "A Brief Instruction on What to Look for and Expect in the Gospels," in *Martin Luther's Basic Theological Writings*, ed. Timothy F. Lull (Minneapolis, MN: Fortress, 1989), 108.

4. Derek Tidball, *The Message of the Cross*, The Bible Speaks Today (Downers Grove, IL: InterVarsity Press, 2001), 24–25.

5. Bruce Waltke observes that the garden of Eden was originally depicted as a kind of temple "from which heavenly waters flow to the rest of the earth. This is a foreshadowing of the life of Christ and his church as temple. The living water of the Spirit now pours out from the temple of believers (cf. John 2:19–22; 7:37–39; 1 Cor. 3:16; 6:19; 2 Cor. 6:16; Eph. 2:21–22; Heb. 3:6)." Bruce K. Waltke with Cathi J. Fredricks, *Genesis: A Commentary* (Grand Rapids: Zondervan, 2001), 101. For a more expansive unpacking of the biblical themes of temple and mission, see especially G. K. Beale, *The Temple and the Church's Mission: A Biblical Theology of the Dwelling Place of God* (Downers Grove, IL: InterVarsity Press, 2004).

6. For some classic studies on humanity as made in God's image, exploring the topic from biblical, historical, and theological perspectives, see G. C. Berkouwer, *Man: The Image of God*, Studies in Dogmatics (Grand Rapids: Eerdmans, 1962); Philip Edgcumbe Hughes, *The True Image: The Origin and Destiny of Man in Christ* (Grand Rapids: Eerdmans, 1989); David Cairns, *The Image of God in Man* (New York: Philosophical Library, 1953); Charles Sherlock, *The Doctrine of Humanity*, Contours of Christian Theology (Downers Grove, IL: InterVarsity Press, 1996); Jürgen Moltmann, *Man: Christian Anthropology in the Conflicts of the Present* (London: SPCK, 1974).

7. E.g., John Owen's approach to the image of God included both a recognition of the importance of faculties as well as relationality; see Kelly M. Kapic, *Communion with God: The Divine and the Human in the Theology of John Owen* (Grand Rapids: Baker, 2007), 35–66. More recently, Anthony Hoekema describes these two dimensions as the "structural and functional" aspects God's image, *Created in God's Image* (Grand Rapids: Eerdmans, 1986), 68–73.

8. Waltke with Fredricks, *Genesis*, 65. Herman Bavinck (*Reformed Dogmatics*, 3:197) similarly quotes Cicero's statement, "Homer attributed human properties to the gods; I would prefer to attribute divine properties to us humans." Likewise Marilynne Robinson notes, "I think anxieties about anthropomorphism are substantially inappropriate in a tradition whose main work has been to assert and ponder human theomorphism." Marilynne Robinson, *The Death of Adam: Essays on Modern Thought* (New York: Picador, 2005), 241.

9. Cf. John Yoder, *The Politics of Jesus: Vicit Agnus Noster* (Grand Rapids: Eerdmans, 1972), 114. This paragraph is deeply influenced by Yoder's exposition of the image.

10. Jürgen Moltmann notes that "Kierkegaard's 'attack on Christianity' in the

nineteenth century, made impressively clear that the rejection of the concept of martyrdom had brought with it the abandonment of the church's understanding of suffering, and meant that the gospel of the cross had lost its meaning and ultimately that established Christianity was bound to lose its eschatological hope. The assimilation of Christianity to bourgeois society always means that the cross is forgotten and hope is lost." Jürgen Moltmann, *The Crucified God: The Cross of Christ as the Foundation and Criticism of Christian Theology* (Minneapolis: Fortress, 1993), 58.

11. Martin Luther, "A Brief Instruction on What to Look for and Expect in the Gospels," 108.

12. Commenting on this passage Jeff Dryden notes that the expression "he suffered" includes "the *entirety* of the passion, including his sufferings and death, but also includes the active obedience of Christ." J. Dryden, *Theology and Ethics in 1 Peter: Paraenetic Strategies for Christian Character Formation* (Tübingen: Mohr Siebeck, 2006), 185.

13. Stott, *The Cross of Christ*, 271.

14. Tidball, *The Message of the Cross*, 301.

15. "Among these good works that the disciples of Jesus have to accomplish, those of self-denial and crossbearing are undoubtedly foremost," writes Herman Bavinck. He adds, "Those who wanted to rally to Jesus' side and follow him had to be prepared to give up everything: marriage (Matt. 19:10–12), the love of family members (10:35–36), their wealth (19:21), indeed even their lives (10:39; 16:25)" (*Reformed Dogmatics*, 4:233).

16. Sociologists of religion Christian Smith, Michael Emerson, and Patricia Snell (see *Passing the Plate*, 197–230) found in a survey of thirty-five Christian denominations in the United States (including Catholics and Protestants, mainline and evangelical churches) that an overwhelming majority (29/35) of these churches have official documents that teach the tithe as a basic gauge, standard, or starting point for Christian giving.

17. See Lev. 27:30–33; Num. 18:8–32; Deut. 14:22–29; 26:12–15; cf. Matt. 23:23; Luke 11:42; 18:12; Heb. 7:4–9. Scholars have vigorously debated the exact number of tithe(s). But Andreas Köstenberger and David Croteau are probably correct to say that the primary key to identifying how many different tithes existed under the Mosaic law is by distinguishing between the diverse purposes associated with the tithe in various passages where the tithe appears in the Pentateuch. See Andreas Köstenberger and David Croteau, " 'Will a Man Rob God?' (Malachi 3:8): A Study of Tithing in the Old and New Testaments," *Bulletin for Biblical Research* 16, no. 1 (2006): 61. Cf. Craig Blomberg, *Neither Poverty nor Riches: A Biblical Theology of Material Possessions* (Downers Grove, IL: InterVarsity Press, 1999), 46.

18. David L. Baker, for example, has a helpful discussion of "scrumping"—that is, the act of entering an orchard without permission and helping oneself to

the fruit (Deut. 23:24–25). The principle that Baker concludes we may take away from this part of the Mosaic law as Christians is that "the needs of the hungry take precedence over the rights of private property, though not without limits. Theft is not defined strictly according to ownership; right of access to satisfy human need is also part of the definition." David L. Baker, *Tight Fists or Open Hands?: Wealth and Poverty in Old Testament Law* (Grand Rapids: Eerdmans, 2009), 249.

19. For helpful analyses of the significance of the tithe for contemporary Christians, see Baker, *Tight Fists or Open Hands*, 239–47; Blomberg, *Neither Poverty nor Riches*, 46–47; Köstenberger and Croteau, "Reconstructing a Biblical Model for Giving," 237–60; David Croteau, "A Biblical and Theological Analysis of Tithing: Toward a Theology of Giving in the New Covenant Era" (Ph.D. diss., Southeastern Baptist Theological Seminary, 2005), 200–273.

20. Croteau, "A Biblical and Theological Analysis of Tithing," 90–91.

21. Alasdair MacIntyre, *After Virtue: A Study in Moral Theory*, 2nd ed. (Notre Dame, IN: University of Notre Dame Press, 1984), 204.

22. Herman Bavinck (*Reformed Dogmatics*, 4:243–44) has similarly observed that John Calvin, in his description of the Christian life, "does not lose himself in a wide-ranging exposition of all sorts of virtues and duties but conceives all of life as a unity controlled by one universal rule [see *Institutes* 3.6–10]. Calvin derives this from Rom. 12:1, where the apostle indicates that it is the duty of believers to offer their bodies as living sacrifices, holy and pleasing to God. The entire life of the Christian is dedicated to the worship of God—we are not our own; we are God's. We belong to God completely and always, in life and in death."

23. Cf. Yoder, *The Politics of Jesus*, 130–31.

24. Bonhoeffer, *The Cost of Discipleship*, 89. Similarly, John Calvin rightly said that Christians are "instructed by the cross to obey, because thus they are taught to live not according to their own whim but according to God's will" (*Institutes*, 3.8.4). Richard Hays makes the same point in his comment that the New Testament offers relatively little detailed information about Jesus' life. But when it does refer to what Jesus did, "the references point, over and over again, to the cross." Richard Hays, *The Moral Vision of the New Testament: Community, Cross, New Creation: A Contemporary Introduction to New Testament Ethics* (San Francisco: HarperSanFrancisco, 1996), 27.

25. Cf. Jürgen Moltmann: "The gospels intentionally direct the gaze of Christians away from the experiences of the risen Christ and the Holy Spirit back to the earthly Jesus and his way to the cross. They represent faith as the call to follow Jesus" (*The Crucified God*, 54). Richard Hays: "While Mark depicts Jesus' death as a vicarious sacrifice, he stresses even more emphatically its exemplary character: Jesus' death on the cross establishes a pattern for his disciples to follow" (*The Moral Vision of the New Testament*, 80). Similarly, Derek Tidball

rightly points out that "no account of the death of Jesus in the gospel of Mark is complete without consideration of it as a model for believers" (*The Message of the Cross*, 148).

26. E.g., Matt. 10:38–39; 16:24–27; Luke 9:23–25; 14:25–43; John 13:13–15; Rom. 15:1–7; Gal. 6:2; Eph. 5:25; Phil. 2:5–11; Heb. 12:1–2.

27. Jesus' death on the cross is most consistently interpreted as a *gift* (John 3:16 [δίδωμι]; Rom. 4:25 [παραδίδωμι]; 5:16 [δώρημα]; 6:23 [χάρισμα]; 8:32 [παραδίδωμι]; Eph. 2:8 [δῶρον]; Matt. 20:28 [δίδωμι]; Mark 10:45 [δίδωμι]; Gal. 1:4 [δίδωμι]; 2:20 [παραδίδωμι]; Eph. 5:2 [παραδίδωμι]; 5:25 [παραδίδωμι]; 2 Thess. 2:16 [δίδωμι]; 1 Tim. 2:6 [δίδωμι]; 2 Tim. 1:8, 9 [δίδωμι]; Titus 2:14 [δίδωμι]). See also Hays, *The Moral Vision of the New Testament*, 197; Michael Gorman, *Cruciformity*, 84–85.

28. "Imitation is not especially a matter of re-enacting *deeds*, but of re-enacting *virtue*." J. Dryden, *Theology and Ethics in 1 Peter: Paraenetic Strategies for Christian Character Formation* (Tübingen: Mohr Siebeck, 2006), 172.

29. In his famed study of the crucifixion, Martin Hengel concludes: "in the death of Jesus of Nazareth God identified himself with the extreme of human wretchedness, which Jesus endured as a representative of us all, in order to bring us to the freedom of the children of God." Martin Hengel, *Crucifixion in the Ancient World and the Folly of the Message of the Cross* (Philadelphia: Fortress, 1977), 89.

30. In a thoughtful article, Jason Hood makes a disquieting observation about the conspicuous neglect of this emphasis, concluding, "*The biblical teaching on the imitation of the crucified Christ is the most neglected aspect of recent work on the New Testament message of the cross*." See his, "The Cross and the New Testament: Two Theses in Conversation with Recent Literature (2000–2007)," *Westminster Theological Journal* 71 (2009): 281–95, italics original.

31. Cf. Schneider, *The Good of Affluence*. See also John Schneider, *Godly Materialism: Rethinking Money and Possessions* (Downers Grove, IL: InterVarsity Press, 1994).

32. For a helpful summary of several key misinterpretations of the *imitatio Christi* throughout history, see Frank Thielman, *Philippians* (Grand Rapid: Zondervan, 1995), 122–25.

33. Schneider, *The Good of Affluence*, 123.

34. Ibid., 124, 126, 149.

35. Ibid., 126.

36. Ibid., 128.

37. Ibid., 125.

38. Richard Hays, *The Moral Vision of the New Testament*, 466.

39. Ibid., 35–36.

40. See Phil. 3:17; 1 Tim. 4:12; Titus 2:7–8; Heb. 6:12; 11; 13:7; 1 Peter 5:2–3; 3 John 11; cf. 1 Thess. 1:6–8; 2:14. John Owen called similar attention to the

importance of learning by example: "It is by all confessed that examples are the most effectual ways of instruction, and, if seasonably proposed, do secretly solicit the mind unto imitation, and almost unavoidably incline it thereunto. But when unto this power which examples have *naturally* and *morally* to instruct and affect our minds, things are peculiarly designed and instituted of God to be our *examples*, he requiring of us that from them we should learn both what to do and what to avoid, there force and efficacy is increased. This the apostle instructs us in at large 1 Cor. x. 6–11. Now, both these concur in the example of holiness that is given us in the person of Christ" (*The Works of John Owen*, 3:509–10).

41. See 1 Cor. 4:15–17; 10:32–11:1; Gal. 4:12; Phil. 3:17; 4:9; 2 Thess. 3:7–9; 2 Tim. 3:10–11; cf. Acts 20:17–35; 1 Thess. 1:6–8.

42. For a helpful chart that carefully catalogs Paul's sufferings, see Gorman, *Cruciformity*, 286–87. In the last chapter we will also pay special attention to how Paul devoted himself to the collection for the poor in Jerusalem. This collection was a major concern of Paul's apostolic ministry.

43. Gordon Fee argues that the language of "imitate me" has "considerable significance" for the "larger question of Pauline ethical instruction." "The lack of specific references to the teaching of Jesus in the Pauline letters has been an ongoing puzzle, the best solution to which lies with this concept.... Paul's actual ethical instruction as it appears in his Epistles rarely uses the *language* of Jesus as it is recorded in the Gospel; but on every page it reflects his example," *The First Epistle to the Corinthians*, New International Commentary on the New Testament (Grand Rapids: Eerdmans, 1987), 187. Cf. Leon Morris, *The Epistles of Paul to the Thessalonians: An Introduction and Commentary*, New International Commentary on the New Testament, rev. ed. (Grand Rapids: Eerdmans, 1984), 144.

44. Gordon Fee, *Paul's Letter to the Philippians* (Grand Rapids: Eerdmans, 1995), 326–37. See also Tidball, *The Message of the Cross*, 223.

45. Gorman, *Cruciformity*, 383.

46. William Easterly, *The White Man's Burden Why the West's Efforts to Aid the Rest Have Done So Much Ill and So Little Good* (New York: Penguin, 2006), 4. For a thoughtful Christian response to some of these problems as they also appear in the context of Christian missions, relief, and development, see Steve Corbett and Brian Fikkert, *When Helping Hurts: How to Alleviate Poverty without Hurting the Poor — and Yourself* (Chicago: Moody Press, 2009).

47. By way of contrast, when complaints about a similar injustice arose in the early church in Jerusalem, the apostles themselves refused to try and exercise their authority to solve the problem on their own (Acts 6:1–7). Evidently the Hellenistic (Gentile) widows, who were a minority in the predominately Jewish church in Jerusalem, were being overlooked when it came to the daily distribution of food. But when complaints arose, instead of trying to solve

the problem from a distance, the apostles appointed seven chosen men filled with the Spirit to administrate the church's resources on behalf of the poor. As a result, the previously disadvantaged community was now responsible for caring for the whole church, both Jew and Gentile. This process of delegation itself demonstrated the apostles' wisdom and humility.

What stands out in the Acts 6 account of the early church's approach to this situation was that every single one of these men appointed to administer the church's funds had a Greek name. An equivalent today in the American church might be, for example, if there was a Hispanic minority whose widows were not being cared for, to have several Hispanic men being given responsibility to administer the church's benevolence budget.

48. Fyodor Dostoevsky, *The Brothers Karamazov* (New York: Knopf, 1992), 57.

49. The "better than" sayings of Proverbs express the same genius we find in Jesus' generosity. For example, Prov. 15:16 deals with the relative value of wealth versus the fear of the Lord. See also 16:16, which compares the value of wisdom and understanding to silver and gold; 17:1, which compares the value of a peaceful household to one of wealth and strife; and 22:1, which compares the value of a good name to great riches. Both personal wealth and personal integrity are affirmed as good and valuable, but when a choice must be made between the two, the fear of the Lord must be chosen and valued far more than wealth. Failure to prioritize God and other people before our personal rights is to fall into idolatry, to elevate the gift above the Giver. The same "better-than" logic of the book of Proverbs is what stands behind the saying of Jesus, "It is more blessed to give than to receive" (Acts 20:35). Cf. other "better-than" proverbs in Prov. 15:17; 16:8, 19, 32; 17:1; 19:1, 22; 28:6. All of these are directly connected to (1) accepting poverty or (2) choosing something better than wealth.

50. Benjamin Warfield, *The Person and Work of Christ* (Philadelphia: Presbyterian and Reformed, 1950), 573.

51. Johnson, *Sharing Possessions*, 40.

52. We are particularly grateful to Jason Hood for many fruitful discussions on the relationship between generosity and the cross.

Chapter 11: Resurrection Faith and Work

1. Richard Gaffin, *"By Faith, Not by Sight": Paul and the Order of Salvation* (Milton Keynes, UK: Paternoster, 2006), 68.

2. Raymond E. Brown, *The Virginal Conception and Bodily Resurrection of Jesus* (New York: Paulist, 1973), 33 [art. 13].

3. N. T. Wright, *Surprised by Hope: Rethinking Heaven, the Resurrection, and the Mission of the Church* (New York: HarperOne, 2008), 67.

4. E.g., John 5:24; 8:51–52; Acts 2:24; Rom. 6:5–14; 1 Cor. 15:12–26; 15:54–57; 2 Tim. 1:10; Heb. 2:9, 14; 1 Peter 3:18; Rev. 2:10–11; 21:4.

5. For helpful studies of the theology and background that guides the leading Protestant Reformers, even amid their diversity, see Timothy George, *Theology of the Reformers* (Nashville, TN: Broadman, 1988); David V. N. Bagchi and David Curtis Steinmetz, *The Cambridge Companion to Reformation Theology*, Cambridge Companions to Religion (Cambridge, UK; New York: Cambridge University Press, 2004); Heiko Augustinus Oberman, *The Reformation: Roots and Ramifications* (Grand Rapids: Eerdmans, 1994); Jaroslav Jan Pelikan, *Reformation of Church and Dogma (1300–1700)* (Chicago: University of Chicago Press, 1984).

6. Westminster Shorter Catechism, #10.

7. For a Protestant treatment unpacking what makes a work "good" and why such actions might be considered only possible for Christians, see Archbishop James Ussher, *A Body of Divinity: Being the Sum and Substance of the Christian Religion* (London: M.F., 1645), discussion under the "36th Head" section; cf. Westminster Confession of Faith 16.7.

8. So writes Calvin, here even reflecting on Christians: "For although this may seem astonishing, yet it is very true that no work springs from us that is absolutely perfect and is not infected by some stain. Hence, since we are all sinners and have several residues of sins, it is always necessary that we be justified by something outside of ourselves. That is to say, we always need Christ, so that his perfection may cover our imperfection, his purity may wash our impurity, his obedience may efface our iniquity; and finally his righteousness may gratuitously credit us with righteousness" (*Instruction in Faith (1537)*, trans. Paul T. Fuhrmann [Louisville: Westminster John Knox, 1992], 45–46 [art. 19]).

9. Leon Morris, "Faith," in J. D. Douglas, N. Hillyer, and F. F. Bruce, *New Bible Dictionary*, 2nd ed. (Leicester, UK: Inter-Varsity Press, 1982), 368 (italics mine).

10. Augustine has a fascinating comment about circumcision. Seeing that Philippians 3 alludes to our justification, Augustine writes, "It's as a result of his [Christ's] resurrection that we are justified, as though we were being circumcised by a flint knife, by rock. That's why he began from there: We are the circumcision (Phil. 3:3). Circumcision by what? By rock. By what rock? By Christ. How? On the eight day—just as the Lord rose again on the Lord's day" (*The Works of Saint Augustine: A Translation for the 21st Century*, 230).

11. For more on the dynamic of the relationship between the law and gospel, see Kelly M. Kapic, "'Evangelical Holiness': Assumptions in John Owen's Theology of Christian Spirituality," in *Life in the Spirit: Spiritual Formation in Theological Perspective*, ed. Jeffrey P. Greenman and George Kalantzis (Downers Grove, IL: InterVarsity Press, 2010).

12. Martin Luther, *A Treatise on Good Works 1520* (Project Gutenberg, www.netlibrary.com), 11.

13. See, e.g., the various treatments of this Greek word in *NIDNTT*, 1:480; also

in *Theological Lexicon of the New Testament*, ed. Ceslas Spicq, trans. James D. Ernest (Peabody, MA: Hendrickson, 1994), under σκύβαλον. Paul does not shy away from sharp language, and he is not nervous about employing more earthy imagery (e.g., Phil 3:2).

14. John Calvin, *Commentaries on the Epistles to the Philippians, Colossians, and Thessalonians*, trans. William Pringle (Grand Rapids: Baker, 1996 repr.), 95.

15. Martin Luther, "The Freedom of a Christian," in *Martin Luther's Basic Theological Writings*, ed. Timothy F. Lull (Minneapolis: Fortress, 1989), 615. Elsewhere Luther states it more strongly: "If one has a gracious God, then everything is good. Furthermore, we say also that if good works do not follow, then the faith is false and not true," see *The Schmalkald Articles*, trans. William R. Russell (Minneapolis: Fortress, 1995), 33 [art.13].

16. Luther, "The Freedom of a Christian," 612. Cf. Calvin, *Instruction in Faith (1537)*, 45–45 (art. 19).

17. See the final part of the next chapter for more on this point.

18. Calvin, *Commentaries on the Epistles to the Philippians, Colossians, and Thessalonians*, 97.

Chapter 12: Resurrection Life in Action

1. From "Seven Stanzas at Easter" in *Telephone Poles and Other Poems* (New York: Knopf, 1963); available at www.iserv.net/~stpats/Updike.htm.

2. Augustine, *The Works of Saint Augustine: A Translation for the 21st Century*, 244 [Sermon 170.10].

3. Cf., Edwin Yamauchi, "Life, Death, and the Afterlife in the Ancient Near East," in *Life in the Face of Death: The Resurrection Message of the New Testament*, ed. Richard N. Longenecker, McMaster New Testament Studies (Grand Rapids: Eerdmans, 1998), 43–44. See also the other stimulating essays in this book for more along these themes of death and resurrection. Cf. Bruce K. Waltke, *An Old Testament Theology*, 965.

4. Cf. Tremper Longman, *Proverbs*, 529. For discussions of Sheol and the grave, see Jon Douglas Levenson, *Resurrection and the Restoration of Israel: The Ultimate Victory of the God of Life* (New Haven, CT: Yale University Press, 2006), 114–15. Levenson's book, embodying the careful conclusions of one of the world's leading Jewish biblical scholars, is now considered the most masterful treatment of the idea of resurrection in the Old Testament — particularly engaging for the Christian reader.

5. It also clarifies Habakkuk 2:4–5: the wicked are characterized as being greedy Sheol, in contrast to the righteous, who "live by ... faith."

6. Hays, *The Moral Vision of the New Testament*, 338–39.

7. Wright, *Surprised by Hope*, 67.

8. Ibid.

9. This number reminds us of Jesus' miracle of feeding the crowds through the loaves and fishes.

10. It should be noted, however, that this is also not about creating a communist utopia, but it is about entering the movement of divine generosity.

11. In the first few centuries of the church, the idea of "private property" was commonly rejected for some of these very reasons. Augustine, for example, writes: "Let us therefore abstain from the possession of private property—or from the love of it, if we cannot abstain from possession—and let us make room for the Lord.... In property which each possesses privately, each necessarily becomes proud.... The flesh of the rich person pushes out against the flesh of the poor person—as if the [rich] flesh had brought anything with it when it was born, or will take anything with it when it dies" (quoted in Charles Avila, *Ownership, Early Christian Teaching* [Maryknoll, NY: Orbis, 1983], 120).

12. Luther, "The Freedom of a Christian," 623.

13. Randy C. Alcorn, *Heaven* (Wheaton, IL: Tyndale, 2004), 111.

14. Martin Luther, "Disputation against Scholastic Theology," in *Martin Luther's Basic Theological Writings*, 16 (#40).

15. We are to live honorably before the watching world; Peter reminds us that "when they speak against you as evildoers, they may see your good deeds and glorify God on the day of visitation" (1 Peter 2:12). We live faithfully in response to God and his call rather than conforming to the demands of the watching world. But in conforming to God, our lives are then testimonies to the watching world.

16. For this point, readers may find it helpful to wrestle through the powerful book by Henri J. M. Nouwen, *Adam, God's Beloved* (Maryknoll, NY: Orbis, 1997). See also Stanley Hauerwas and Jean Vanier, *Living Gently in a Violent World: The Prophetic Witness of Weakness*, Resources for Reconciliation (Downers Grove, IL: InterVarsity Press, 2008); and John Swinton and Brian Brock, *Theology, Disability, and the New Genetics: Why Science Needs the Church* (London; New York: T&T Clark, 2007).

17. Such self-elected good works include "running to the convent, singing, reading, playing the organ, saying the mass, praying matins, vespers, and other hours, founding and ornamenting churches, altars, convents, gathering chimes, jewels, vestments, gems and treasures, going to Rome and to the saints, curtsying and bowing the knees, praying the rosary and the psalter" (Luther, *A Treatise on Good Works*, 5).

18. In many ways this is the story of the slave Onesimus, who was formerly "useless" but freed in the gospel, he became "useful to you and to me" (Philem. 11). Philemon was no longer Onesimus's lord, Jesus was; and thus his work was done ultimately to Christ, not merely an earthly master (cf. vv. 15–16).

19. This was the original language of the letter, but no ill was meant by it. Rather, the author was trying to make the point that Sue's mother no longer had the

opportunities to express her gifts and abilities for the sake of others as she once had done.

Chapter 13: Receiving Life Together

1. Calvin, *Institutes*, 4.1.3.
2. Heidelberg Catechsim Q. & A. 55, as reprinted in Philip Schaff, *The Creeds of Christendom: The Evangelical Protestant Creeds* (Grand Rapids: Baker, 1966 repr.), 3:325.
3. Marilynne Robinson, *The Death of Adam: Essays on Modern Thought* (New York: Picador, 2005), 234.
4. For more on this type of worry, begin with Karl Barth, *The Church and the Churches*, new ed. (Grand Rapids: Eerdmans, 2005), esp. 19 – 30.
5. Gustaf Aulén, *The Faith of the Christian Church*, trans. Eric H. Wahlstrom (Philadelphia: Muhlenberg, 1960), 304.
6. While there can be debates about what "this rock" is a reference to (e.g., the apostolic confession of faith, Peter, etc.), our point here is that Jesus declares the church to be his, "my church."
7. Calvin, *Institutes*, 4.1.3. I was brought back to this section of Calvin and these quotes in particular in the excellent essay by John Webster, "The Church and the Perfection of God," in *The Community of the Word: Toward an Evangelical Ecclesiology*, ed. Mark Husbands and Daniel J. Treier (Downers Grove, IL: InterVarsity Press, 2005), 75 – 95 (esp. 77, 91). See also Webster's essay "The Visible Attests the Invisible" in the same volume (pp. 96 – 113), and John Webster, *Word and Church: Essays in Christian Dogmatics* (Edinburgh; New York: T&T Clark, 2001), esp. 211 – 30.
8. Christoph Schwöbel, "The Creature of the Word: Recovering the Ecclesiology of the Reformers," in *On Being the Church: Essays on the Christian Community*, ed. Colin E. Gunton and Daniel W. Hardy (Edinburgh: T&T Clark, 1989), 110 – 55 (quote on 122).
9. Bonhoeffer, *Life Together*, 30.
10. Cf. "You can't commend what you don't cherish," John Piper, *Let The Nations Be Glad! The Supremacy of God in Missions* (Grand Rapids: Baker, 2003), 17.
11. This is one of the reasons God has given his church the two primary offices of pastor and deacon, one excelling in the ministry of the Word and the other in works of mercy. One should note, however, that the most basic requirements for pastors (1 Tim. 3:2; Titus 1:7 – 8) include hospitality.
12. Craig S. Keener, *1 – 2 Corinthians*, New Cambridge Bible Commentary (Cambridge: Cambridge University Press, 2005), 203.
13. John Koenig, *New Testament Hospitality: Partnership with Strangers as Promise and Mission*, Overtures to Biblical Theology 17 (Philadelphia: Fortress, 1985), 10.
14. Ibid., 15. Here Koenig draws on ancient sources gathered by C. G. Montefiore

and M. Loewe, *A Rabbinic Anthology* (Philadelphia: Jewish Publication Society of America, 1963), 28–82, 415. Koenig also notes that the *First Epistle of Clement*, an early Christian document from the last decade of the first century, "also reflects the contemporary Jewish understanding of Abraham as supreme practitioner of hospitality. See chap. X."

15. Commenting on Rom. 15:3 in context Richard Hays notes that "Paul assumes without explanation that his readers will understand his citation of Psalm 69:9b ('The insults of those who insult you have fallen on me') as an allusion to the passion of Jesus. Once we recognize that allusion, Paul's point comes into focus: just as the crucified Messiah took upon himself suffering for the sake of others, so the 'powerful' in the Roman church should welcome the others even if it means putting up with their 'weaknesses'" (*The Moral Vision of the New Testament*, 28).

16. C. S. Lewis, *Reflections on the Psalms* (New York: Harcourt Brace, 1958), 9.

17. John Calvin, *Commentary on Matthew* 25:40 (Pringle ed. and trans., 181); CO 45, 689. Quoted in Bonnie Pattison, *Poverty in the Theology of John Calvin* (Eugene, OR: Wipf & Stock, 2006), 314.

18. See Kapic, *Communion with God*, 94, n. 14.

Chapter 14: Giving Life Together

1. Chrysostom, *The Gospel of Matthew*, Homily 78.3 (*Nicene and Post Nicene Fathers*, series 1; 10:472). Cited in Manlio Simonetti, *Matthew 14–28*, Ancient Christian Commentary on Scripture—New Testament 1b (Downers Grove, IL: InterVarsity Press, 2002), 228–29. This is a homily based on the parable of the talents in Matthew 25:14–30.

2. This crucial theme is masterfully handled throughout the magisterial work of Christopher J. H. Wright, *The Mission of God*), esp. 191–221. Some have recently raised questions about the translation and significance for understanding of this text, notably R. W. L. Moberly, *The Theology of the Book of Genesis* (Cambridge: Cambridge University Press, 2009), 141–61; Moberly, *The Bible, Theology, and Faith: A Study of Abraham and Jesus* (Cambridge: Cambridge University Press, 2000), 123–24. But here I am sympathetic with those who see this passage as significant not simply for understanding Genesis, but the rest of Scripture, e.g., Gerhard von Rad, *Genesis: A Commentary*, trans. John H. Marks, rev. ed.; Old Testamebnt Library (London: SCM, 1972), 152–54; Richard Bauckham, *Bible and Mission: Christian Witness in a Postmodern World* (Grand Rapids: Baker, 2003), 28. Additionally, Patrick Miller helpfully argues that one should not simply choose between "intrinsic" and "instrumental" views of "election" in the Old Testament, because there are plenty of texts that treat election in each of these different ways. See Miller's extended response to Joel S. Kaminsky's *Yet I Loved Jacob: Reclaiming the Biblical Concept of Election* (Nashville: Abingdon, 2007), published in *Review of*

Biblical Literature 3 (2008). Miller is largely in line with the classic critical essay on this passage by Hans Walter Wolff, "The Kerygma of the Yahwist," *Interpretation* 20/2 (1966): 131–58, esp. 137ff.

3. Wright, *The Mission of God*, 253.

4. Charles H. H. Scobie, *The Ways of Our God: An Approach to Biblical Theology* (Grand Rapids: Eerdmans, 2003), 520, 530 (cf. 509–40). Cf. Joachim Jeremias, *Jesus' Promise to the Nations* (Philadelphia: Fortress, 1982), 60.

5. For background on translation of v. 17, which literally could be translated "if anyone is in Christ—new creation!" see the helpful discussion in Hays, *The Moral Vision of the New Testament*, 20.

6. Christine D. Pohl, *Making Room: Recovering Hospitality as a Christian Tradition* (Grand Rapids: Eerdmans, 1999), 34.

7. Rodney Stark, *The Rise of Christianity: A Sociologist Reconsiders History* (Princeton, NJ: Princeton University Press, 1996), 82.

8. For this, see the entire chapter in ibid., 76–94.

9. Ibid., 82, 84.

10. Emperor Julian, *Epistle to Pagan High Priests*, quoted in James Hunter, *To Change the World: The Irony, Tragedy, and Possibility of Christianity in the Late Modern World* (New York: Oxford, 2010), 55–56. Hunter adds (p. 55): "It was by stressing their relationship with the socially and economically marginal that the [Christian] bishops projected a form of authority within the city that *outflanked* the traditional [pagan] leadership of the notables."

11. Similar stories could be told throughout the history of the church. It is worth noting, for example, that to properly understand the beginning of the Reformation, one needs to appreciate that Luther's 95 theses were originally focused not on justification by faith alone, but they were concerned with the abuse and injustice of indulgences, which took particular advantage of the poor. This was Luther beginning to work out his lived theology, and that is why it resonated so quickly with the populace. Cf. Richard Hordern, "Luther's Attitude towards Poverty: Theology and Social Reform," in *Festschrift: A Tribute to Dr. William Hordern*, ed. Walter Freitag (Saskatoon: University of Saskatchewan Press, 1985), 94–108. Similarly, it would surprise many people to learn how concerned Calvin was with the poor and how much he worked to advocate their cause and help them in their need. See Bonnie L. Pattison, *Poverty in the Theology of John Calvin*, Princeton Theological Monograph Series 69 (Eugene, OR: Wipf & Stock, 2006). She provides not only a detailed discussion of Calvin on these themes, but also background from the Patristic through the Reformation period (pp. 11–122) before focusing on Calvin in particular.

12. Scot McKnight, "Collection for the Saints," in *Dictionary of Paul and His Letters*, ed. Gerald F. Hawthorne, Ralph P. Martin, and Daniel G. Reid (Downers Grove, IL: InterVarsity Press, 1993), 143–47 (quote from 143). He concludes, "It is hard to imagine any campaign more embracing of the northern Mediter-

ranean and any project that occupied Paul's attention more than this collection for the saints." So also Keith Nickle notes, "If the events which resulted in the launching of this project are taken into account, the time involved spanned the entire period of his known public missionary activity from Antioch to Rome"; Keith Fullerton Nickle, *The Collection: A Study in Paul's Strategy,* Studies in Biblical Theology 48 (London: SCM Press, 1966), esp. 104–11.

13. Major studies on the collection, besides those footnoted elsewhere, include: Dieter Georgi, *Remembering the Poor: The History of Paul's Collection for Jerusalem* (Nashville: Abingdon, 1992); Burkhard Beckheuer, *Paulus und Jerusalem* (Bern: P. Lang, 1997); Verlyn D. Verbrugge, *Paul's Style of Church Leadership Illustrated by His Instructions to the Corinthians on the Collection* (San Francisco: Mellen Research Univ. Press, 1992); Stephan Joubert, *Paul as Benefactor* (Tübingen: Mohr Siebeck, 2000); David Downs, *The Offering of the Gentiles: Paul's Collection for Jerusalem in Its Chronological, Cultural, and Cultic Contexts* (Tübingen: Mohr Siebeck, 2008).

14. Dunn, *The Theology of Paul the Apostle,* 707. See also Nickle, *The Collection,* esp. 104–11.

15. N. T. Wright, *Paul: In Fresh Perspective* (Minneapolis: Fortress, 2005), 167.

16. Dunn notes "It was delivery of the collection which took him back to Jerusalem for the last time [Rom. 15:31].... And in the event it was the reaction to that visit (and the collection?) which triggered the sequence which ended in his journey to Rome and eventual execution" (Dunn, *The Theology of Paul the Apostle,* 707).

17. Jason Hood concludes that Paul's "return to Judea to deliver the collection takes priority over Paul's visit to Rome. As he explains to the Romans (Rom. 15), this visit was to be the great launch of gospel ministry in the western half of the Empire all the way to Spain. We do not know if Paul achieved this mission, but we do know that he delivered the collection. *The collection was so vital that its delivery was at that moment a more urgent matter for Paul than his desire to evangelize and plant churches on the missionary frontier* among those who were 'without hope and without God in the world,' as he describes them in Ephesians 2:12." Jason Hood, "Theology in Action: Paul and Christian Social Concern," in *Transforming the World? The Gospel and Social Responsibility,* eds. J. Grant and D. Hughes (Leicester: Inter-Varsity Press, 2009), 132.

18. Craig Blomberg argues: "Paul's primary motivation would then have been simply to alleviate this human need in keeping with the principles of compassion that permeate God's Word" (Blomberg, *Neither Poverty Nor Riches,* 188–89).

19. Calvin, *Institutes,* 4.4.6.

20. Martin Luther, *Commentary on Galatians* (Grand Rapids: Kregel, 1987), 55. Luther is here commenting on Galatians 2:10.

21. N. T. Wright, *Paul: In Fresh Perspective* (Minneapolis: Fortress, 2005), 167.

22. Michael Gorman, *Apostle of the Crucified Lord* (Grand Rapids; Eerdmans,2004), 313.

23. Verbrugge argues (*Paul's Style of Church Leadership*, 294–330), especially in the light of Romans 15:25–29, that unity in the church was the main motivating factor for Paul in spearheading the Collection in his Gentile churches.

24. Nickle, *The Collection*, 109.

25. The following list is adapted from ibid., 109–10. See also Dunn, *The Theology of Paul the Apostle*, 707–8; Gorman, *Apostle of the Crucified Lord*, 313–14.

26. See Johannes Munck, *Paul and the Salvation of Mankind* (Atlanta: John Knox, 1959); Scot McKnight, "Collection for the Saints," 146; Nickle, *The Collection*, 129–42; Scot McKnight, *A Light among the Gentiles: Jewish Missionary Activity in the Second Temple Period* (Minneapolis: Fortress, 1991), esp. 47–48; F. F. Bruce, "Paul and Jerusalem," *Tyndale Bulletin* 19 (1968): 22–25.

27. For more on this theme, see again chapter 1, where Rom. 11:36 is discussed at length.

28. For more on this term, see Jürgen Goetzmann's carefully constructed article in *NIDNTT*, 2:253–56.

Scripture Index

Subject Index

NIV Stewardship Study Bible

Discover God's Design for Life, the Environment, Finances, Generosity, and Eternity

The *NIV Stewardship Study Bible* uses a variety of engaging features to lead individuals through a comprehensive study of what it means to be managers entrusted with the resources of God. Through 366 Exploring Stewardship notes, profiles of individuals, notes on challenges to stewardship, quotes on stewardship from respected Christians throughout the ages, and other articles and helps, the *NIV Stewardship Study Bible* projects a positive picture of the privilege that we have to manage what God has given us to his glory and to the building of his kingdom.

More than just money, this Bible emphasizes stewardly responsibility in all areas of life, including relationships, creation care, money management, institutions, and caring for the poor. It's been pulled together with the purpose of changing perceptions about what the word "stewardship" means—not something intended to be draining and guilt-inducing, but rather motivating, empowering, and uplifting.

The *NIV Stewardship Study Bible* has been endorsed by Crown Ministries, Dave Ramsey, Good $ense ministries, the Barnabas Foundation, Prison Fellowship, and various other programs and ministries that seek to encourage responsible stewardship among Christians. Kelly M. Kapic also served as an editor on this resource. This Bible will be a natural "next step" for individuals and groups who benefit from these ministries and take part in their programs.

Available in stores and online!

ZONDERVAN®
.com

Share Your Thoughts

With the Author: Your comments will be forwarded to the author when you send them to *zauthor@zondervan.com*.

With Zondervan: Submit your review of this book by writing to *zreview@zondervan.com*.

Free Online Resources at
www.zondervan.com

Zondervan AuthorTracker: Be notified whenever your favorite authors publish new books, go on tour, or post an update about what's happening in their lives at www.zondervan.com/authortracker.

Daily Bible Verses and Devotions: Enrich your life with daily Bible verses or devotions that help you start every morning focused on God. Visit www.zondervan.com/newsletters.

Free Email Publications: Sign up for newsletters on Christian living, academic resources, church ministry, fiction, children's resources, and more. Visit www.zondervan.com/newsletters.

Zondervan Bible Search: Find and compare Bible passages in a variety of translations at www.zondervanbiblesearch.com.

Other Benefits: Register yourself to receive online benefits like coupons and special offers, or to participate in research.

ZONDERVAN®

ZONDERVAN.com/
AUTHORTRACKER
follow your favorite authors